PRIDE AND PREJUDICE

First published 2011
by SelfMadeHero
A division of Metro Media Ltd
5 Upper Wimpole Street
London W1G 6BP
www.selfmadehero.com

Adaptor: Ian Edginton
Illustrator: Robert Deas
Editorial Assistance and Cover Typography: Lizzie Kaye
Marketing Director: Doug Wallace
Publishing Director: Emma Hayley
With thanks to: Nick de Somogyi and Jane Laporte

A CIP record for this book is available from the British Library

ISBN: 978-1-906838-30-0

10 9 8 7 6 5 4 3 2 1

Printed and bound in China

PRIDE AND PREJUDICE

ADAPTED FROM THE ORIGINAL NOVEL BY
JANE AUSTEN
ILLUSTRATED BY
ROBERT DEAS
TEXT ADAPTED BY
IAN EDGINTON

SELF MADE HERO

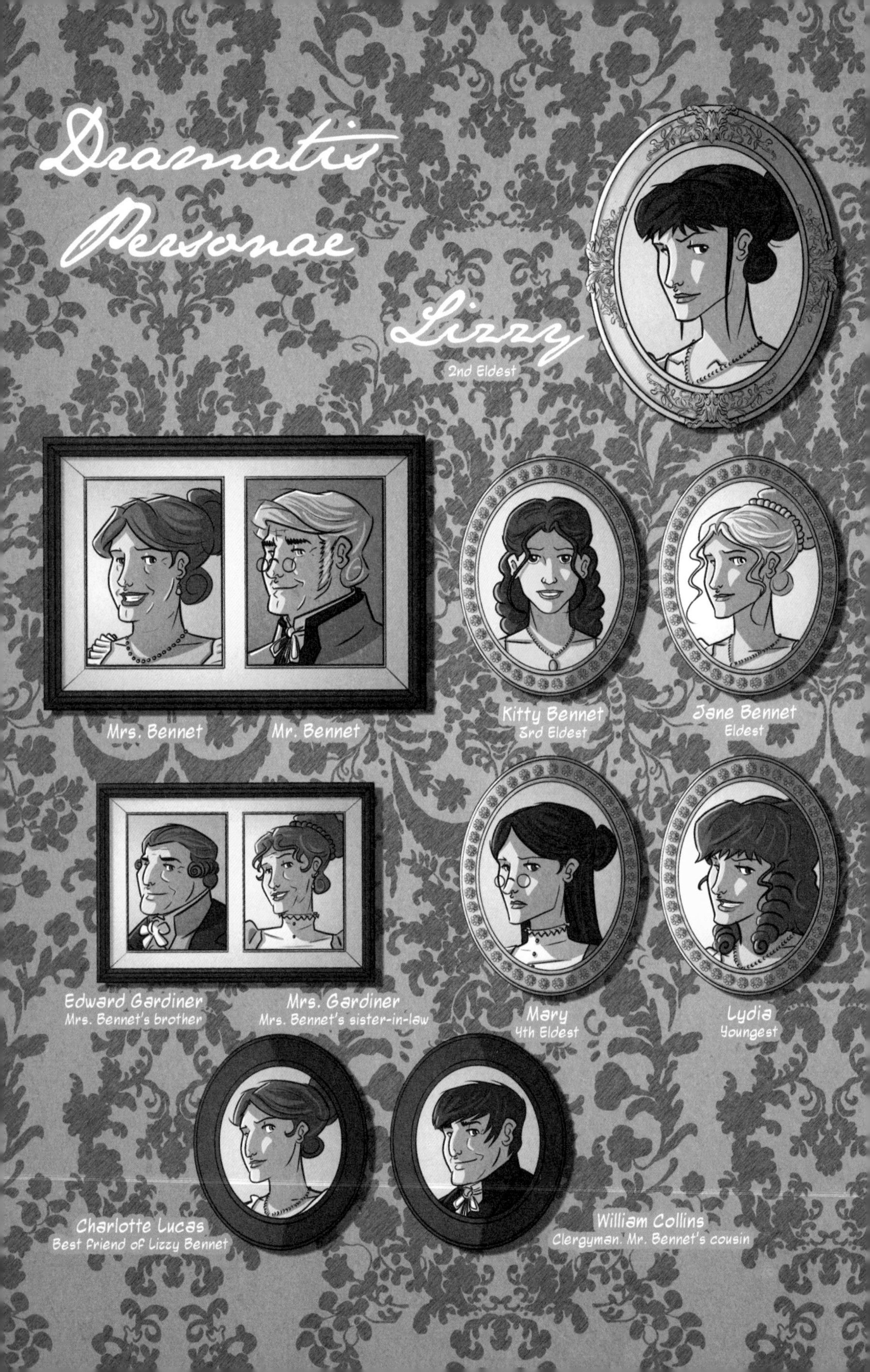
Dramatis Personae
Lizzy
2nd Eldest
Mrs. Bennet
Mr. Bennet
Kitty Bennet
3rd Eldest
Jane Bennet
Eldest
Edward Gardiner
Mrs. Bennet's brother
Mrs. Gardiner
Mrs. Bennet's sister-in-law
Mary
4th Eldest
Lydia
Youngest
Charlotte Lucas
Best friend of Lizzy Bennet
William Collins
Clergyman. Mr. Bennet's cousin

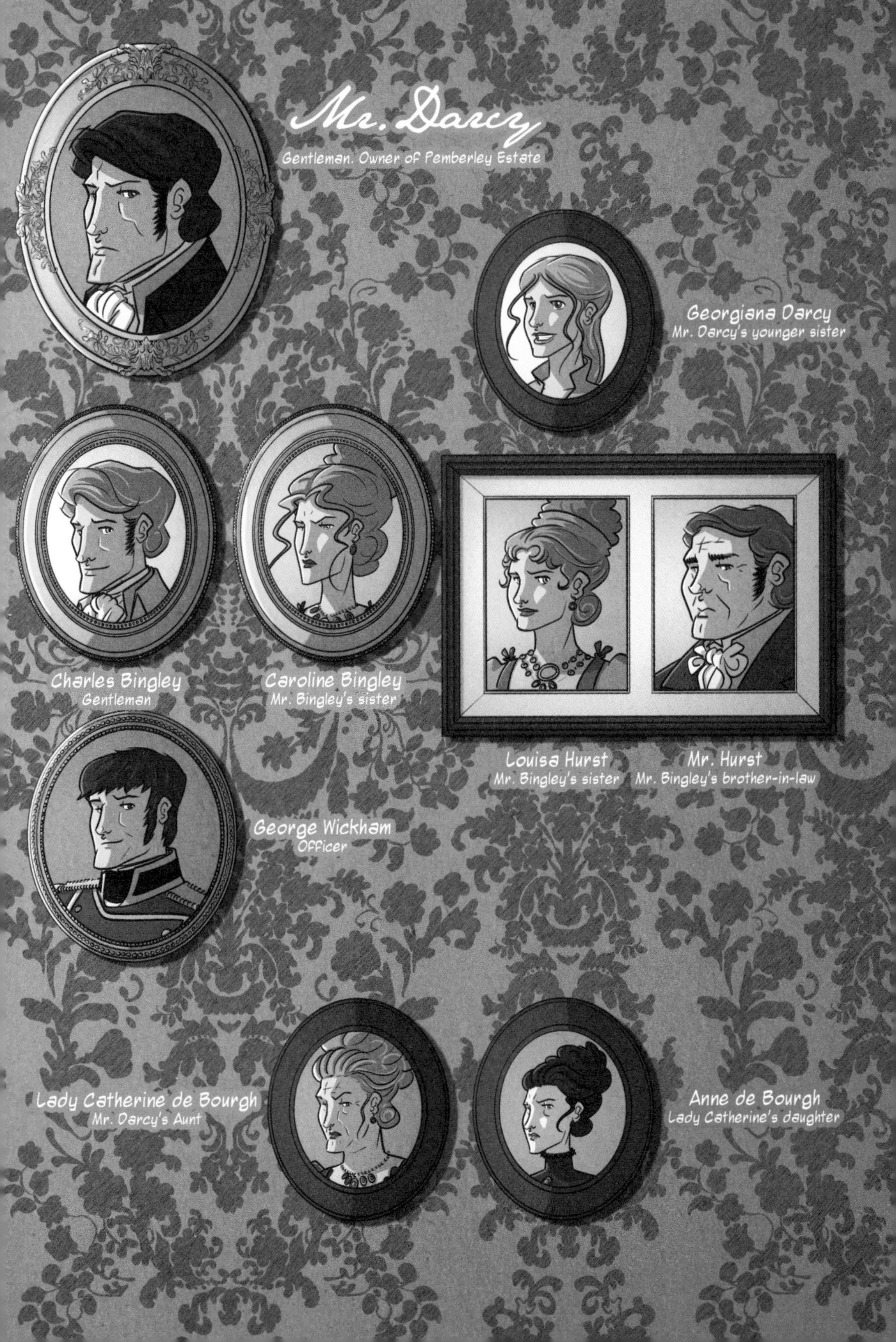
Mr. Darcy
Gentleman. Owner of Pemberley Estate
Georgiana Darcy
Mr. Darcy's younger sister
Charles Bingley
Gentleman
Caroline Bingley
Mr. Bingley's sister
Louisa Hurst
Mr. Bingley's sister
Mr. Hurst
Mr. Bingley's brother-in-law
George Wickham
Officer
Lady Catherine de Bourgh
Mr. Darcy's Aunt
Anne de Bourgh
Lady Catherine's daughter

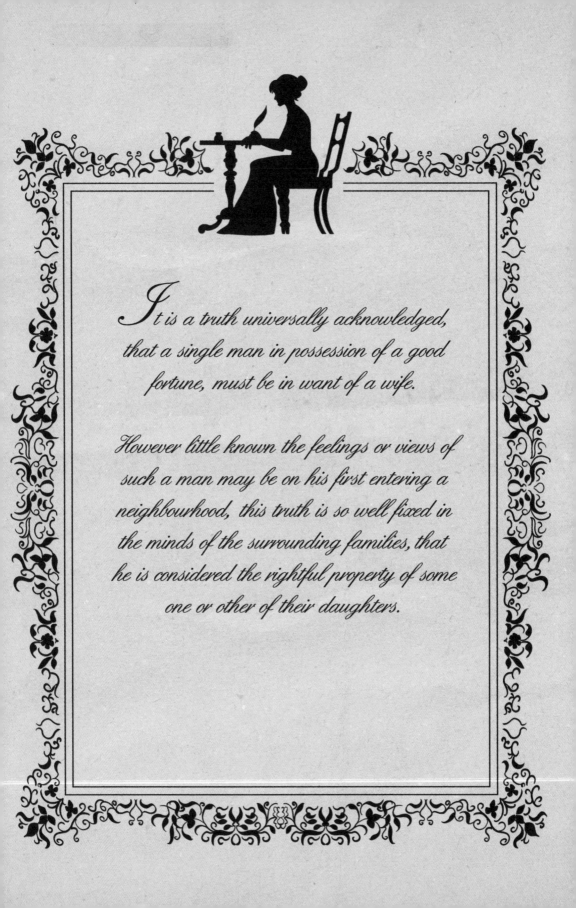

It is a truth universally acknowledged, that a single man in possession of a good fortune, must be in want of a wife.

However little known the feelings or views of such a man may be on his first entering a neighbourhood, this truth is so well fixed in the minds of the surrounding families, that he is considered the rightful property of some one or other of their daughters.

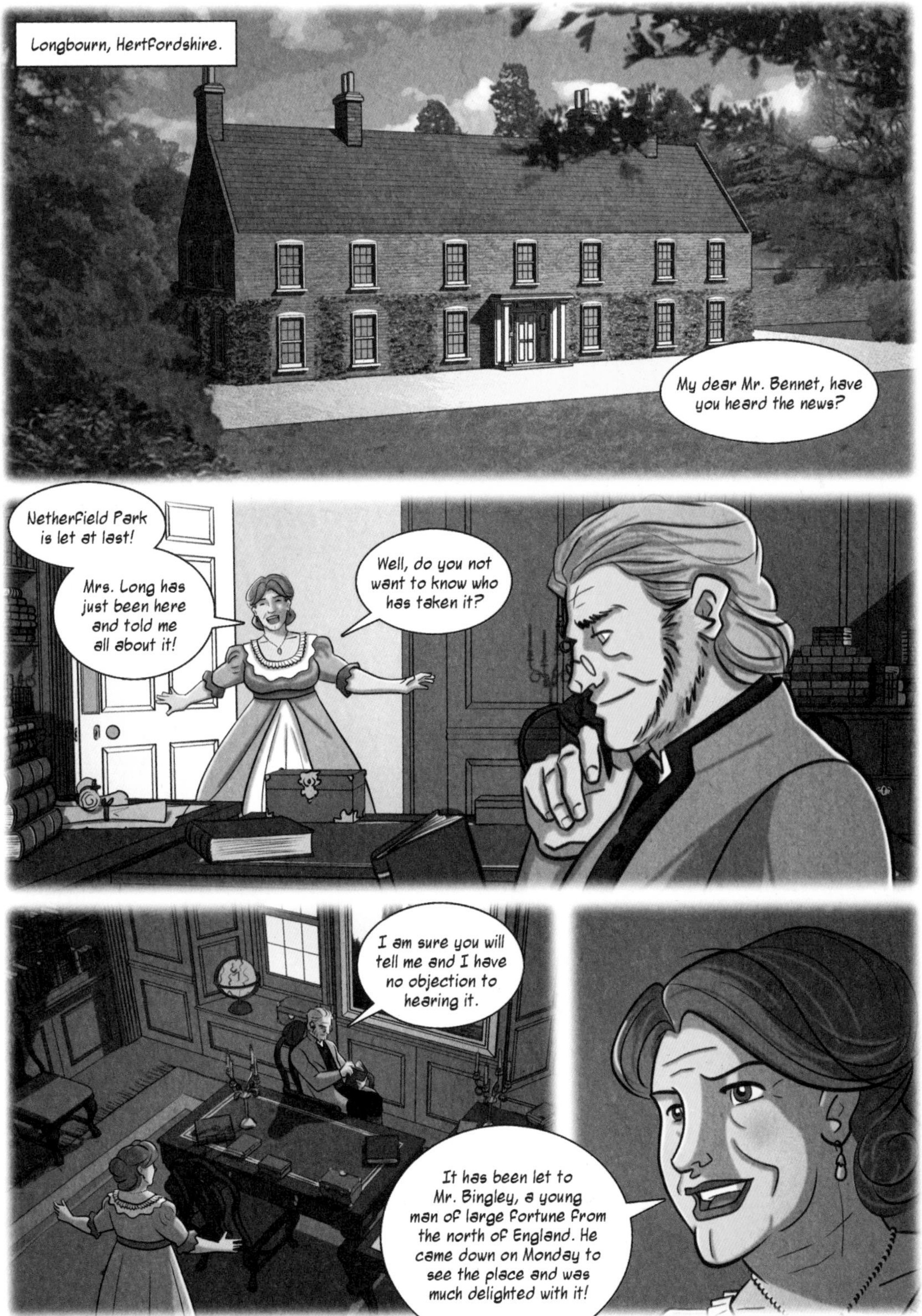
Longbourn, Hertfordshire.
My dear Mr. Bennet, have you heard the news?
Netherfield Park is let at last!
Mrs. Long has just been here and told me all about it!
Well, do you not want to know who has taken it?
I am sure you will tell me and I have no objection to hearing it.
It has been let to Mr. Bingley, a young man of large fortune from the north of England. He came down on Monday to see the place and was much delighted with it!

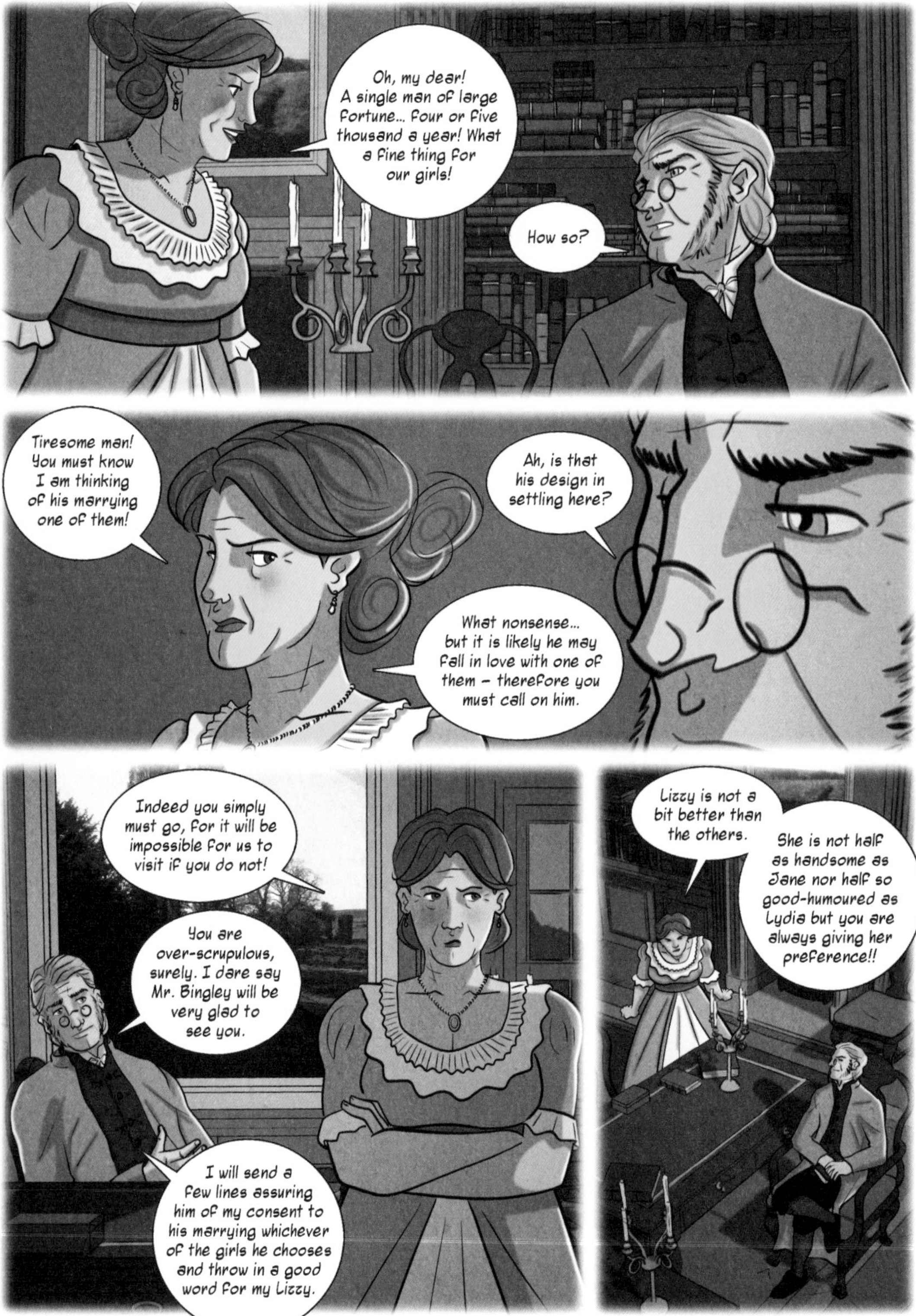

Oh, my dear! A single man of large fortune... four or five thousand a year! What a fine thing for our girls!
How so?
Tiresome man! You must know I am thinking of his marrying one of them!
Ah, is that his design in settling here?
What nonsense... but it is likely he may fall in love with one of them – therefore you must call on him.
Indeed you simply must go, for it will be impossible for us to visit if you do not!
You are over-scrupulous, surely. I dare say Mr. Bingley will be very glad to see you.
I will send a few lines assuring him of my consent to his marrying whichever of the girls he chooses and throw in a good word for my Lizzy.
Lizzy is not a bit better than the others.
She is not half as handsome as Jane nor half so good-humoured as Lydia but you are always giving her preference!!

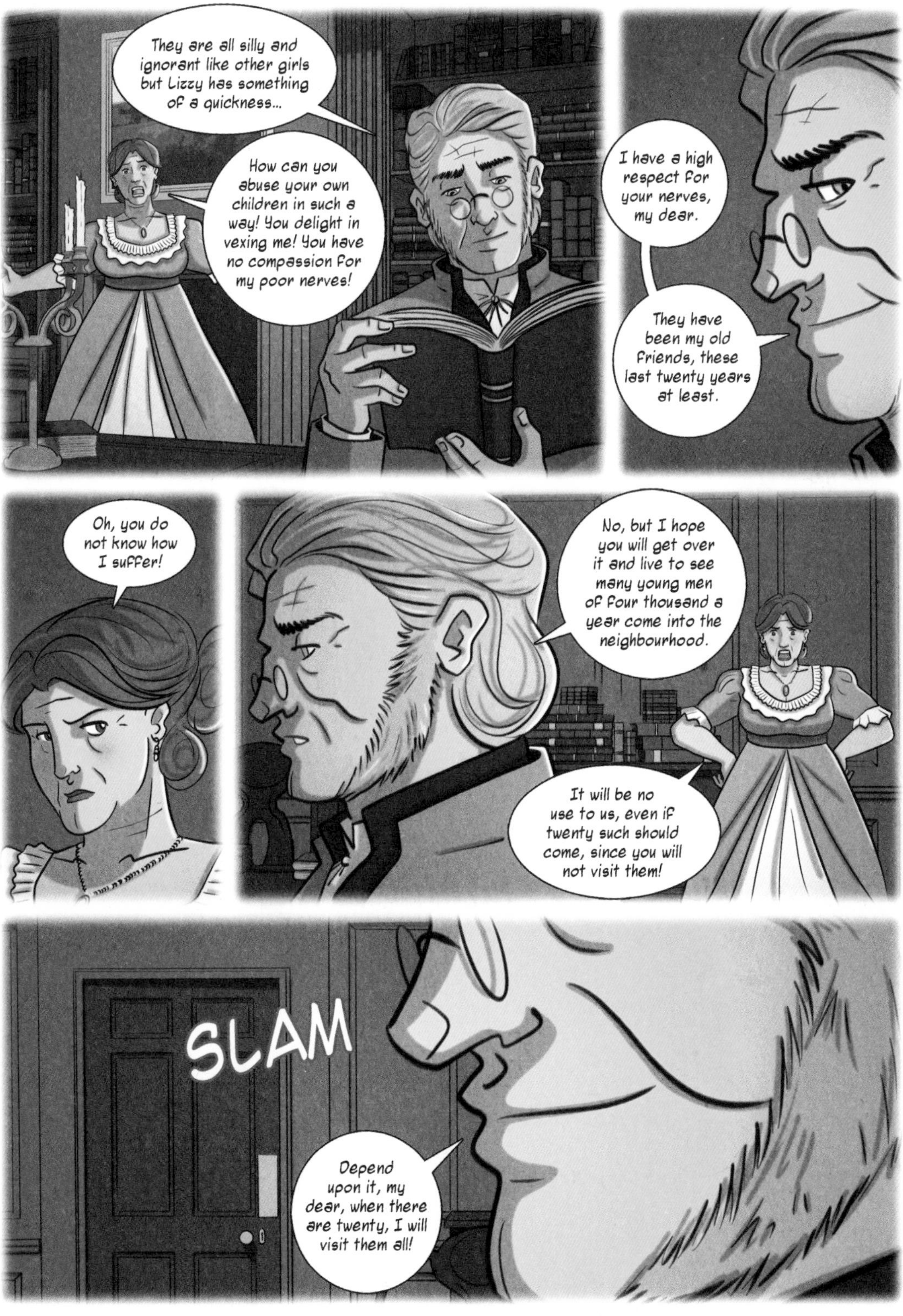
They are all silly and ignorant like other girls but Lizzy has something of a quickness...
How can you abuse your own children in such a way! You delight in vexing me! You have no compassion for my poor nerves!
I have a high respect for your nerves, my dear.
They have been my old friends, these last twenty years at least.
Oh, you do not know how I suffer!
No, but I hope you will get over it and live to see many young men of four thousand a year come into the neighbourhood.
It will be no use to us, even if twenty such should come, since you will not visit them!
SLAM
Depend upon it, my dear, when there are twenty, I will visit them all!

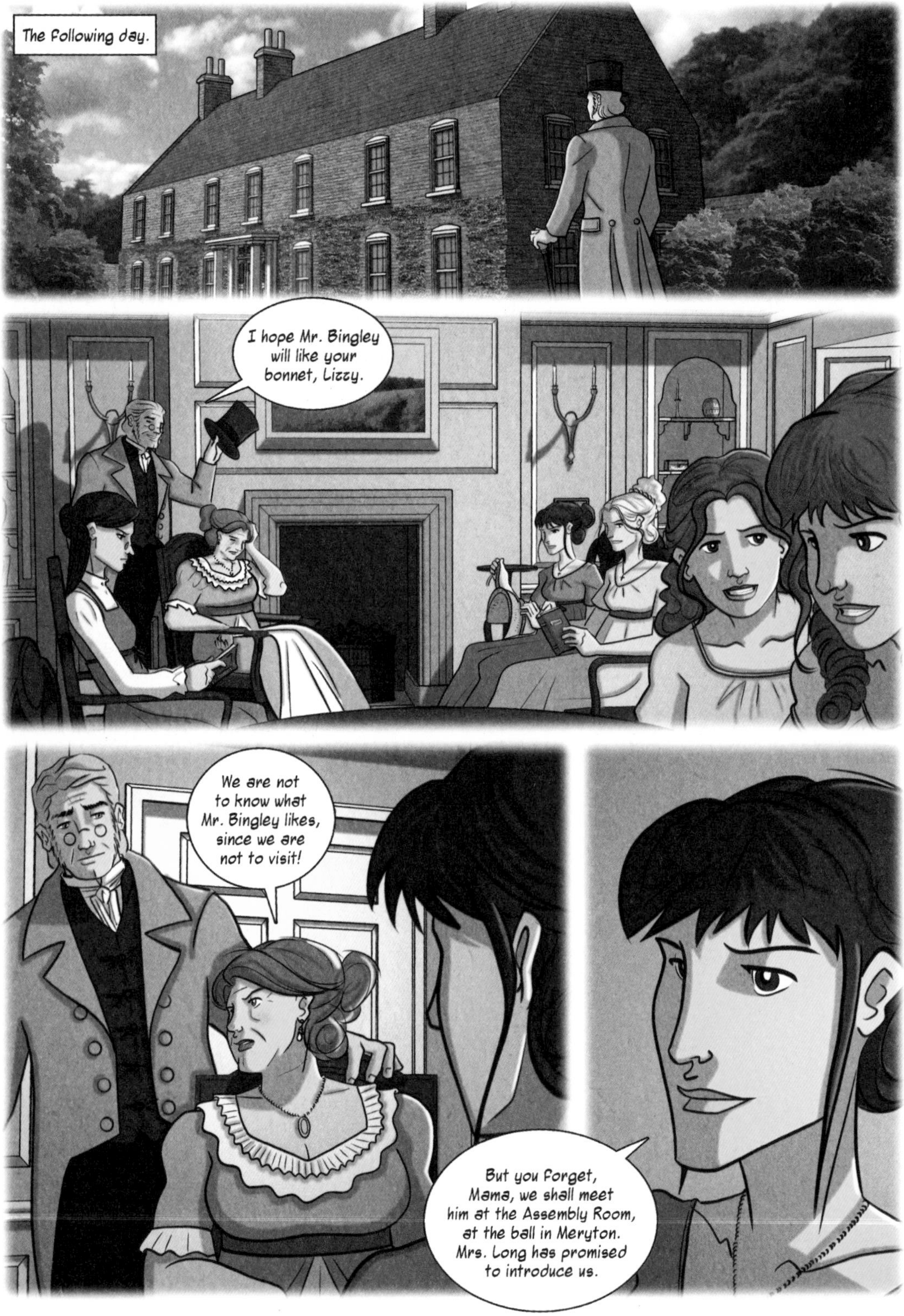
The following day.
I hope Mr. Bingley will like your bonnet, Lizzy.
We are not to know what Mr. Bingley likes, since we are not to visit!
But you forget, Mama, we shall meet him at the Assembly Room, at the ball in Meryton. Mrs. Long has promised to introduce us.

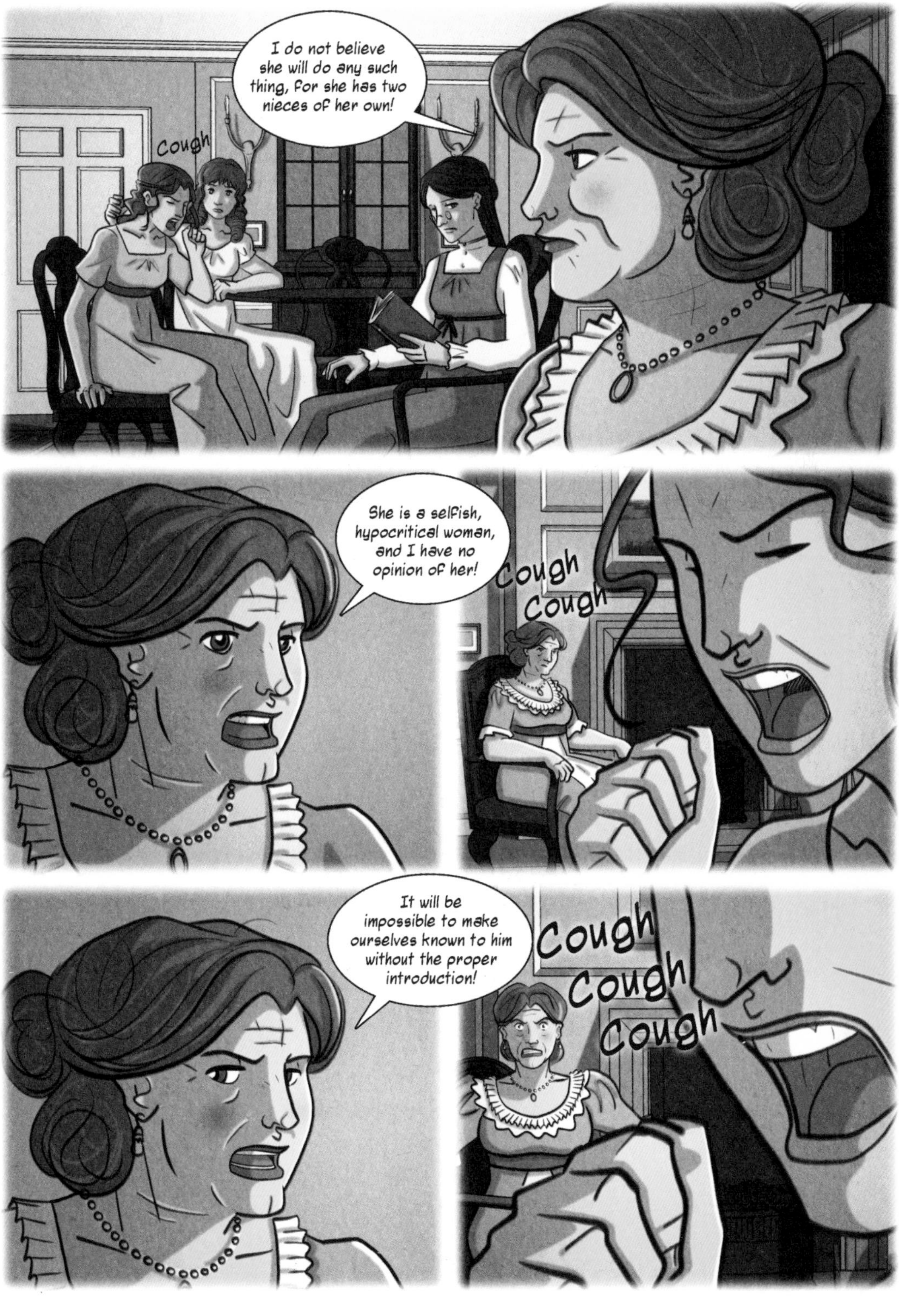
I do not believe she will do any such thing, for she has two nieces of her own!
Cough
She is a selfish, hypocritical woman, and I have no opinion of her!
Cough
Cough
It will be impossible to make ourselves known to him without the proper introduction!
Cough
Cough
Cough

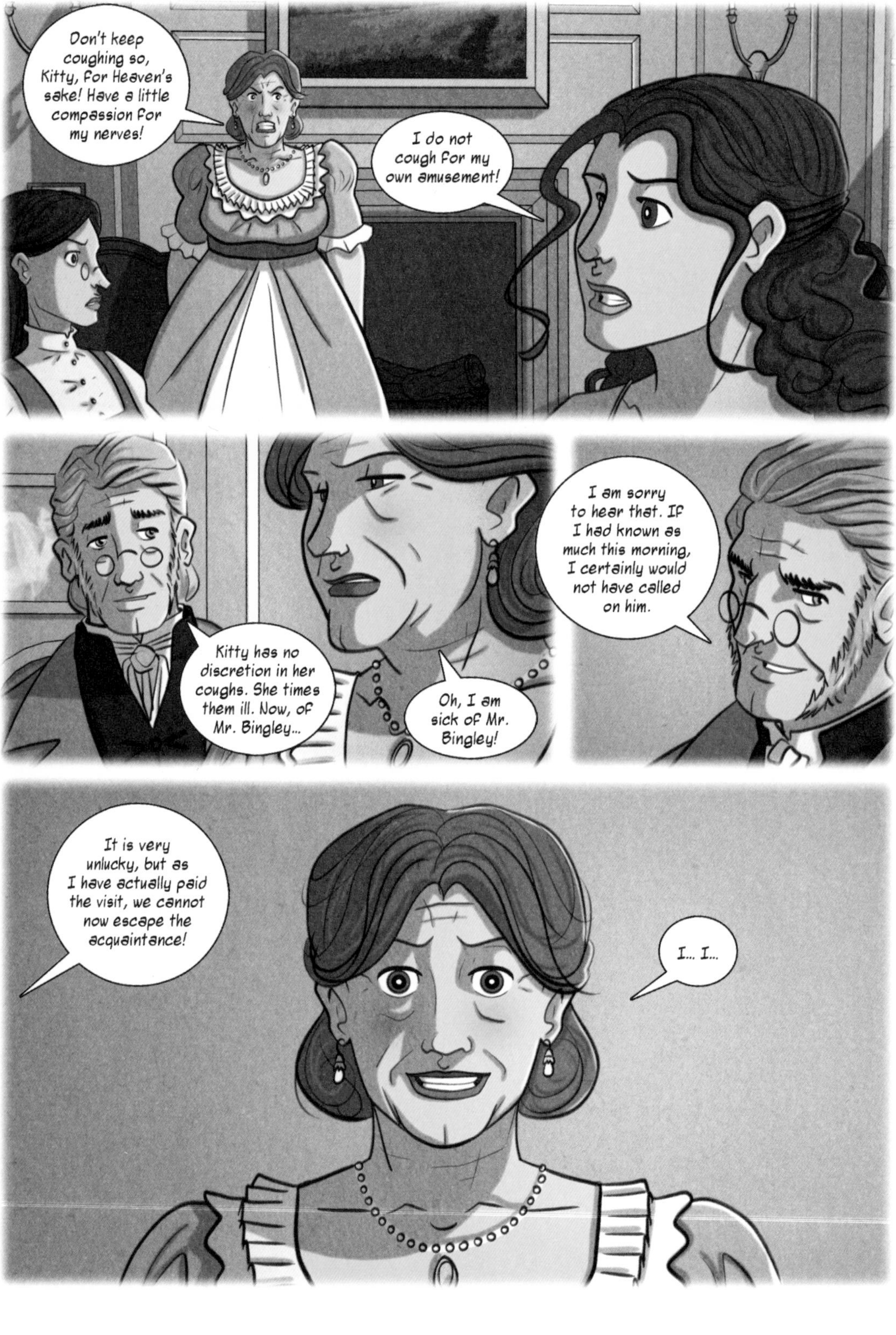
Don't keep coughing so, Kitty, for Heaven's sake! Have a little compassion for my nerves!
I do not cough for my own amusement!
Kitty has no discretion in her coughs. She times them ill. Now, of Mr. Bingley...
Oh, I am sick of Mr. Bingley!
I am sorry to hear that. If I had known as much this morning, I certainly would not have called on him.
It is very unlucky, but as I have actually paid the visit, we cannot now escape the acquaintance!
I... I...

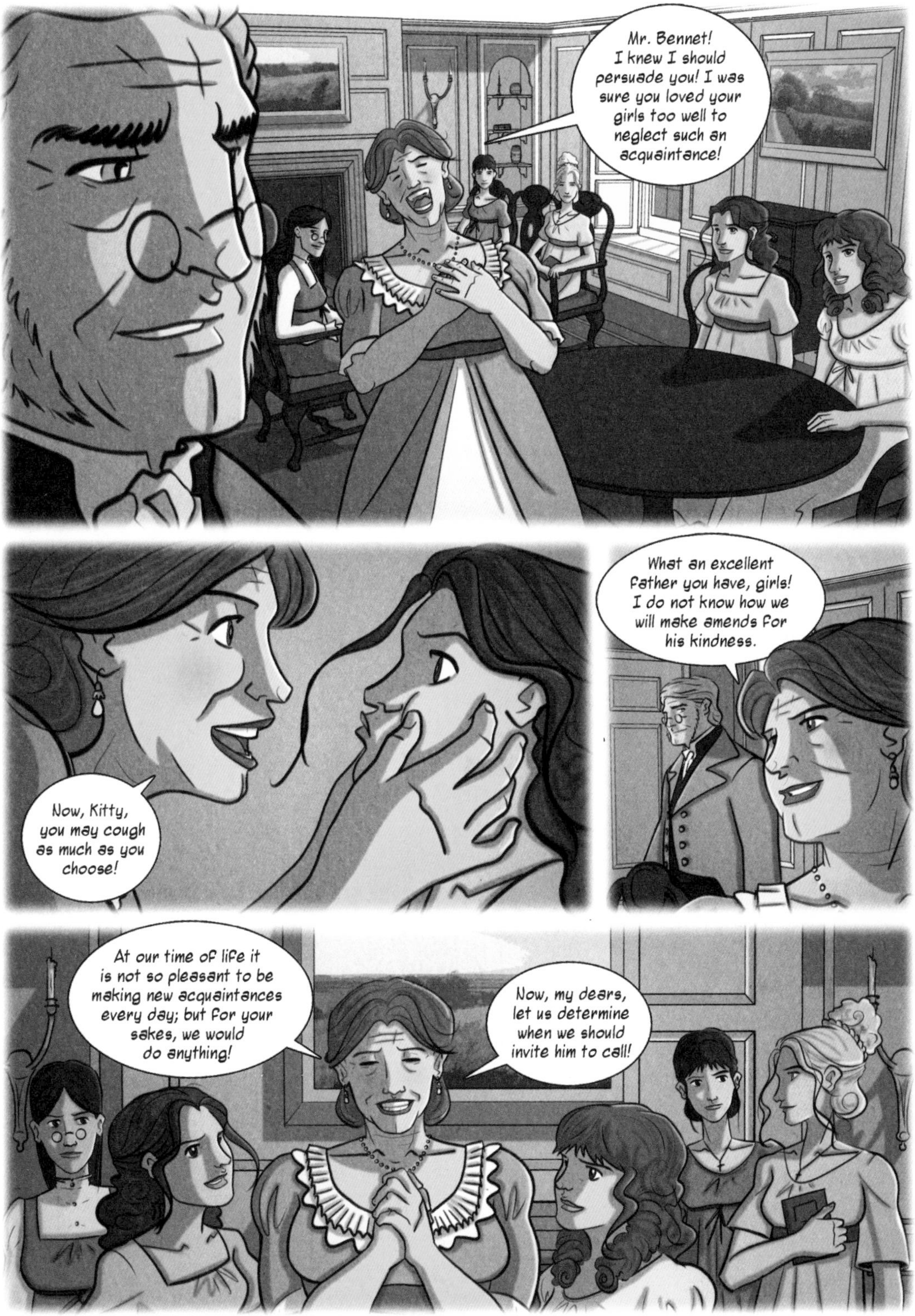
Mr. Bennet! I knew I should persuade you! I was sure you loved your girls too well to neglect such an acquaintance!
Now, Kitty, you may cough as much as you choose!
What an excellent father you have, girls! I do not know how we will make amends for his kindness.
At our time of life it is not so pleasant to be making new acquaintances every day; but for your sakes, we would do anything!
Now, my dears, let us determine when we should invite him to call!

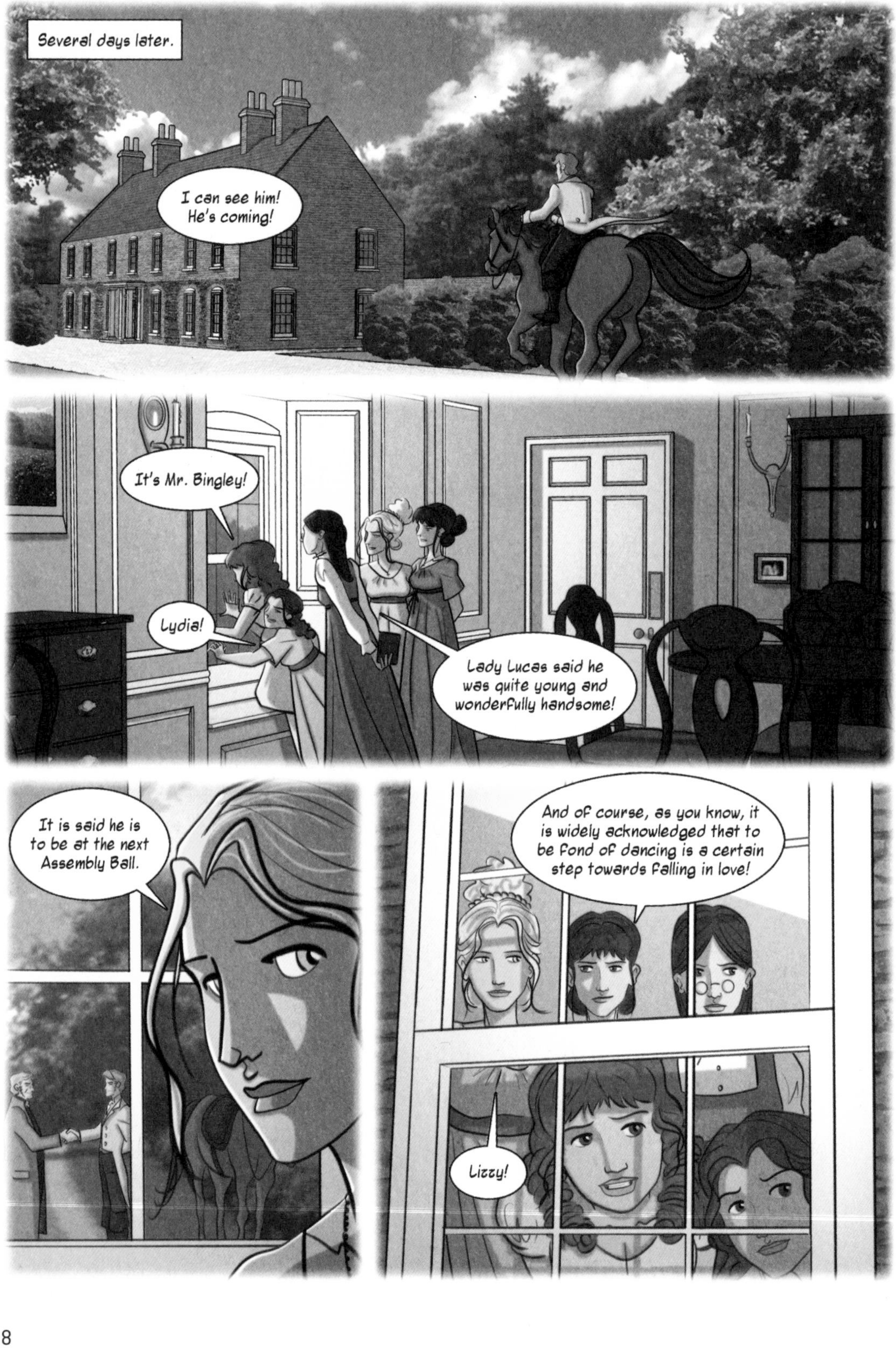
Several days later.
I can see him! He's coming!
It's Mr. Bingley!
Lydia!
Lady Lucas said he was quite young and wonderfully handsome!
It is said he is to be at the next Assembly Ball.
And of course, as you know, it is widely acknowledged that to be fond of dancing is a certain step towards falling in love!
Lizzy!

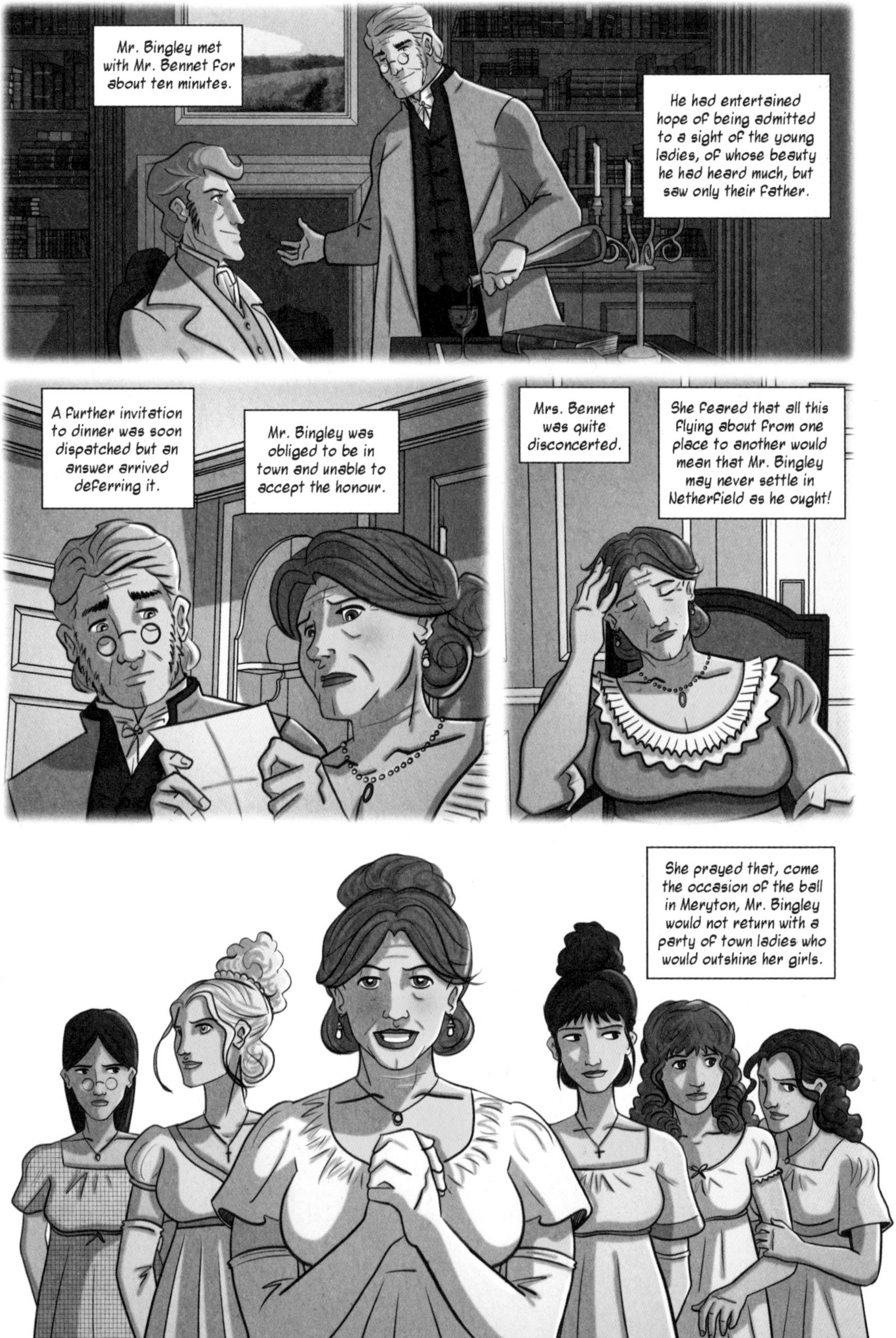
Mr. Bingley met with Mr. Bennet for about ten minutes.
He had entertained hope of being admitted to a sight of the young ladies, of whose beauty he had heard much, but saw only their father.
A further invitation to dinner was soon dispatched but an answer arrived deferring it.
Mr. Bingley was obliged to be in town and unable to accept the honour.
Mrs. Bennet was quite disconcerted.
She feared that all this flying about from one place to another would mean that Mr. Bingley may never settle in Netherfield as he ought!
She prayed that, come the occasion of the ball in Meryton, Mr. Bingley would not return with a party of town ladies who would outshine her girls.

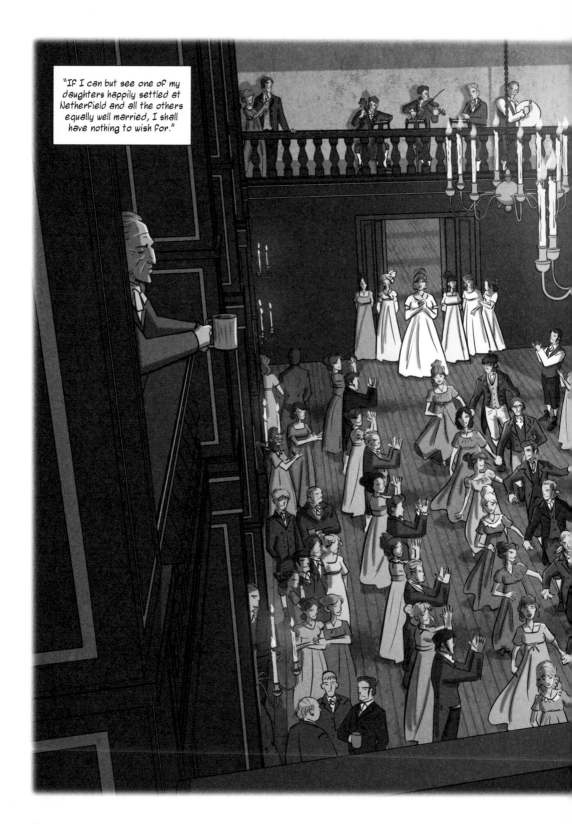

"If I can but see one of my daughters happily settled at Netherfield and all the others equally well married, I shall have nothing to wish for."

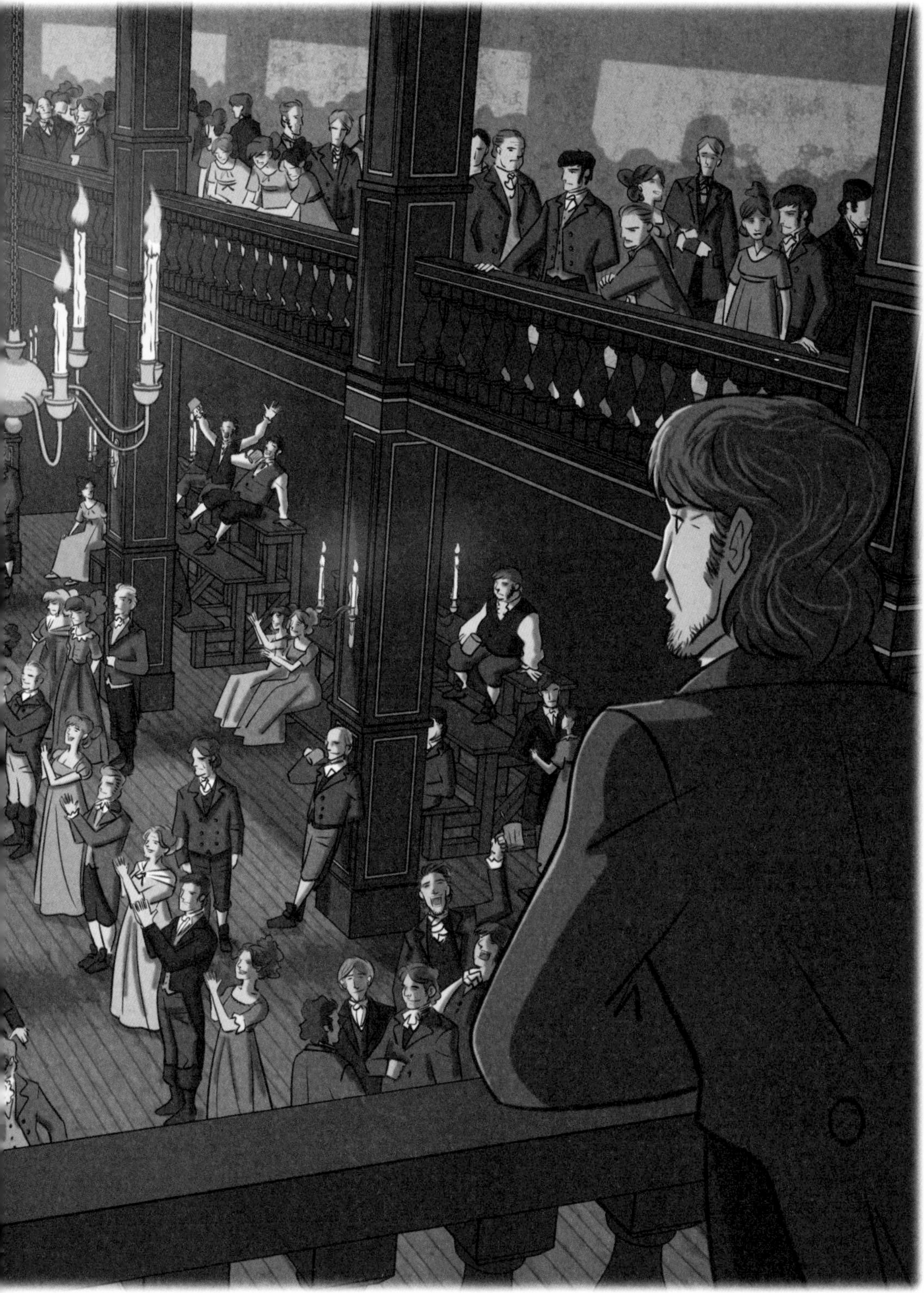

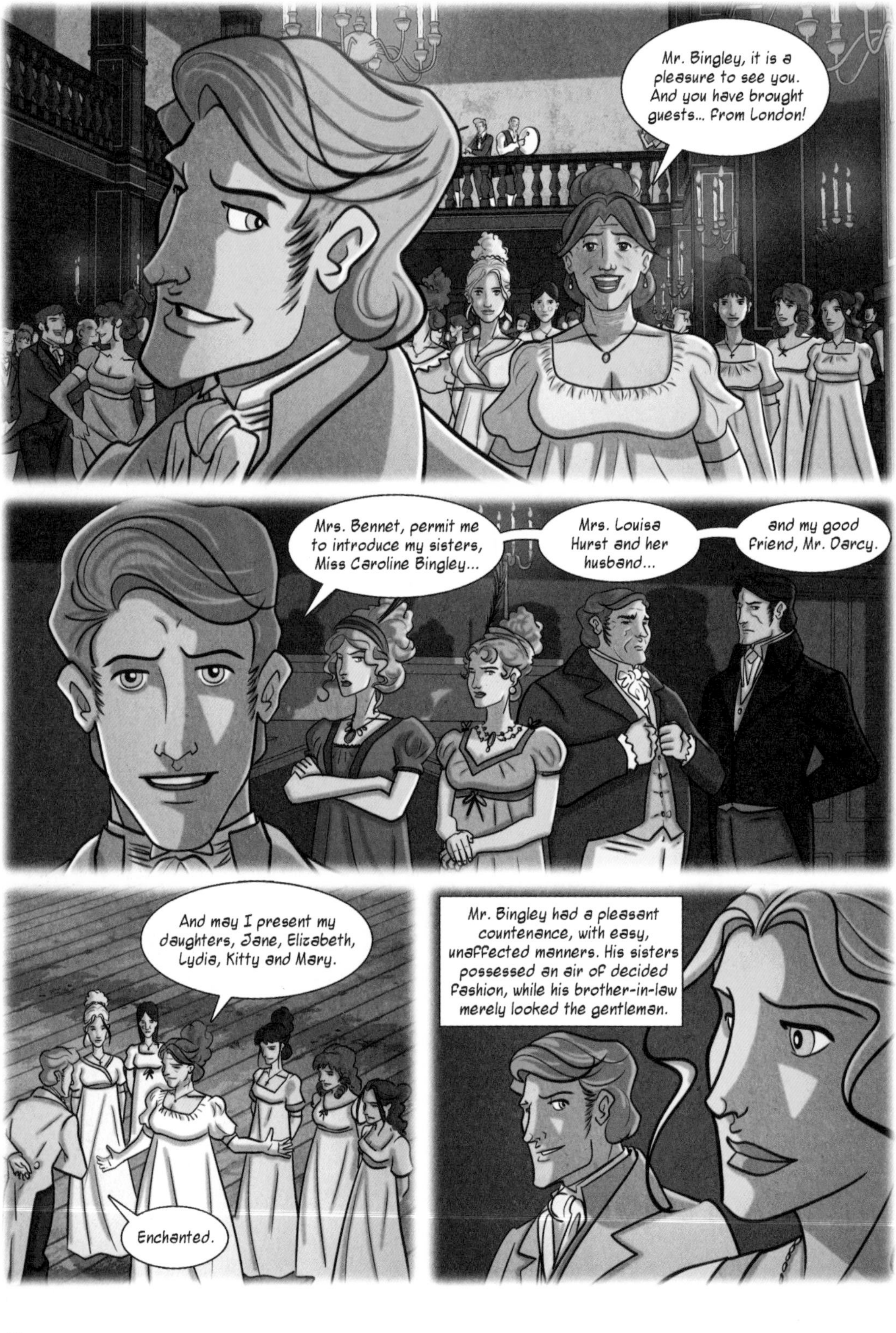
Mr. Bingley, it is a pleasure to see you. And you have brought guests... from London!
Mrs. Bennet, permit me to introduce my sisters, Miss Caroline Bingley...
Mrs. Louisa Hurst and her husband...
and my good friend, Mr. Darcy.
And may I present my daughters, Jane, Elizabeth, Lydia, Kitty and Mary.
Enchanted.
Mr. Bingley had a pleasant countenance, with easy, unaffected manners. His sisters possessed an air of decided fashion, while his brother-in-law merely looked the gentleman.

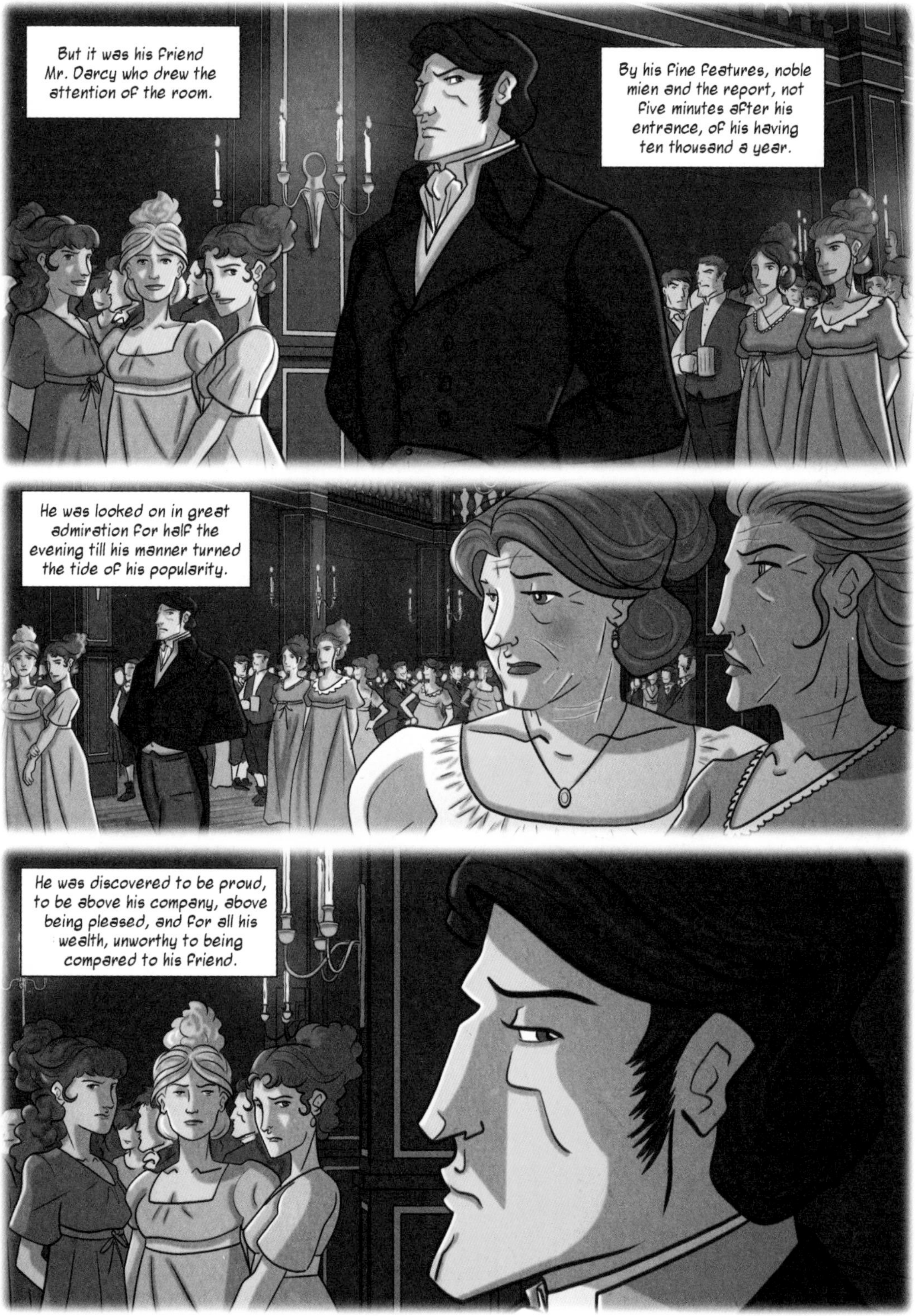
But it was his friend Mr. Darcy who drew the attention of the room.
By his fine features, noble mien and the report, not five minutes after his entrance, of his having ten thousand a year.
He was looked on in great admiration for half the evening till his manner turned the tide of his popularity.
He was discovered to be proud, to be above his company, above being pleased, and for all his wealth, unworthy to being compared to his friend.

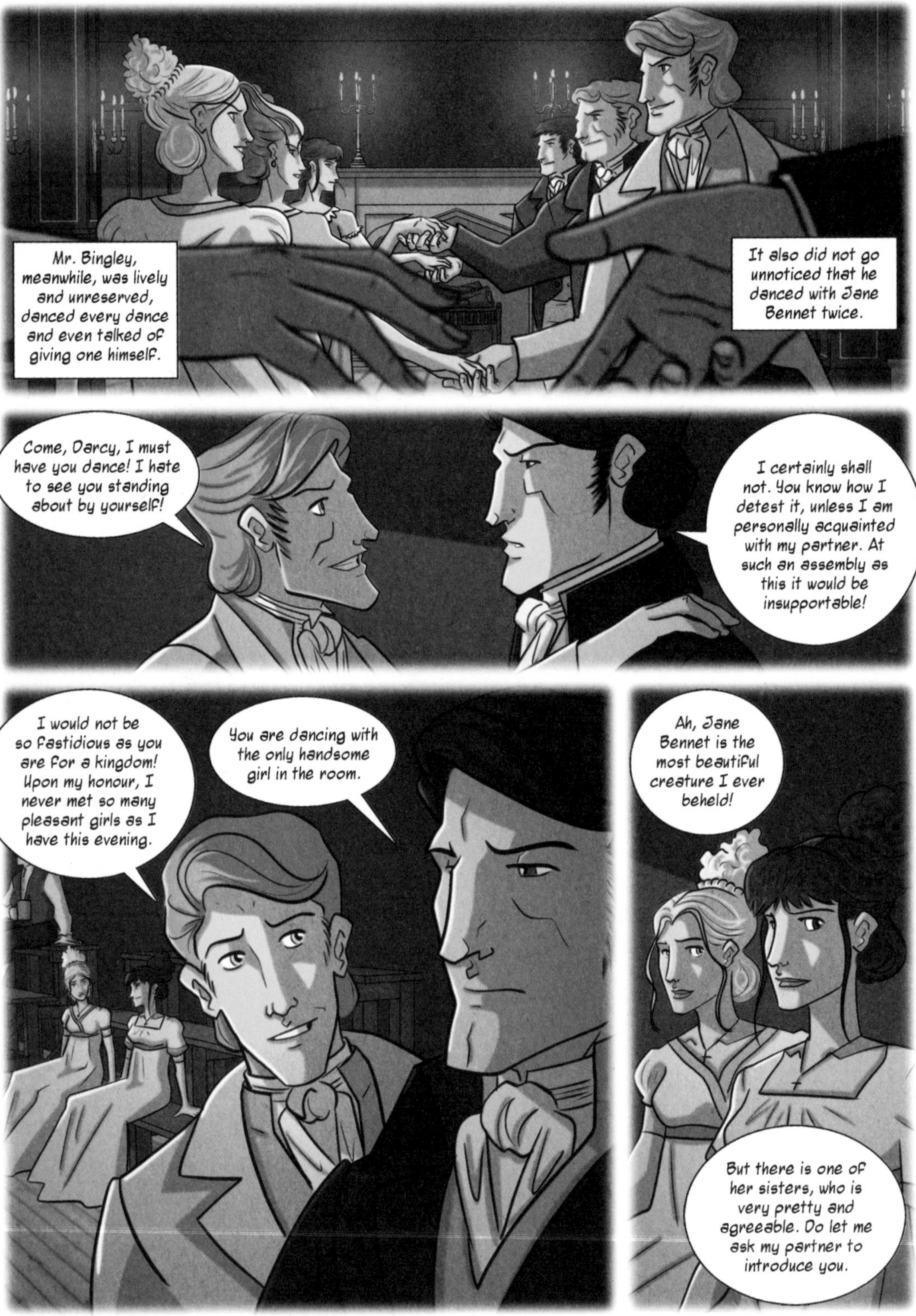
Mr. Bingley, meanwhile, was lively and unreserved, danced every dance and even talked of giving one himself.
It also did not go unnoticed that he danced with Jane Bennet twice.
Come, Darcy, I must have you dance! I hate to see you standing about by yourself!
I certainly shall not. You know how I detest it, unless I am personally acquainted with my partner. At such an assembly as this it would be insupportable!
I would not be so fastidious as you are for a kingdom! Upon my honour, I never met so many pleasant girls as I have this evening.
You are dancing with the only handsome girl in the room.
Ah, Jane Bennet is the most beautiful creature I ever beheld!
But there is one of her sisters, who is very pretty and agreeable. Do let me ask my partner to introduce you.

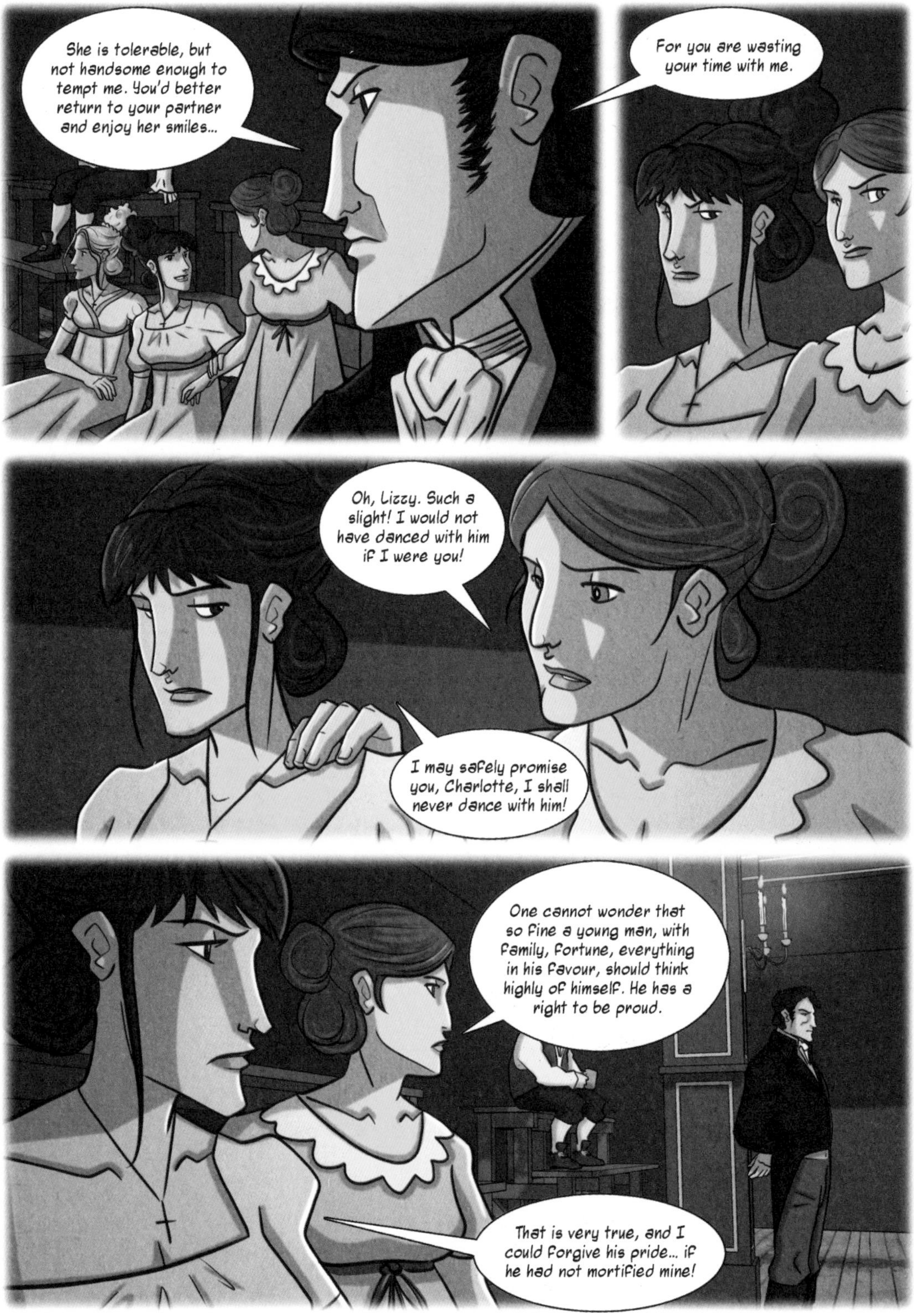
She is tolerable, but not handsome enough to tempt me. You'd better return to your partner and enjoy her smiles...
For you are wasting your time with me.
Oh, Lizzy. Such a slight! I would not have danced with him if I were you!
I may safely promise you, Charlotte, I shall never dance with him!
One cannot wonder that so fine a young man, with family, fortune, everything in his favour, should think highly of himself. He has a right to be proud.
That is very true, and I could forgive his pride... if he had not mortified mine!

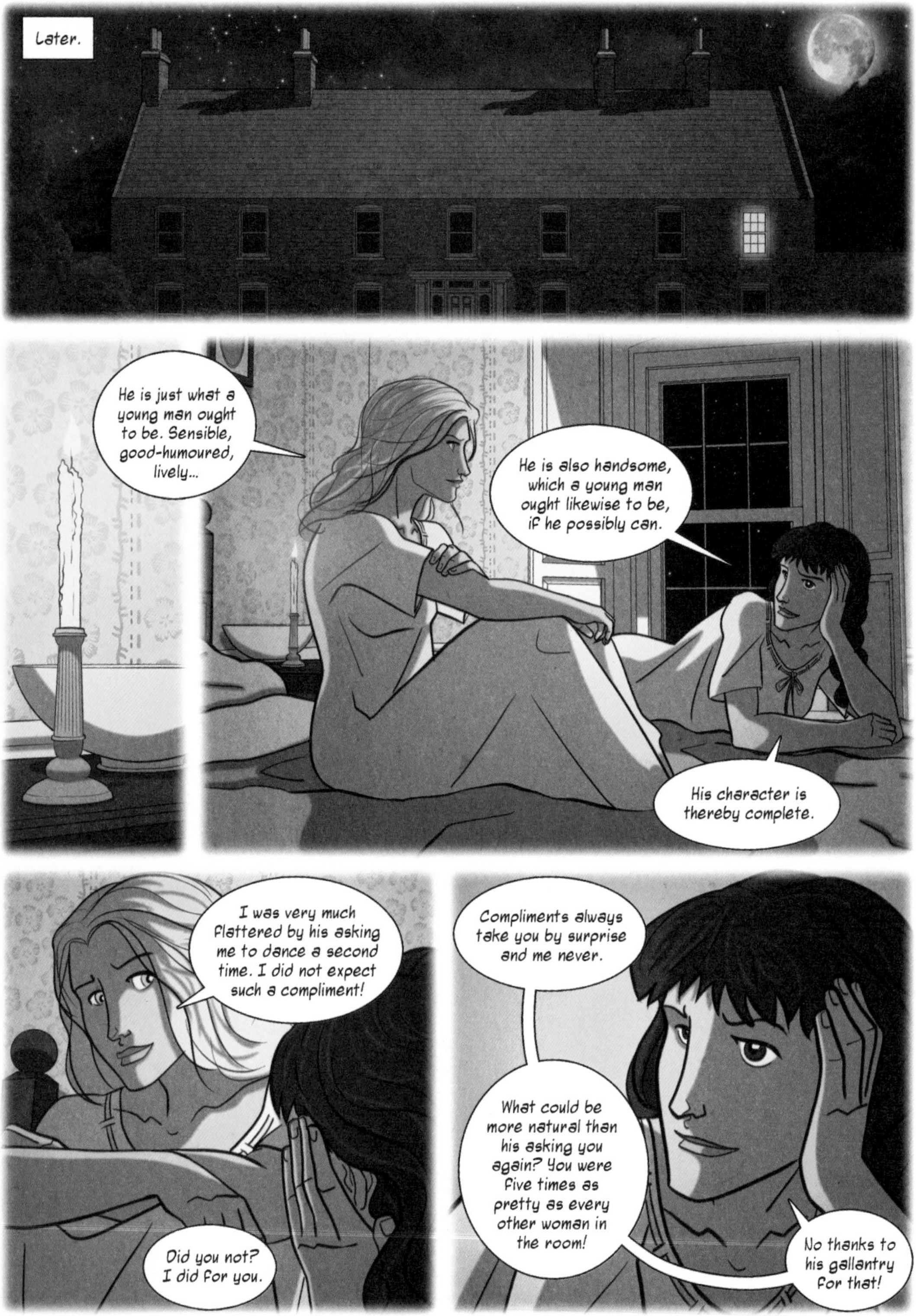

Later.
He is just what a young man ought to be. Sensible, good-humoured, lively...
He is also handsome, which a young man ought likewise to be, if he possibly can.
His character is thereby complete.
I was very much flattered by his asking me to dance a second time. I did not expect such a compliment!
Did you not? I did for you.
Compliments always take you by surprise and me never.
What could be more natural than his asking you again? You were five times as pretty as every other woman in the room!
No thanks to his gallantry for that!

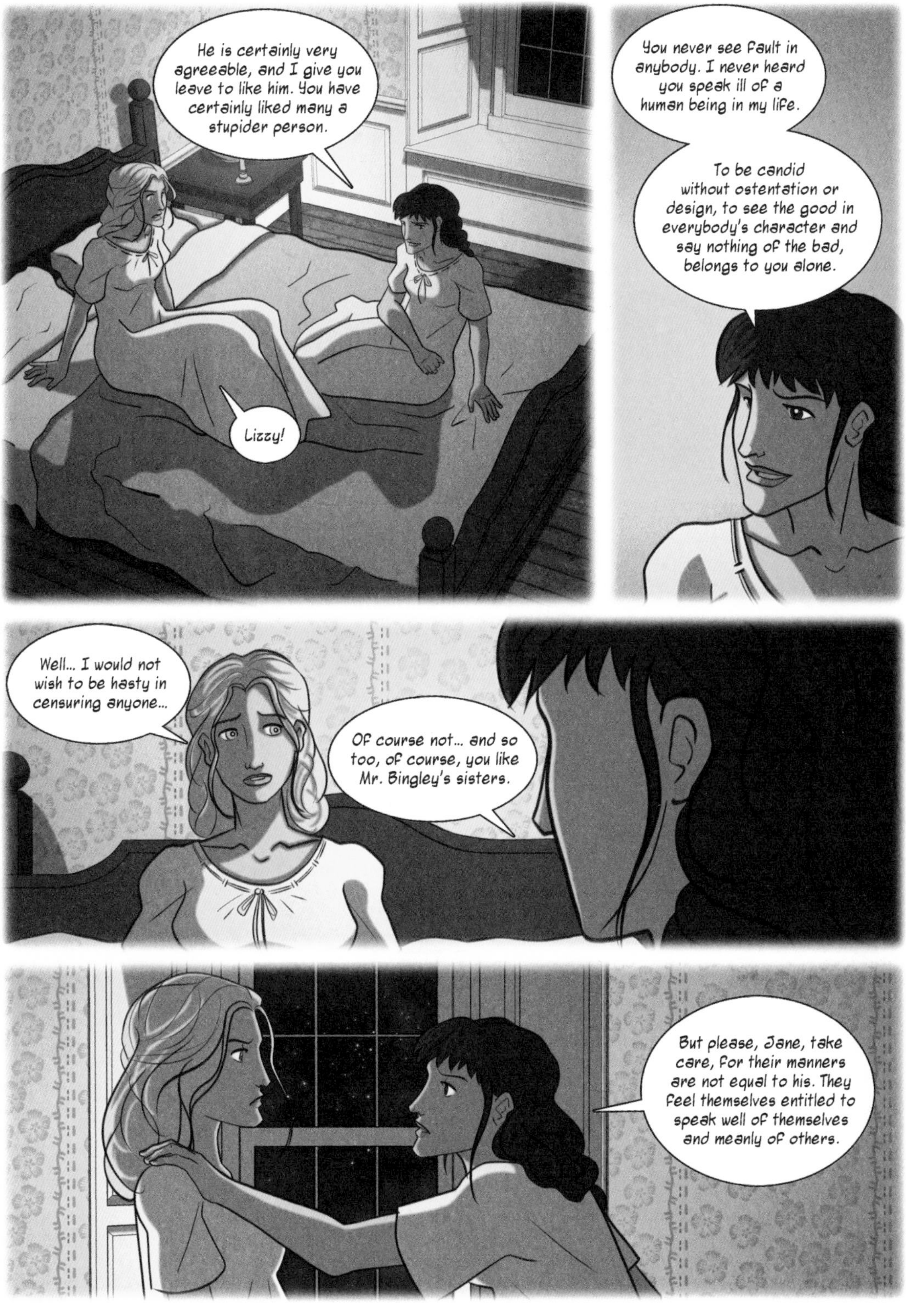
He is certainly very agreeable, and I give you leave to like him. You have certainly liked many a stupider person.
Lizzy!
You never see fault in anybody. I never heard you speak ill of a human being in my life.
To be candid without ostentation or design, to see the good in everybody's character and say nothing of the bad, belongs to you alone.
Well... I would not wish to be hasty in censuring anyone...
Of course not... and so too, of course, you like Mr. Bingley's sisters.
But please, Jane, take care, for their manners are not equal to his. They feel themselves entitled to speak well of themselves and meanly of others.

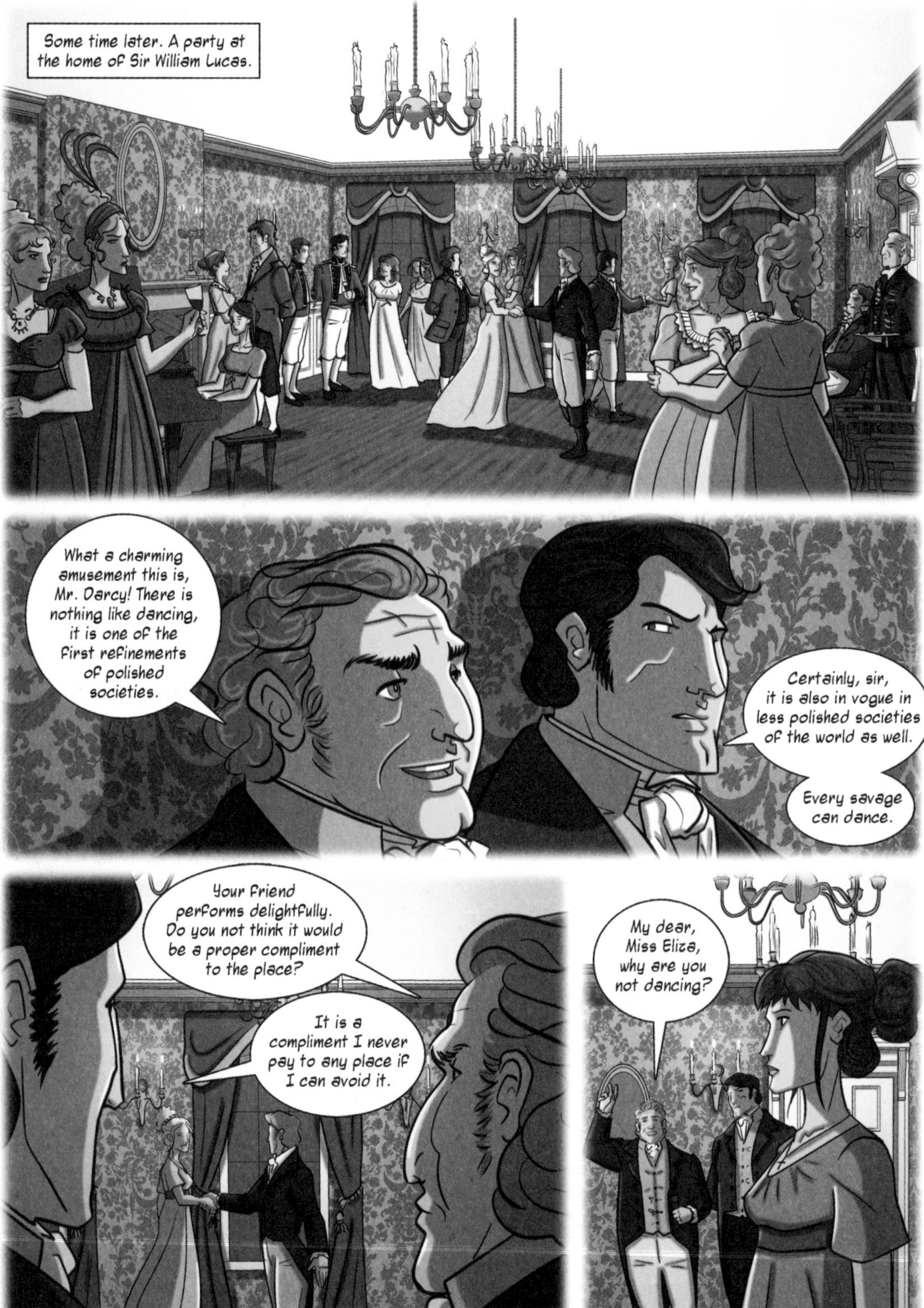
Some time later. A party at the home of Sir William Lucas.
What a charming amusement this is, Mr. Darcy! There is nothing like dancing, it is one of the first refinements of polished societies.
Certainly, sir, it is also in vogue in less polished societies of the world as well.
Every savage can dance.
Your friend performs delightfully. Do you not think it would be a proper compliment to the place?
It is a compliment I never pay to any place if I can avoid it.
My dear, Miss Eliza, why are you not dancing?

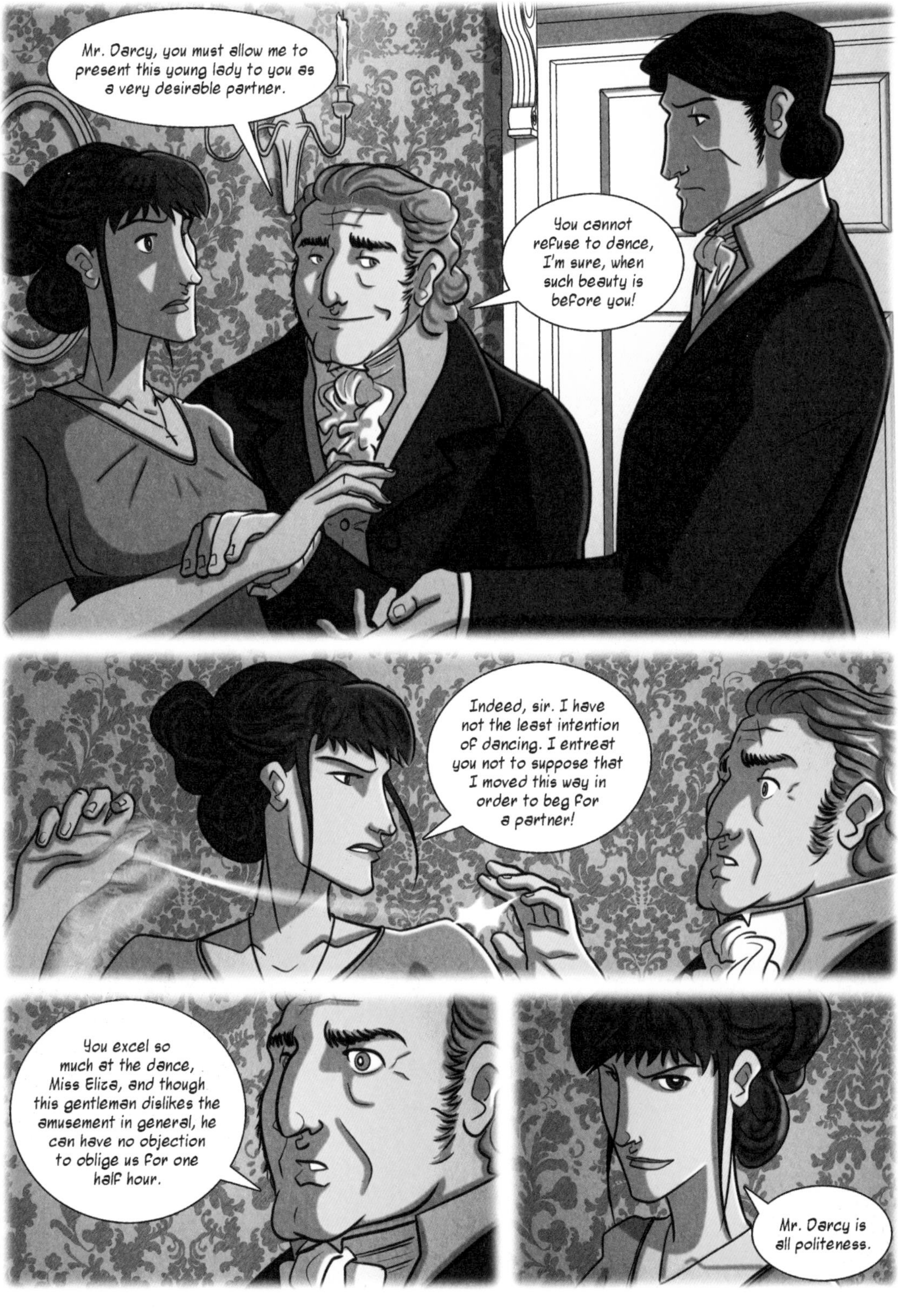
Mr. Darcy, you must allow me to present this young lady to you as a very desirable partner.
You cannot refuse to dance, I'm sure, when such beauty is before you!
Indeed, sir. I have not the least intention of dancing. I entreat you not to suppose that I moved this way in order to beg for a partner!
You excel so much at the dance, Miss Eliza, and though this gentleman dislikes the amusement in general, he can have no objection to oblige us for one half hour.
Mr. Darcy is all politeness.

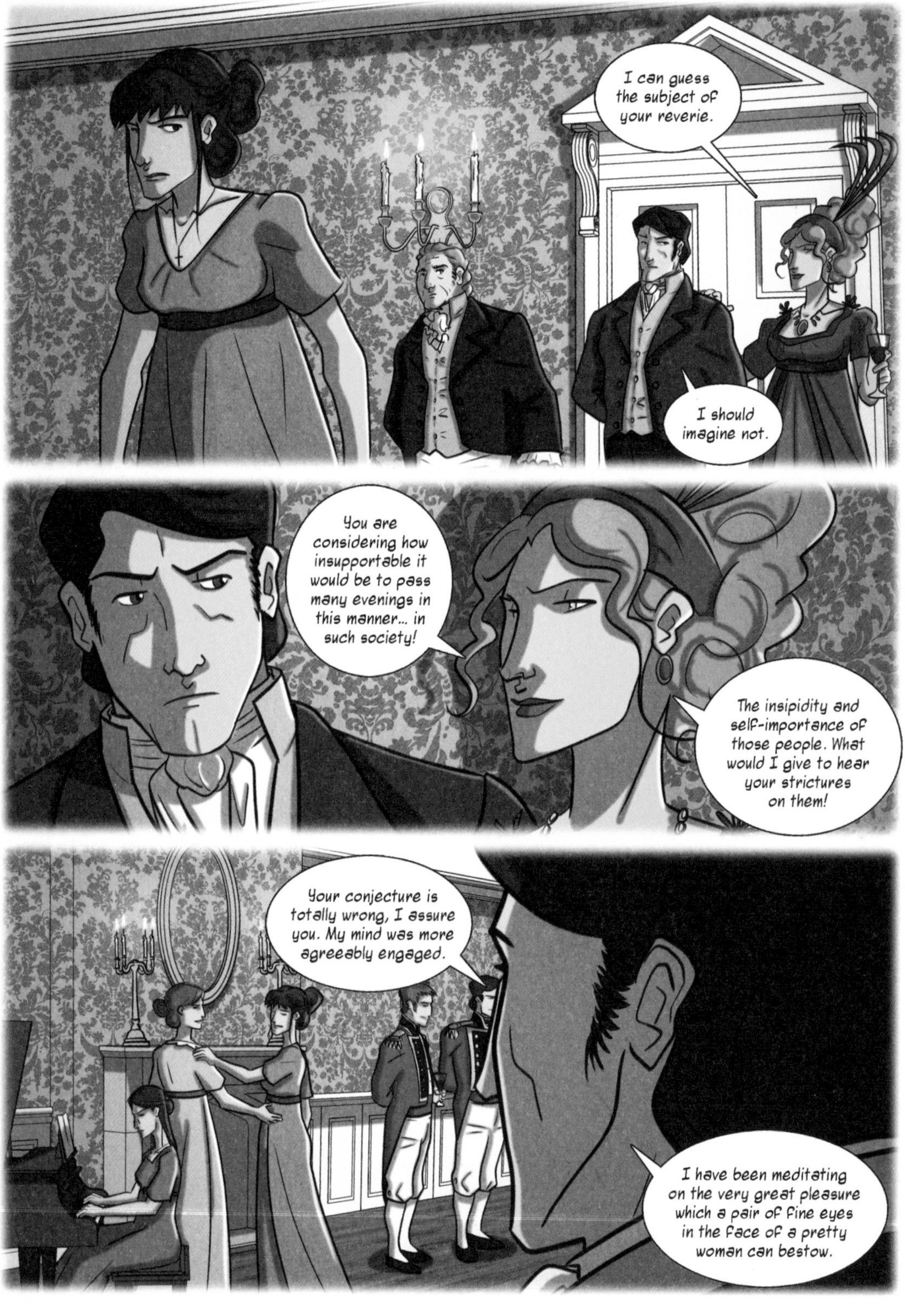
I can guess the subject of your reverie.
I should imagine not.
You are considering how insupportable it would be to pass many evenings in this manner... in such society!
The insipidity and self-importance of those people. What would I give to hear your strictures on them!
Your conjecture is totally wrong, I assure you. My mind was more agreeably engaged.
I have been meditating on the very great pleasure which a pair of fine eyes in the face of a pretty woman can bestow.

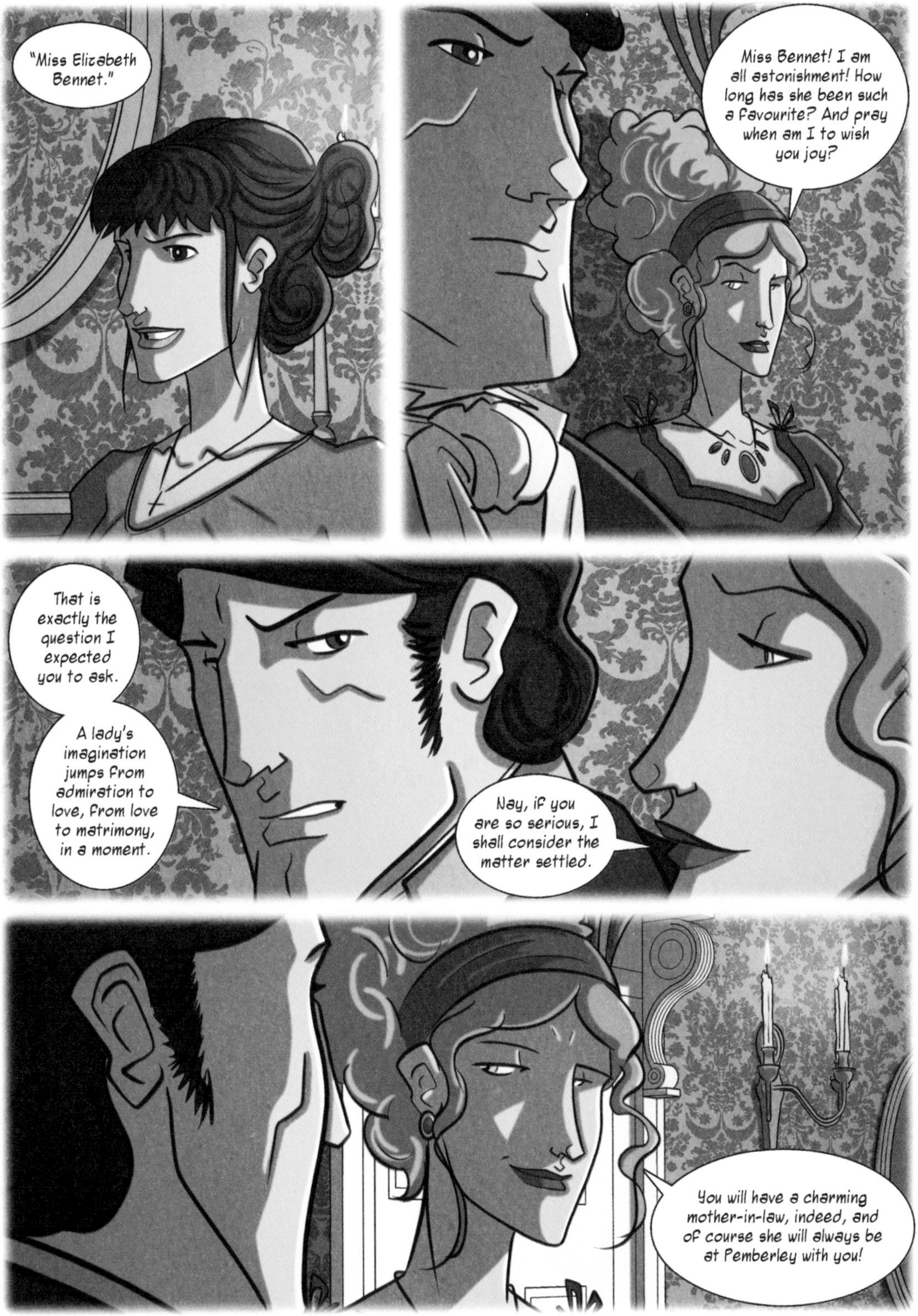
"Miss Elizabeth Bennet."
Miss Bennet! I am all astonishment! How long has she been such a favourite? And pray when am I to wish you joy?
That is exactly the question I expected you to ask.
A lady's imagination jumps from admiration to love, from love to matrimony, in a moment.
Nay, if you are so serious, I shall consider the matter settled.
You will have a charming mother-in-law, indeed, and of course she will always be at Pemberley with you!

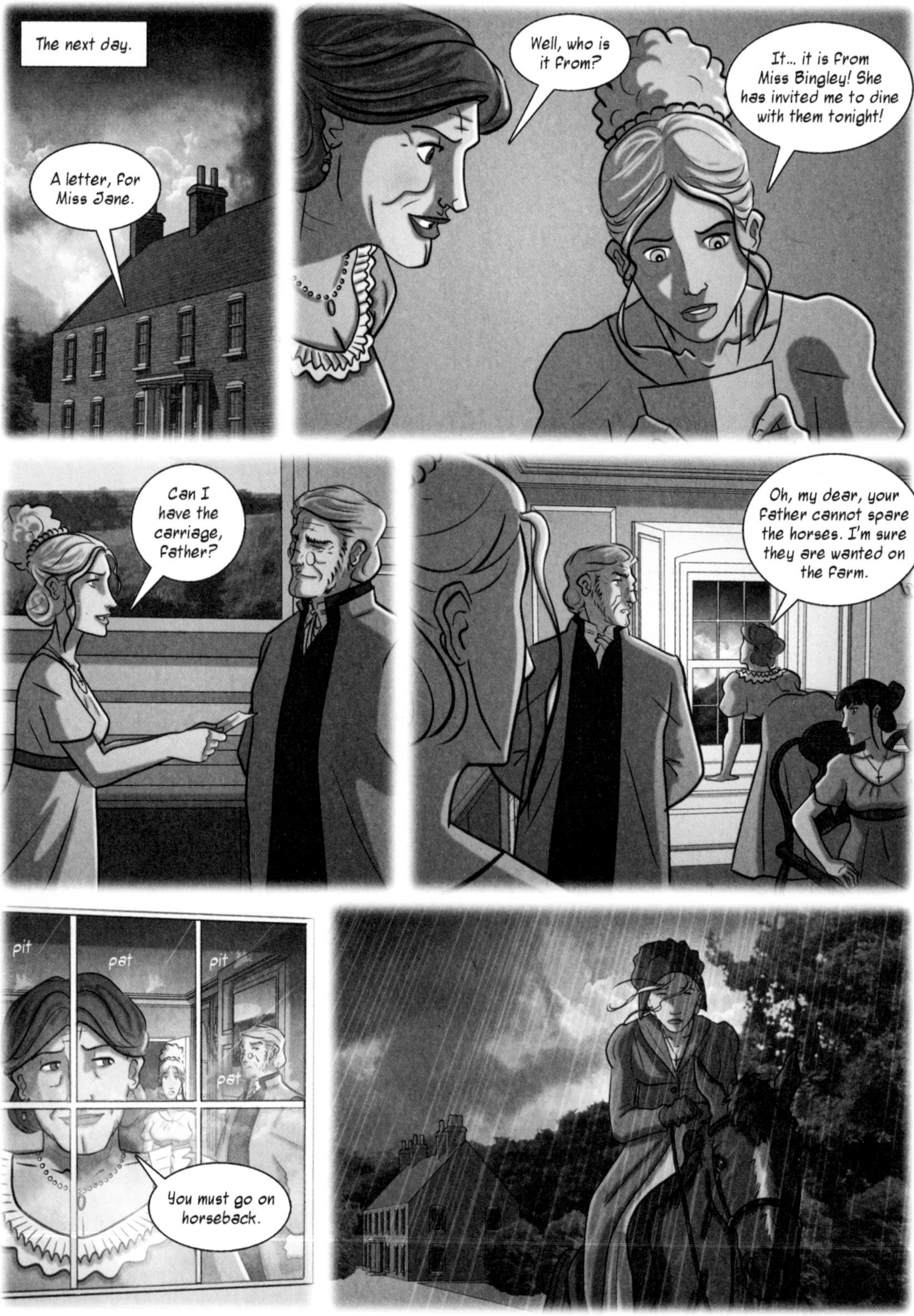
The next day.
A letter, for Miss Jane.
Well, who is it from?
It... it is from Miss Bingley! She has invited me to dine with them tonight!
Can I have the carriage, father?
Oh, my dear, your father cannot spare the horses. I'm sure they are wanted on the farm.
pit
pat
pit
pat
You must go on horseback.

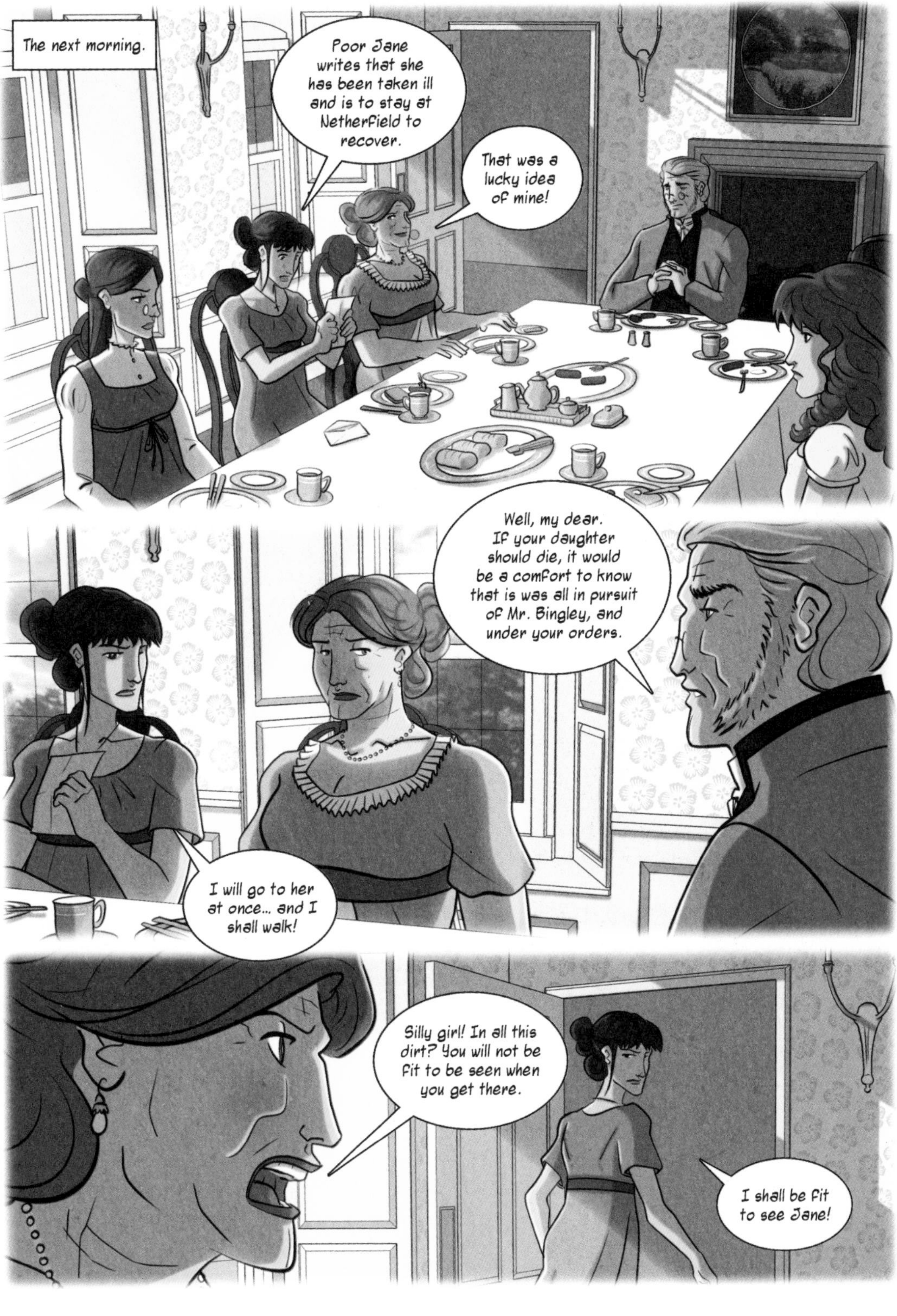
The next morning.
Poor Jane writes that she has been taken ill and is to stay at Netherfield to recover.
That was a lucky idea of mine!
Well, my dear. If your daughter should die, it would be a comfort to know that is was all in pursuit of Mr. Bingley, and under your orders.
I will go to her at once... and I shall walk!
Silly girl! In all this dirt? You will not be fit to be seen when you get there.
I shall be fit to see Jane!

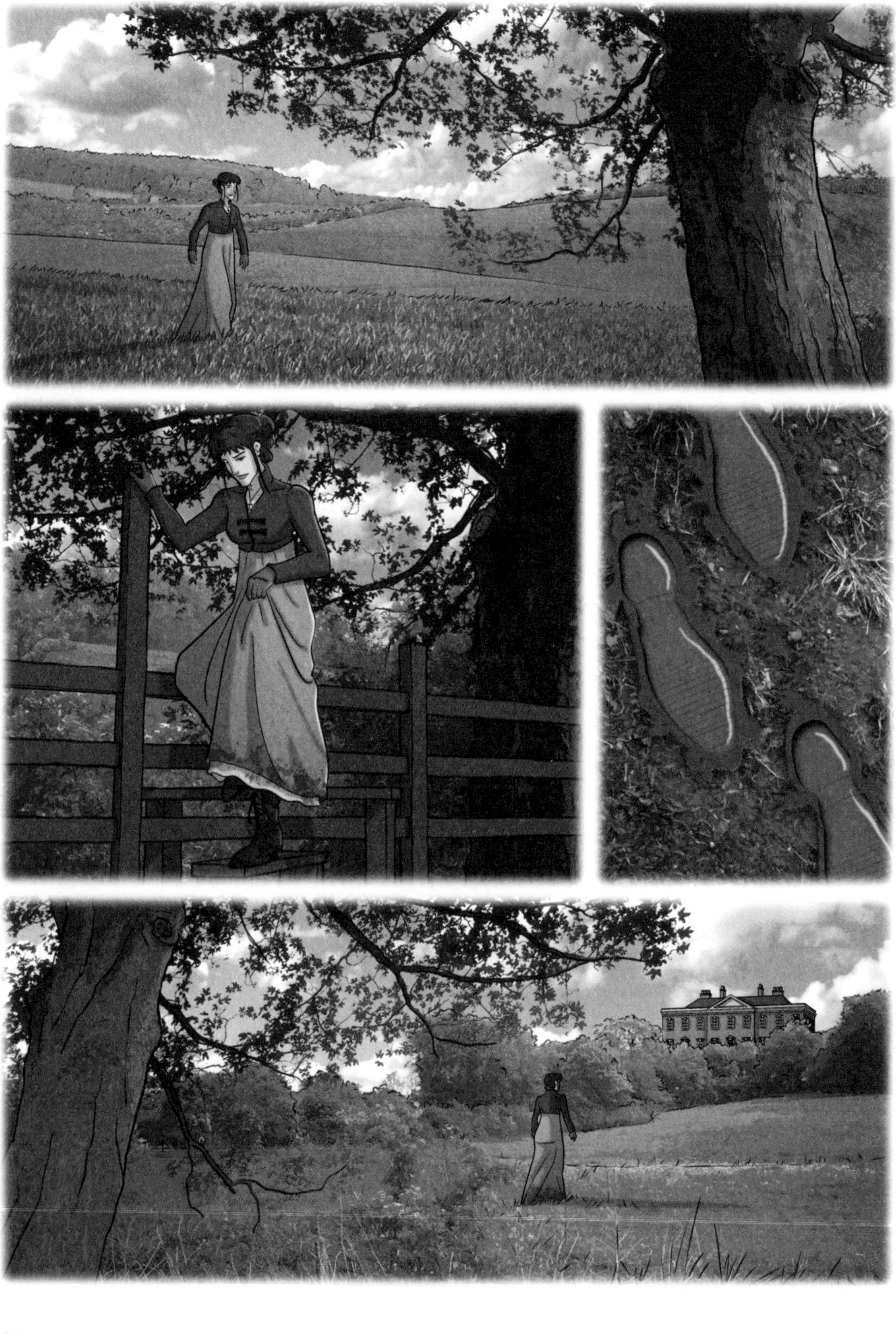

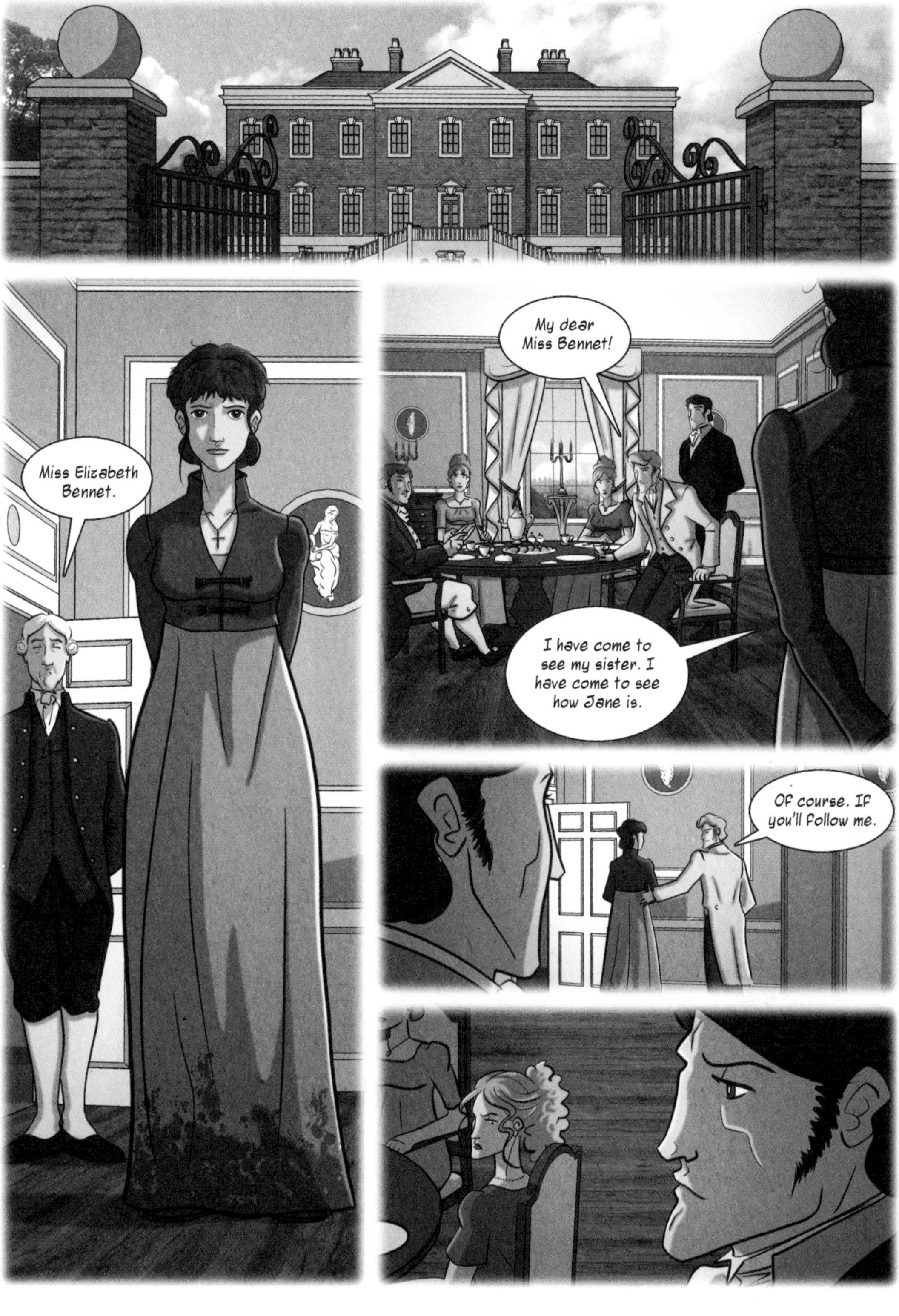
Miss Elizabeth Bennet.
My dear Miss Bennet!
I have come to see my sister. I have come to see how Jane is.
Of course. If you'll follow me.

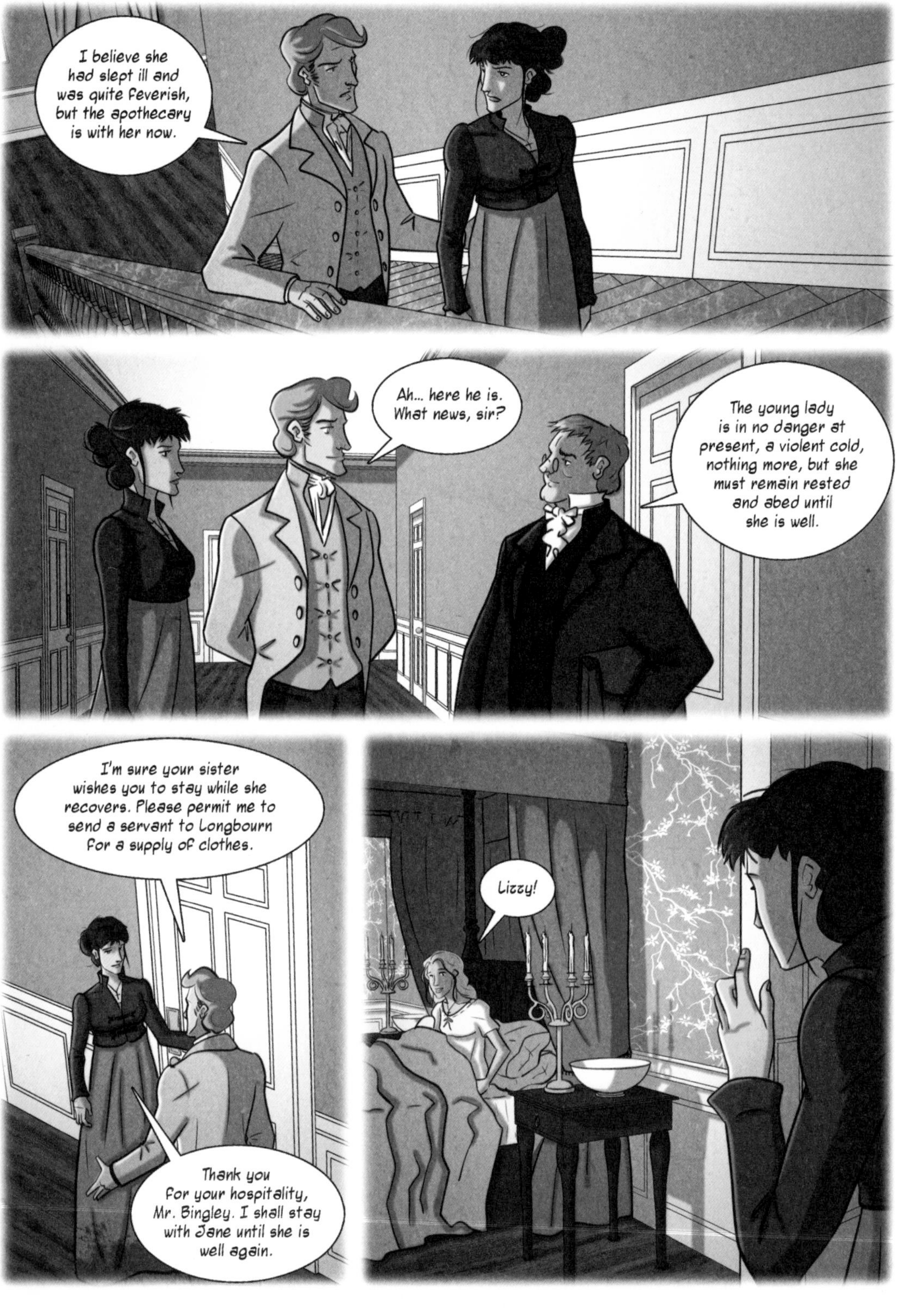
I believe she had slept ill and was quite feverish, but the apothecary is with her now.
Ah... here he is. What news, sir?
The young lady is in no danger at present, a violent cold, nothing more, but she must remain rested and abed until she is well.
I'm sure your sister wishes you to stay while she recovers. Please permit me to send a servant to Longbourn for a supply of clothes.
Thank you for your hospitality, Mr. Bingley. I shall stay with Jane until she is well again.
Lizzy!

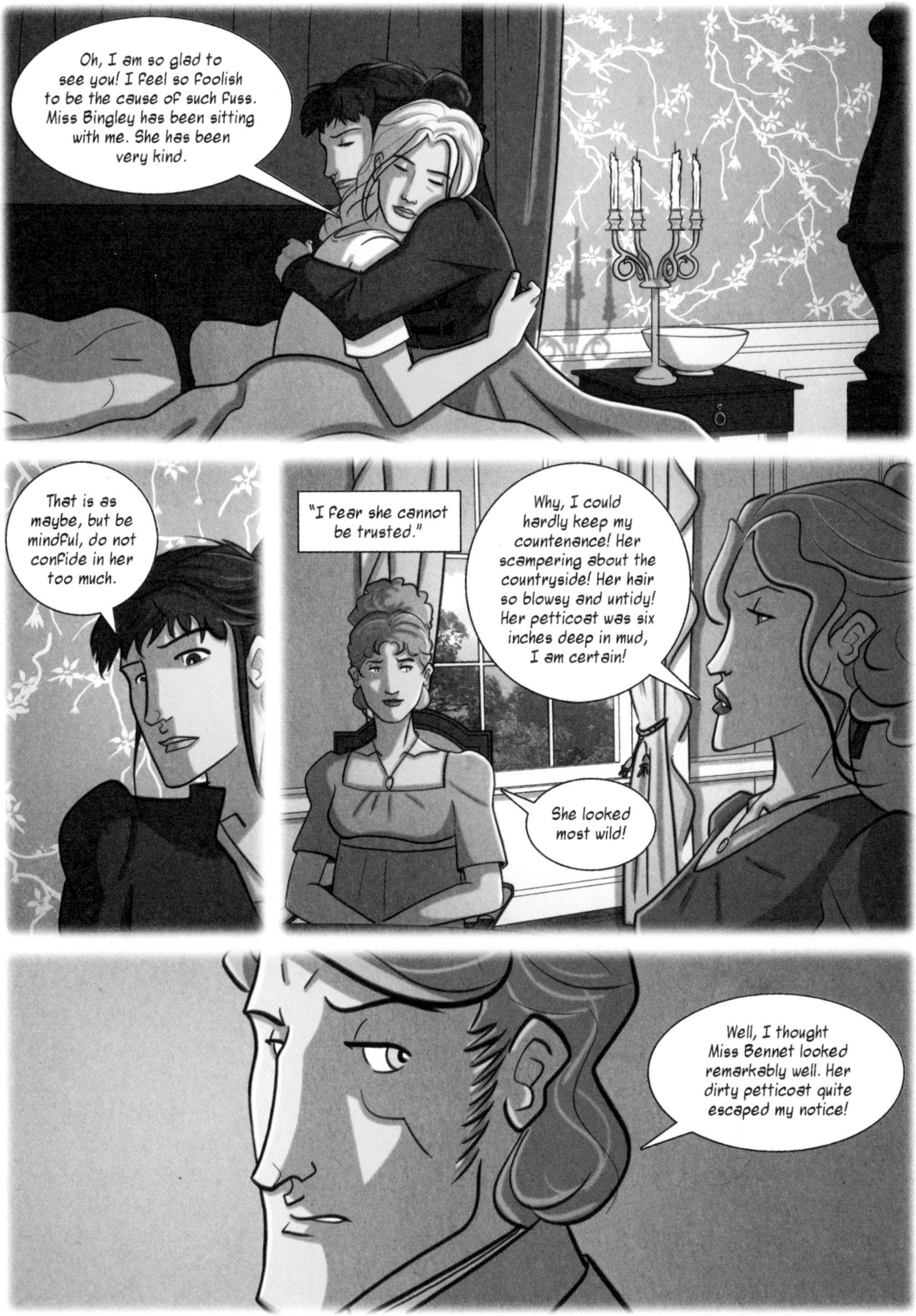
Oh, I am so glad to see you! I feel so foolish to be the cause of such fuss. Miss Bingley has been sitting with me. She has been very kind.
That is as maybe, but be mindful, do not confide in her too much.
"I fear she cannot be trusted."
Why, I could hardly keep my countenance! Her scampering about the countryside! Her hair so blowsy and untidy! Her petticoat was six inches deep in mud, I am certain!
She looked most wild!
Well, I thought Miss Bennet looked remarkably well. Her dirty petticoat quite escaped my notice!

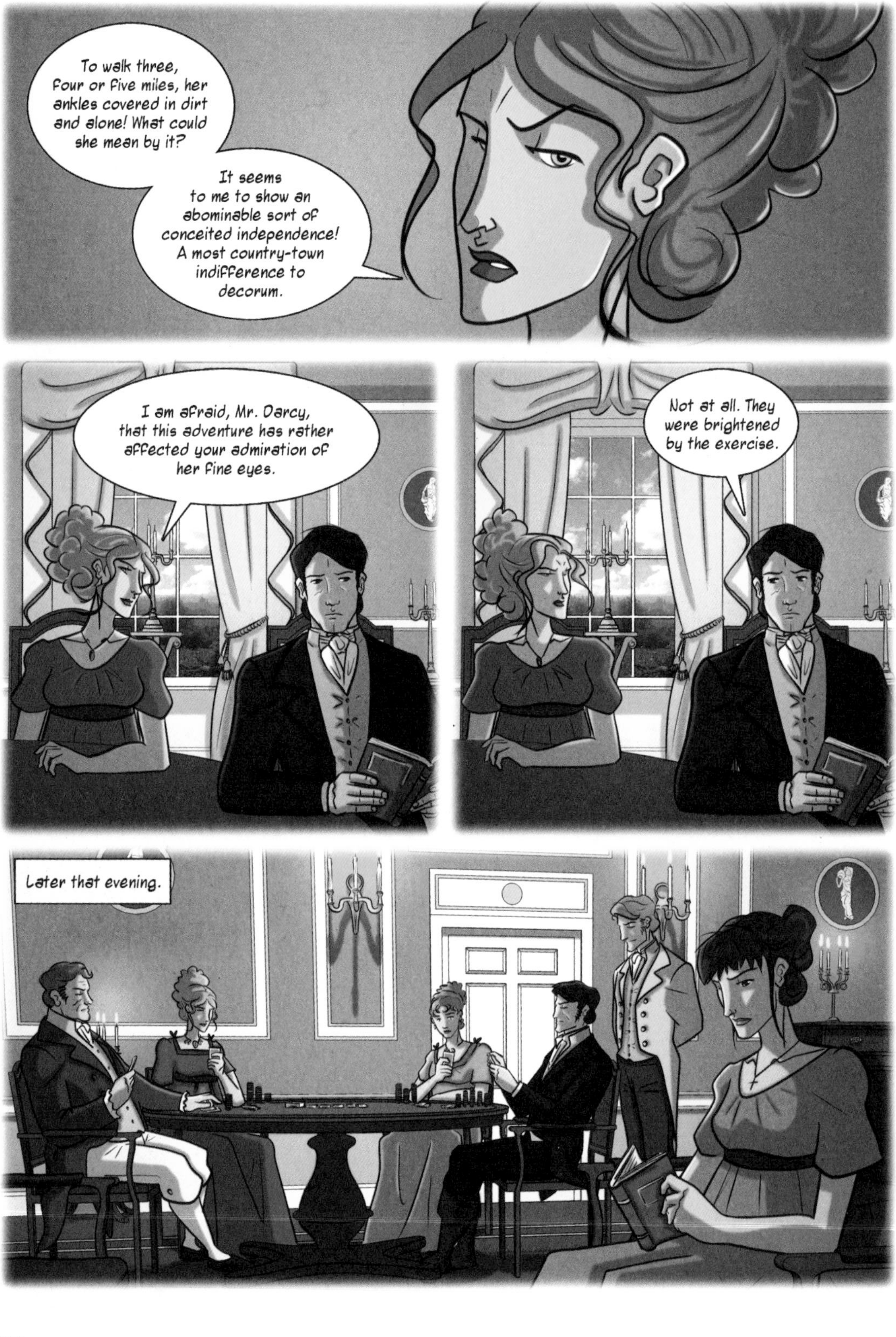
To walk three, four or five miles, her ankles covered in dirt and alone! What could she mean by it?
It seems to me to show an abominable sort of conceited independence! A most country-town indifference to decorum.
I am afraid, Mr. Darcy, that this adventure has rather affected your admiration of her fine eyes.
Not at all. They were brightened by the exercise.
Later that evening.

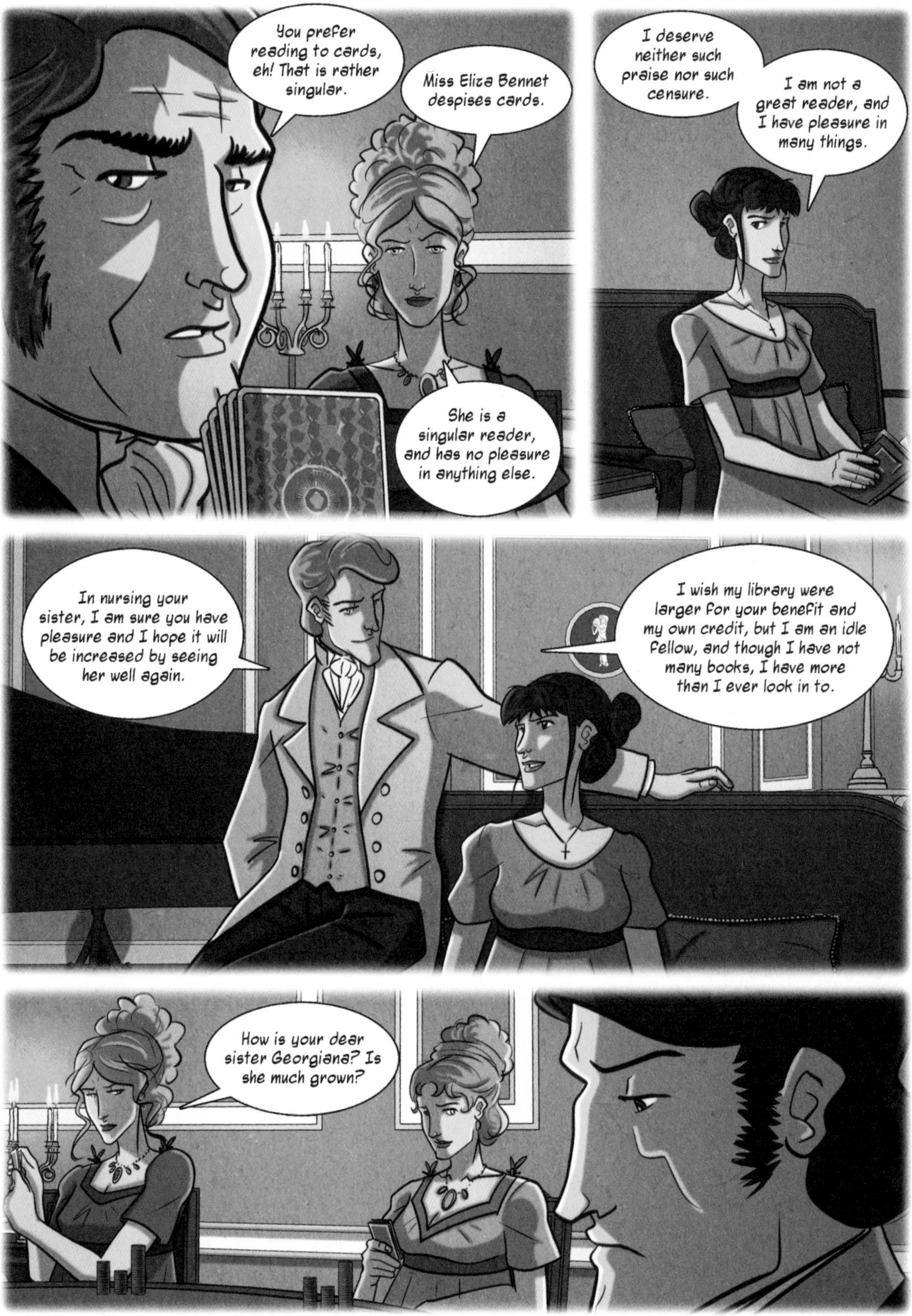
You prefer reading to cards, eh! That is rather singular.
Miss Eliza Bennet despises cards.
She is a singular reader, and has no pleasure in anything else.
I deserve neither such praise nor such censure.
I am not a great reader, and I have pleasure in many things.
In nursing your sister, I am sure you have pleasure and I hope it will be increased by seeing her well again.
I wish my library were larger for your benefit and my own credit, but I am an idle fellow, and though I have not many books, I have more than I ever look in to.
How is your dear sister Georgiana? Is she much grown?

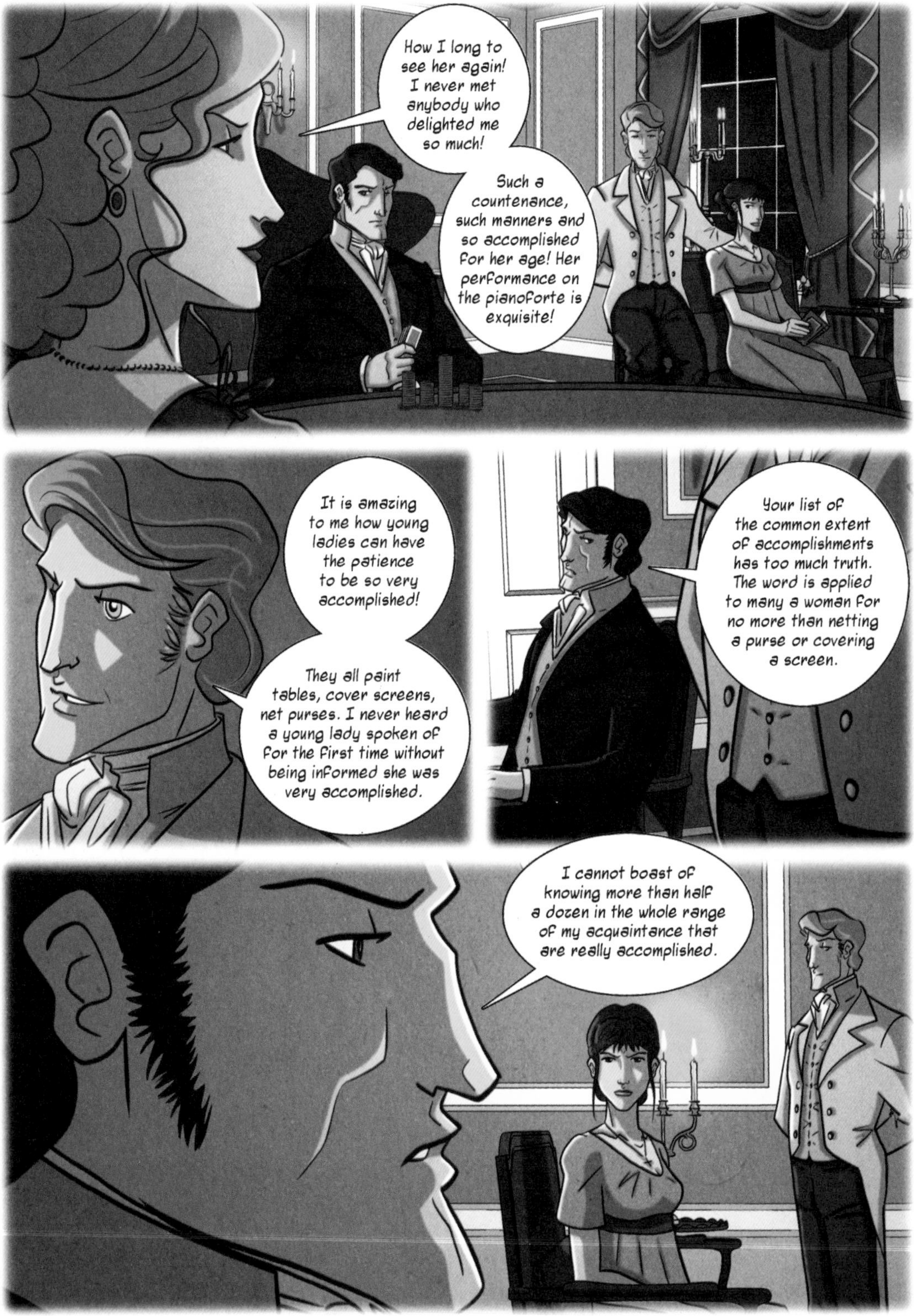
How I long to see her again! I never met anybody who delighted me so much!
Such a countenance, such manners and so accomplished for her age! Her performance on the pianoforte is exquisite!
It is amazing to me how young ladies can have the patience to be so very accomplished!
They all paint tables, cover screens, net purses. I never heard a young lady spoken of for the first time without being informed she was very accomplished.
Your list of the common extent of accomplishments has too much truth. The word is applied to many a woman for no more than netting a purse or covering a screen.
I cannot boast of knowing more than half a dozen in the whole range of my acquaintance that are really accomplished.

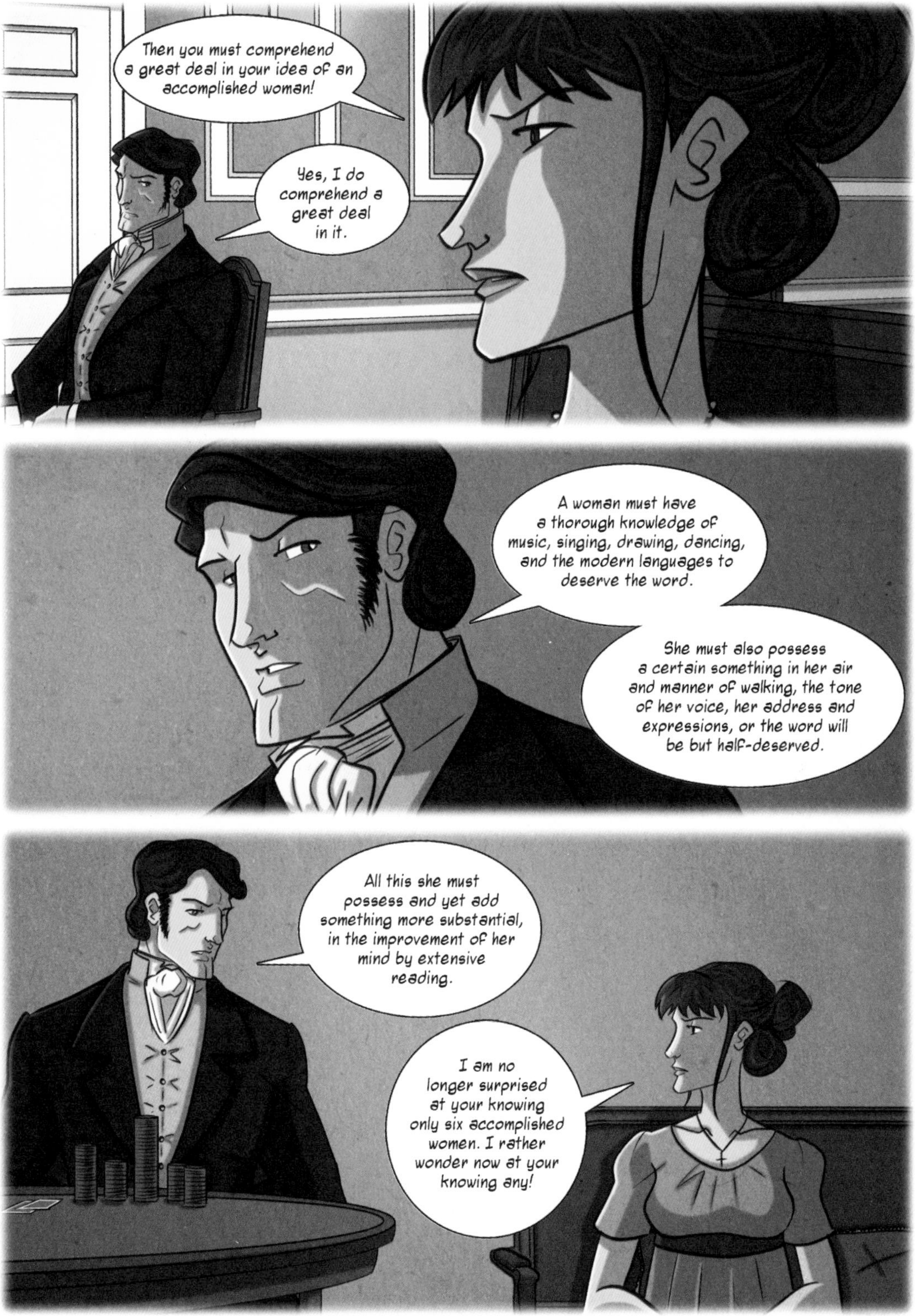
Then you must comprehend a great deal in your idea of an accomplished woman!
Yes, I do comprehend a great deal in it.
A woman must have a thorough knowledge of music, singing, drawing, dancing, and the modern languages to deserve the word.
She must also possess a certain something in her air and manner of walking, the tone of her voice, her address and expressions, or the word will be but half-deserved.
All this she must possess and yet add something more substantial, in the improvement of her mind by extensive reading.
I am no longer surprised at your knowing only six accomplished women. I rather wonder now at your knowing any!

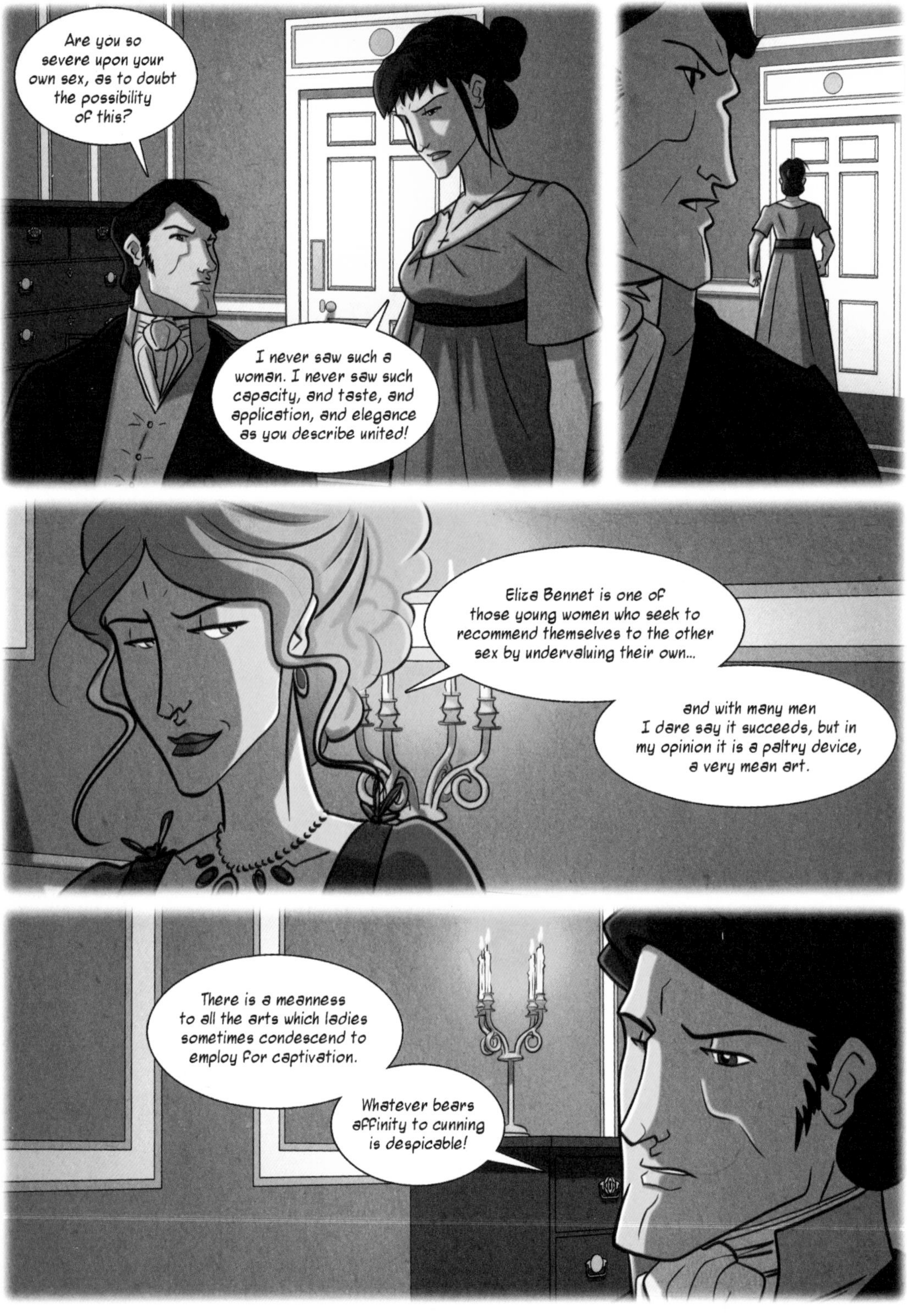
Are you so severe upon your own sex, as to doubt the possibility of this?
I never saw such a woman. I never saw such capacity, and taste, and application, and elegance as you describe united!
Eliza Bennet is one of those young women who seek to recommend themselves to the other sex by undervaluing their own...
and with many men I dare say it succeeds, but in my opinion it is a paltry device, a very mean art.
There is a meanness to all the arts which ladies sometimes condescend to employ for captivation.
Whatever bears affinity to cunning is despicable!

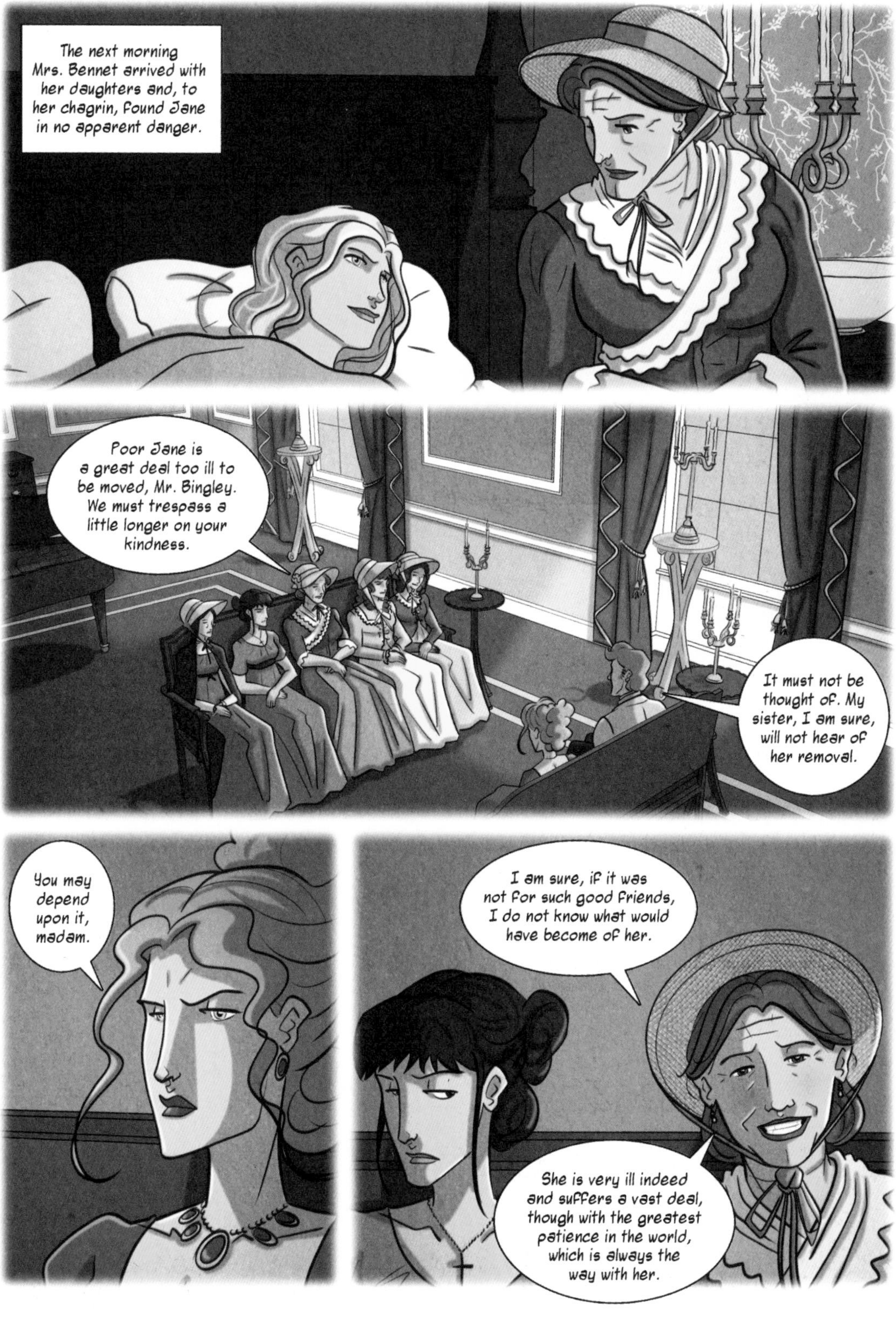
The next morning Mrs. Bennet arrived with her daughters and, to her chagrin, found Jane in no apparent danger.
Poor Jane is a great deal too ill to be moved, Mr. Bingley. We must trespass a little longer on your kindness.
It must not be thought of. My sister, I am sure, will not hear of her removal.
You may depend upon it, madam.
I am sure, if it was not for such good friends, I do not know what would have become of her.
She is very ill indeed and suffers a vast deal, though with the greatest patience in the world, which is always the way with her.

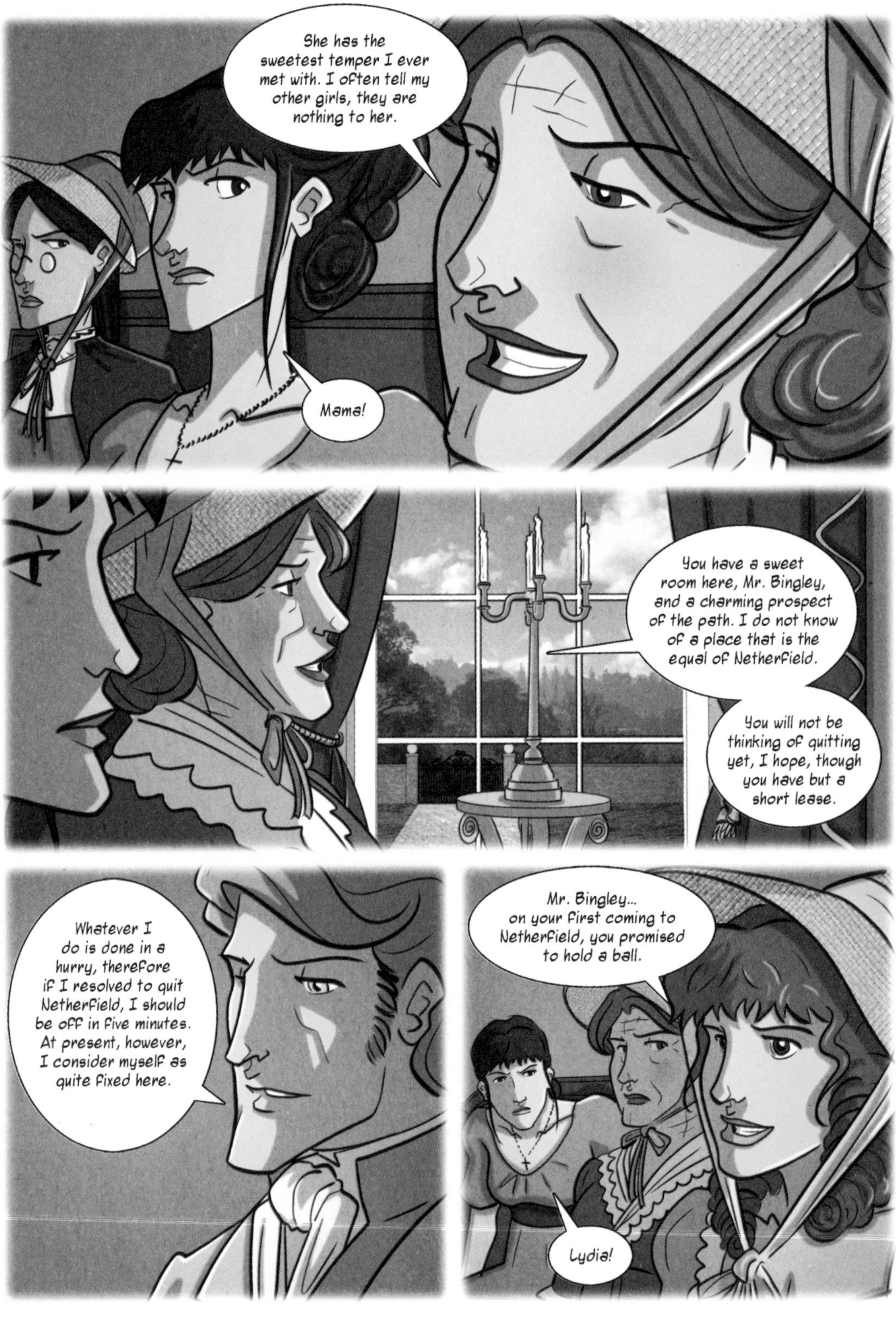
She has the sweetest temper I ever met with. I often tell my other girls, they are nothing to her.
Mama!
You have a sweet room here, Mr. Bingley, and a charming prospect of the path. I do not know of a place that is the equal of Netherfield.
You will not be thinking of quitting yet, I hope, though you have but a short lease.
Whatever I do is done in a hurry, therefore if I resolved to quit Netherfield, I should be off in five minutes. At present, however, I consider myself as quite fixed here.
Mr. Bingley... on your first coming to Netherfield, you promised to hold a ball.
Lydia!

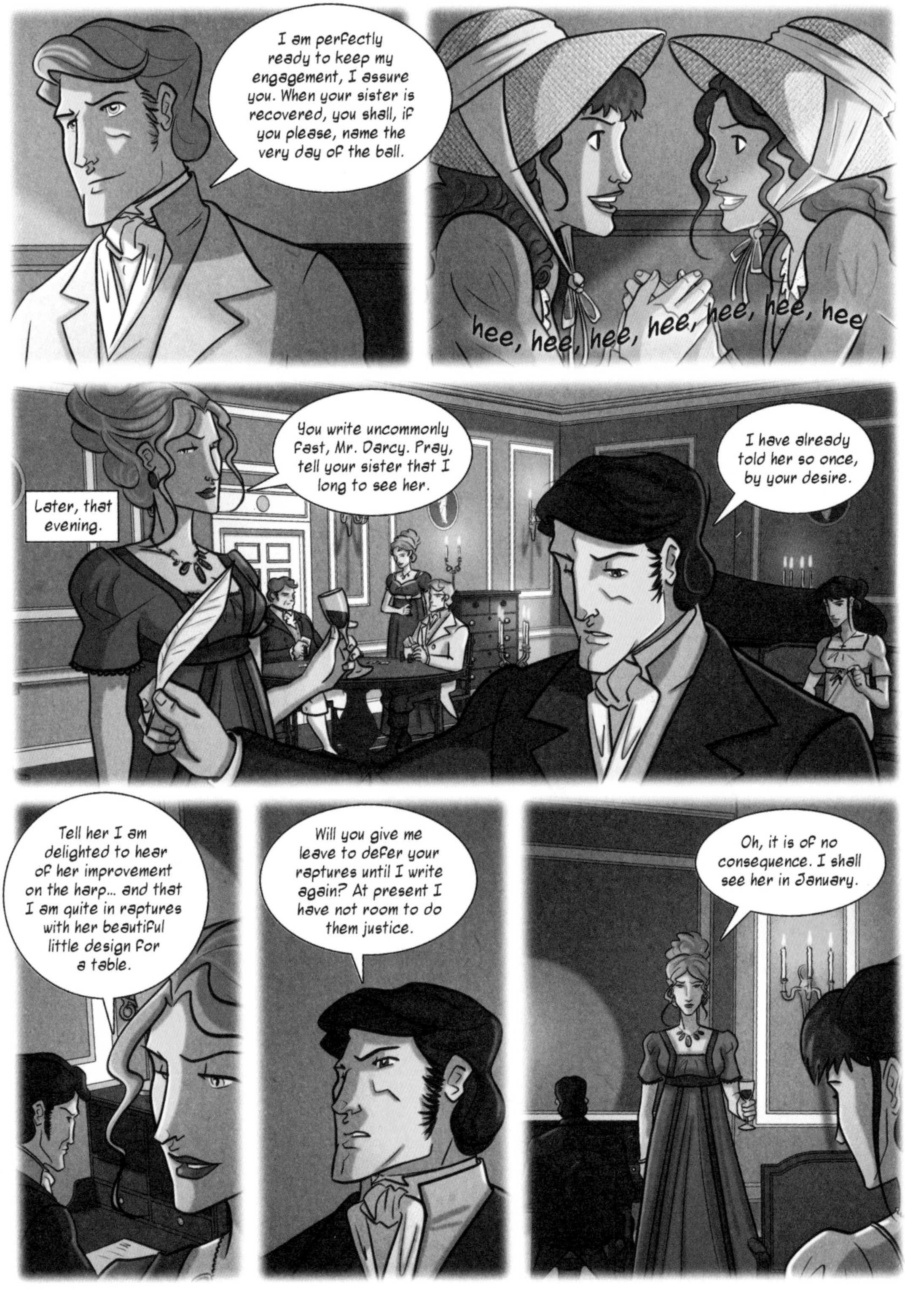
I am perfectly ready to keep my engagement, I assure you. When your sister is recovered, you shall, if you please, name the very day of the ball.
hee, hee, hee, hee, hee, hee, hee
Later, that evening.
You write uncommonly fast, Mr. Darcy. Pray, tell your sister that I long to see her.
I have already told her so once, by your desire.
Tell her I am delighted to hear of her improvement on the harp... and that I am quite in raptures with her beautiful little design for a table.
Will you give me leave to defer your raptures until I write again? At present I have not room to do them justice.
Oh, it is of no consequence. I shall see her in January.

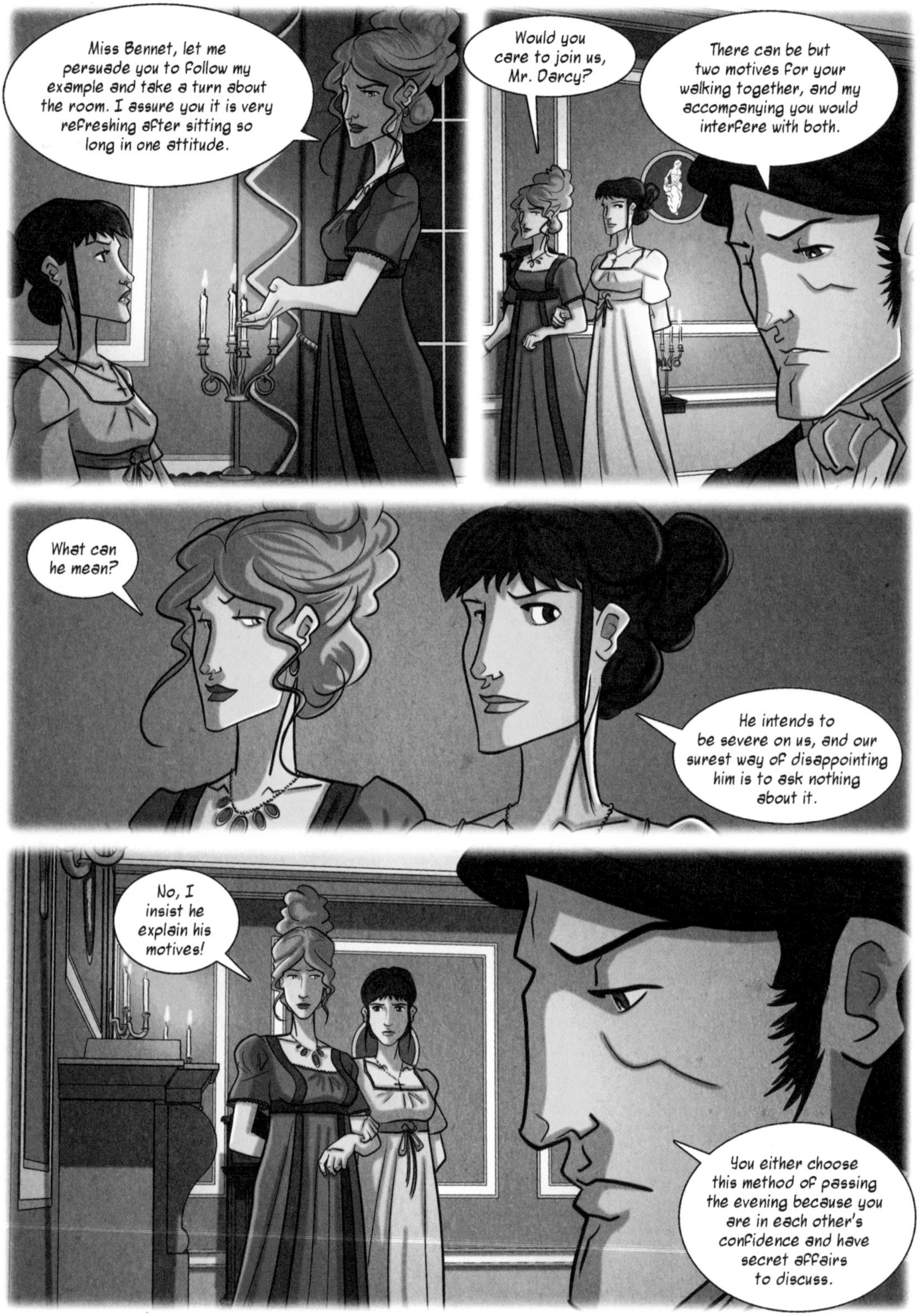
Miss Bennet, let me persuade you to follow my example and take a turn about the room. I assure you it is very refreshing after sitting so long in one attitude.
Would you care to join us, Mr. Darcy?
There can be but two motives for your walking together, and my accompanying you would interfere with both.
What can he mean?
He intends to be severe on us, and our surest way of disappointing him is to ask nothing about it.
No, I insist he explain his motives!
You either choose this method of passing the evening because you are in each other's confidence and have secret affairs to discuss.

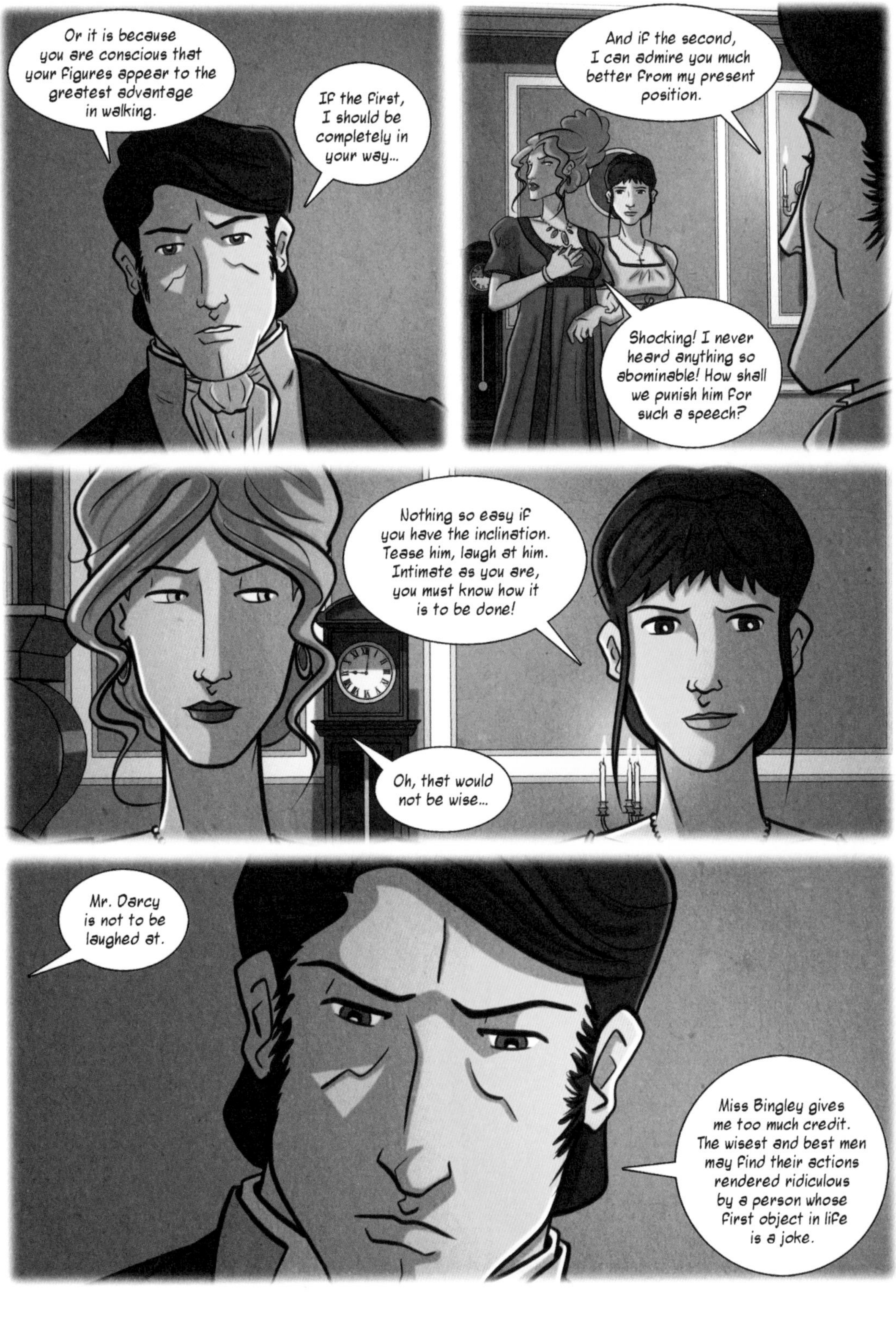
Or it is because you are conscious that your figures appear to the greatest advantage in walking.
If the first, I should be completely in your way...
And if the second, I can admire you much better from my present position.
Shocking! I never heard anything so abominable! How shall we punish him for such a speech?
Nothing so easy if you have the inclination. Tease him, laugh at him. Intimate as you are, you must know how it is to be done!
Oh, that would not be wise...
Mr. Darcy is not to be laughed at.
Miss Bingley gives me too much credit. The wisest and best men may find their actions rendered ridiculous by a person whose first object in life is a joke.

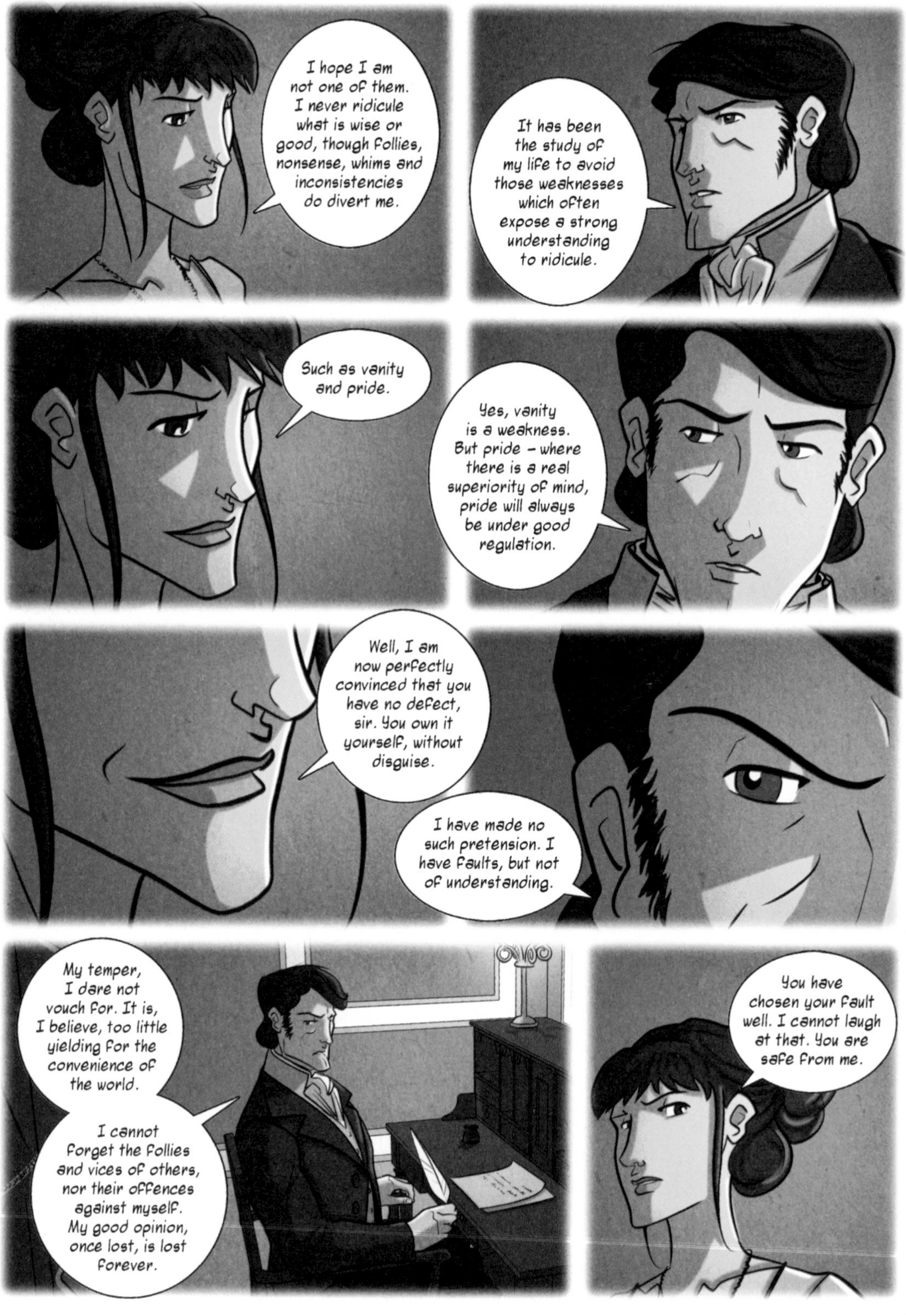
I hope I am not one of them. I never ridicule what is wise or good, though follies, nonsense, whims and inconsistencies do divert me.
It has been the study of my life to avoid those weaknesses which often expose a strong understanding to ridicule.
Such as vanity and pride.
Yes, vanity is a weakness. But pride – where there is a real superiority of mind, pride will always be under good regulation.
Well, I am now perfectly convinced that you have no defect, sir. You own it yourself, without disguise.
I have made no such pretension. I have faults, but not of understanding.
My temper, I dare not vouch for. It is, I believe, too little yielding for the convenience of the world.
I cannot forget the follies and vices of others, nor their offences against myself. My good opinion, once lost, is lost forever.
You have chosen your fault well. I cannot laugh at that. You are safe from me.

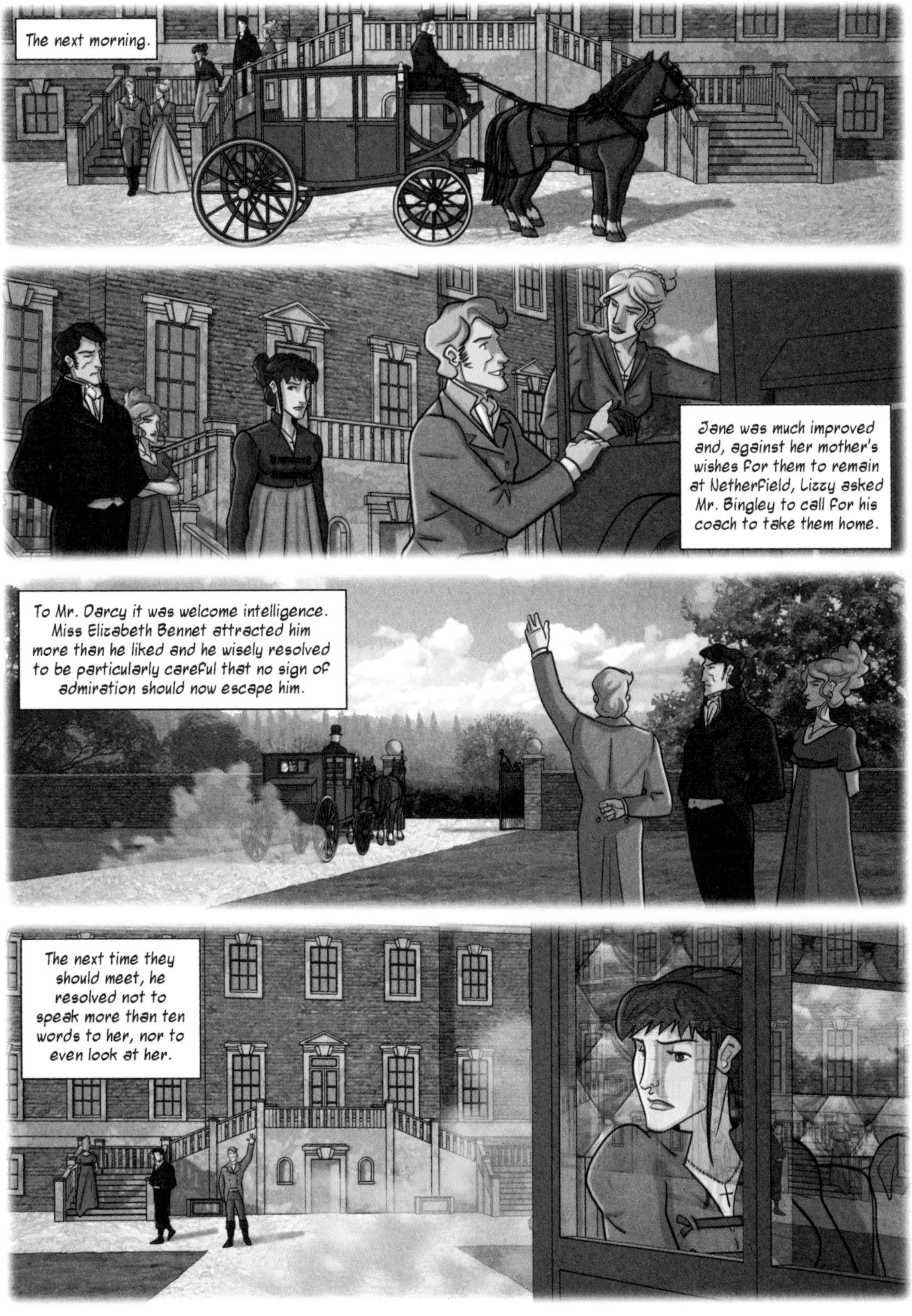
The next morning.
Jane was much improved and, against her mother's wishes for them to remain at Netherfield, Lizzy asked Mr. Bingley to call for his coach to take them home.
To Mr. Darcy it was welcome intelligence. Miss Elizabeth Bennet attracted him more than he liked and he wisely resolved to be particularly careful that no sign of admiration should now escape him.
The next time they should meet, he resolved not to speak more than ten words to her, nor to even look at her.

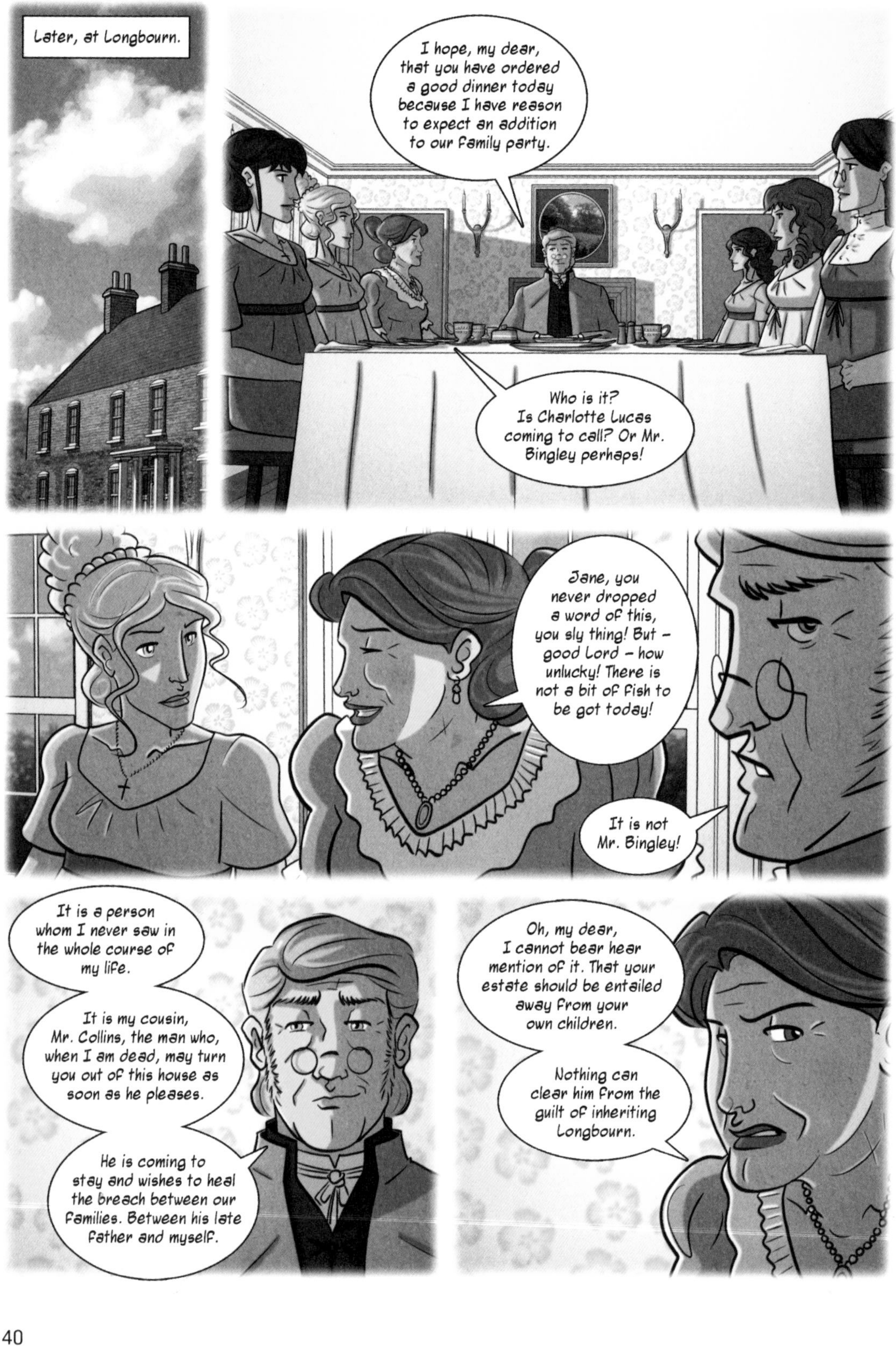
Later, at Longbourn.
I hope, my dear, that you have ordered a good dinner today because I have reason to expect an addition to our family party.
Who is it? Is Charlotte Lucas coming to call? Or Mr. Bingley perhaps!
Jane, you never dropped a word of this, you sly thing! But – good Lord – how unlucky! There is not a bit of fish to be got today!
It is not Mr. Bingley!
It is a person whom I never saw in the whole course of my life.
It is my cousin, Mr. Collins, the man who, when I am dead, may turn you out of this house as soon as he pleases.
He is coming to stay and wishes to heal the breach between our families. Between his late father and myself.
Oh, my dear, I cannot bear hear mention of it. That your estate should be entailed away from your own children.
Nothing can clear him from the guilt of inheriting Longbourn.

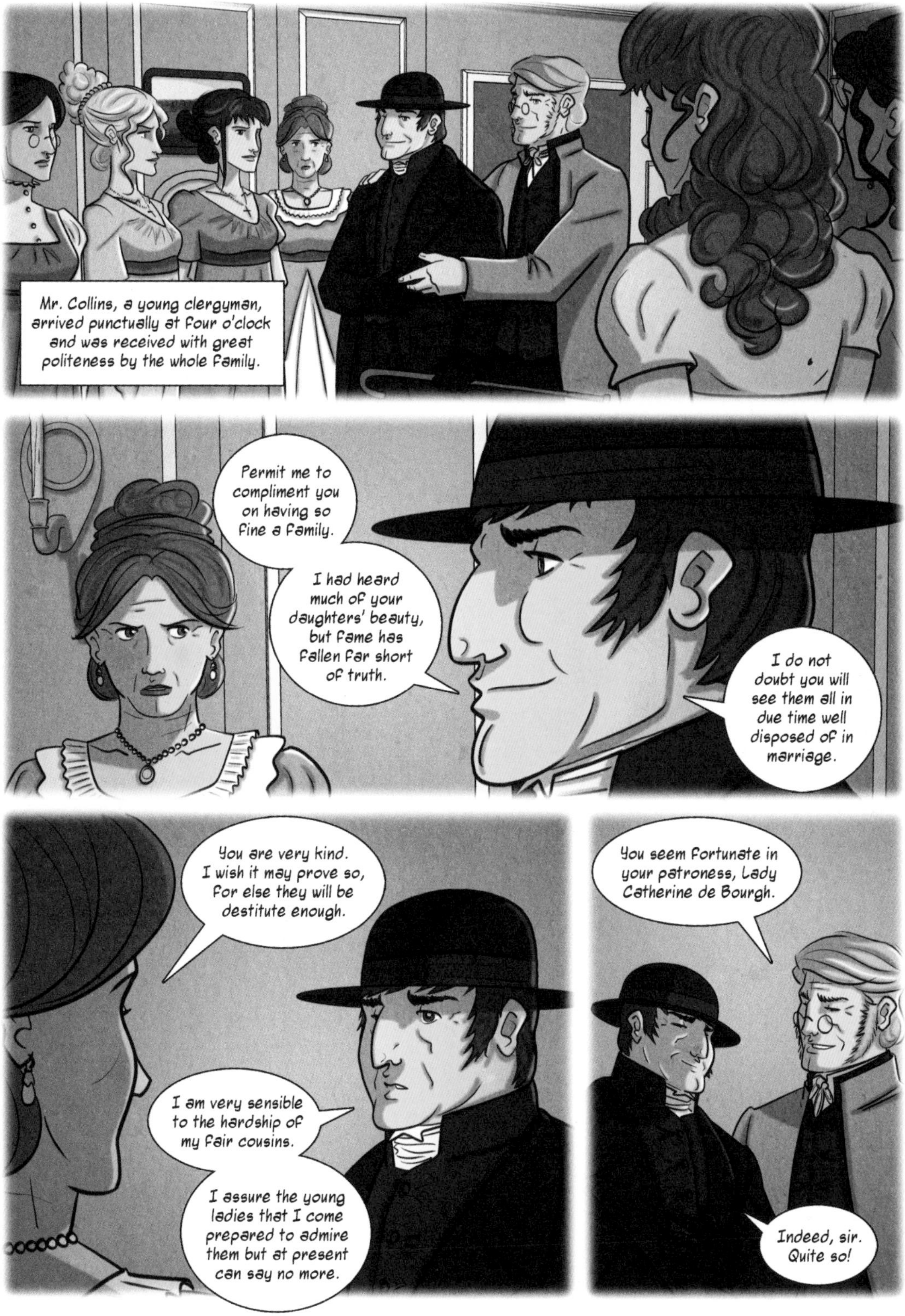
Mr. Collins, a young clergyman, arrived punctually at four o'clock and was received with great politeness by the whole family.
Permit me to compliment you on having so fine a family.
I had heard much of your daughters' beauty, but fame has fallen far short of truth.
I do not doubt you will see them all in due time well disposed of in marriage.
You are very kind. I wish it may prove so, for else they will be destitute enough.
I am very sensible to the hardship of my fair cousins.
I assure the young ladies that I come prepared to admire them but at present can say no more.
You seem fortunate in your patroness, Lady Catherine de Bourgh.
Indeed, sir. Quite so!

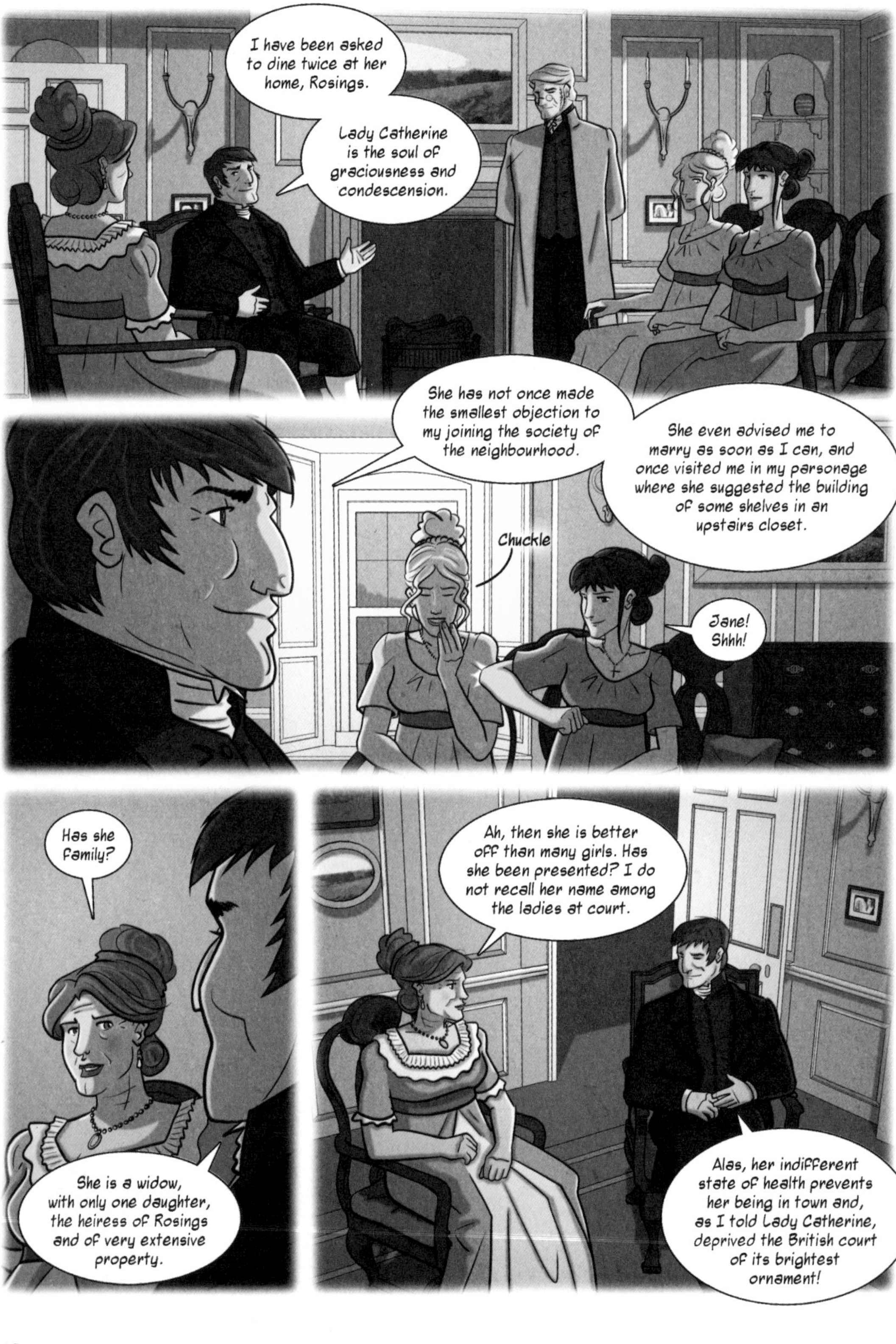
I have been asked to dine twice at her home, Rosings.
Lady Catherine is the soul of graciousness and condescension.
She has not once made the smallest objection to my joining the society of the neighbourhood.
She even advised me to marry as soon as I can, and once visited me in my parsonage where she suggested the building of some shelves in an upstairs closet.
Chuckle
Jane! Shhh!
Has she family?
She is a widow, with only one daughter, the heiress of Rosings and of very extensive property.
Ah, then she is better off than many girls. Has she been presented? I do not recall her name among the ladies at court.
Alas, her indifferent state of health prevents her being in town and, as I told Lady Catherine, deprived the British court of its brightest ornament!

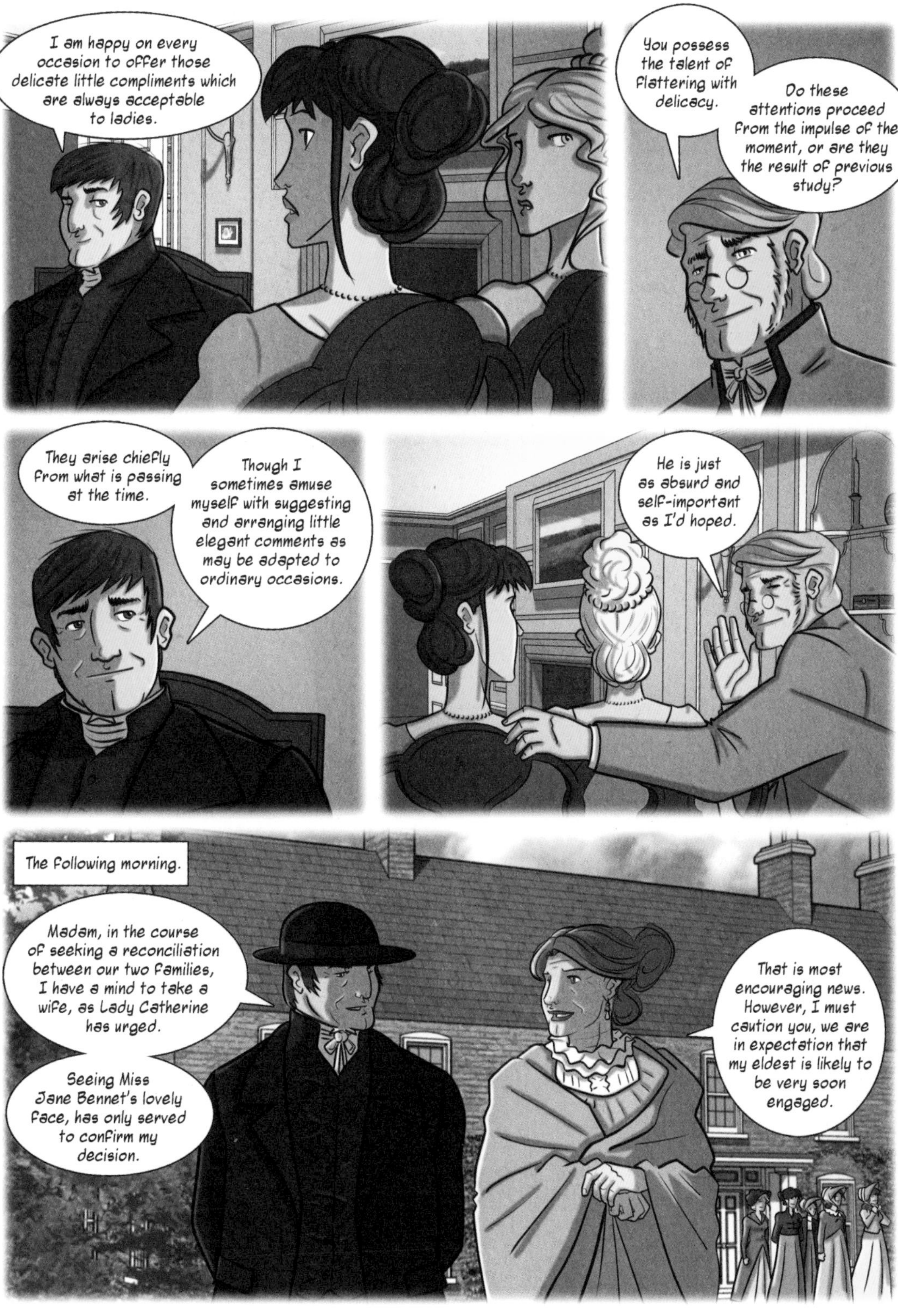

I am happy on every occasion to offer those delicate little compliments which are always acceptable to ladies.
You possess the talent of flattering with delicacy.
Do these attentions proceed from the impulse of the moment, or are they the result of previous study?
They arise chiefly from what is passing at the time.
Though I sometimes amuse myself with suggesting and arranging little elegant comments as may be adapted to ordinary occasions.
He is just as absurd and self-important as I'd hoped.
The following morning.
Madam, in the course of seeking a reconciliation between our two families, I have a mind to take a wife, as Lady Catherine has urged.
Seeing Miss Jane Bennet's lovely face, has only served to confirm my decision.
That is most encouraging news. However, I must caution you, we are in expectation that my eldest is likely to be very soon engaged.

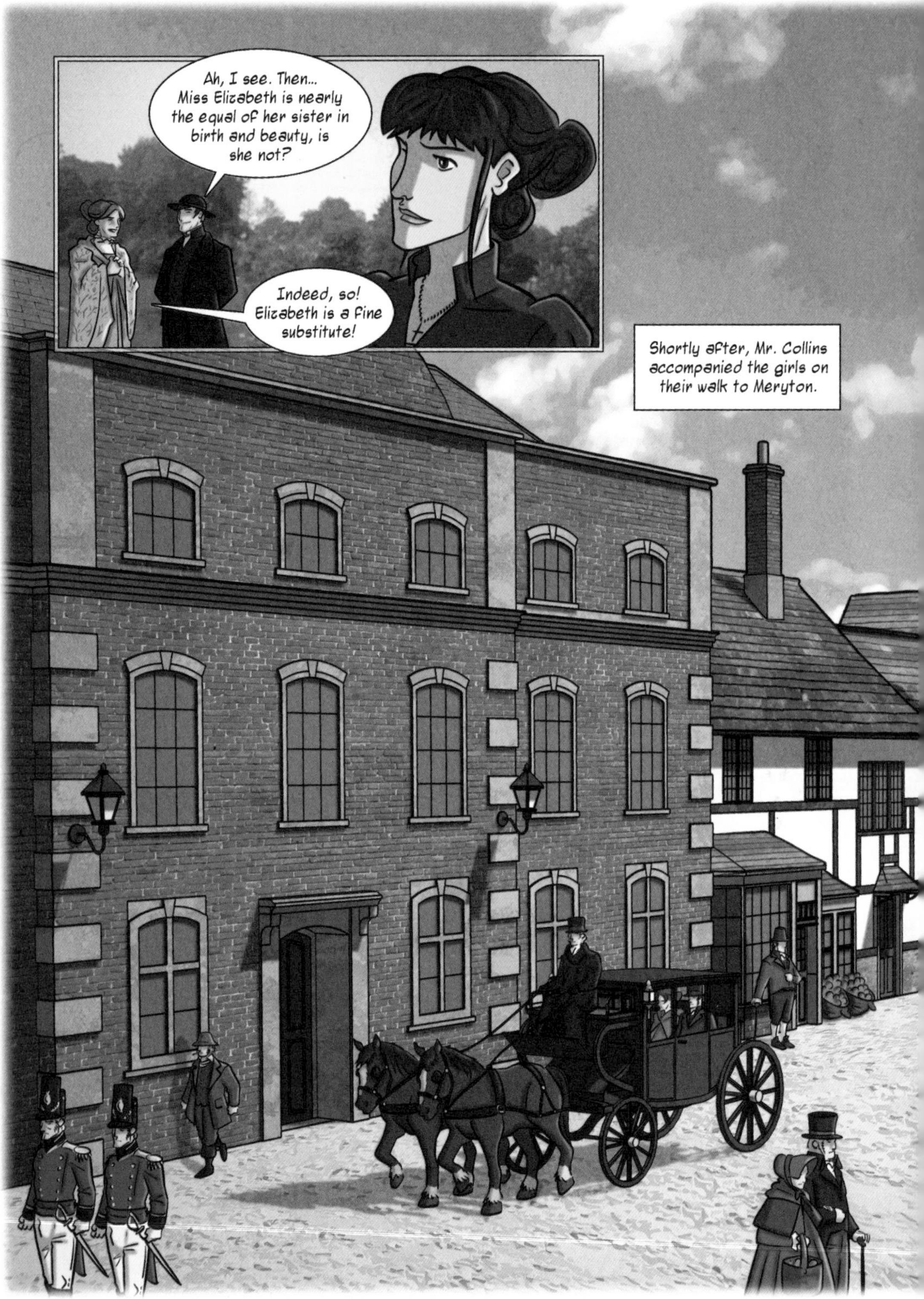
Ah, I see. Then... Miss Elizabeth is nearly the equal of her sister in birth and beauty, is she not?
Indeed, so! Elizabeth is a fine substitute!
Shortly after, Mr. Collins accompanied the girls on their walk to Meryton.

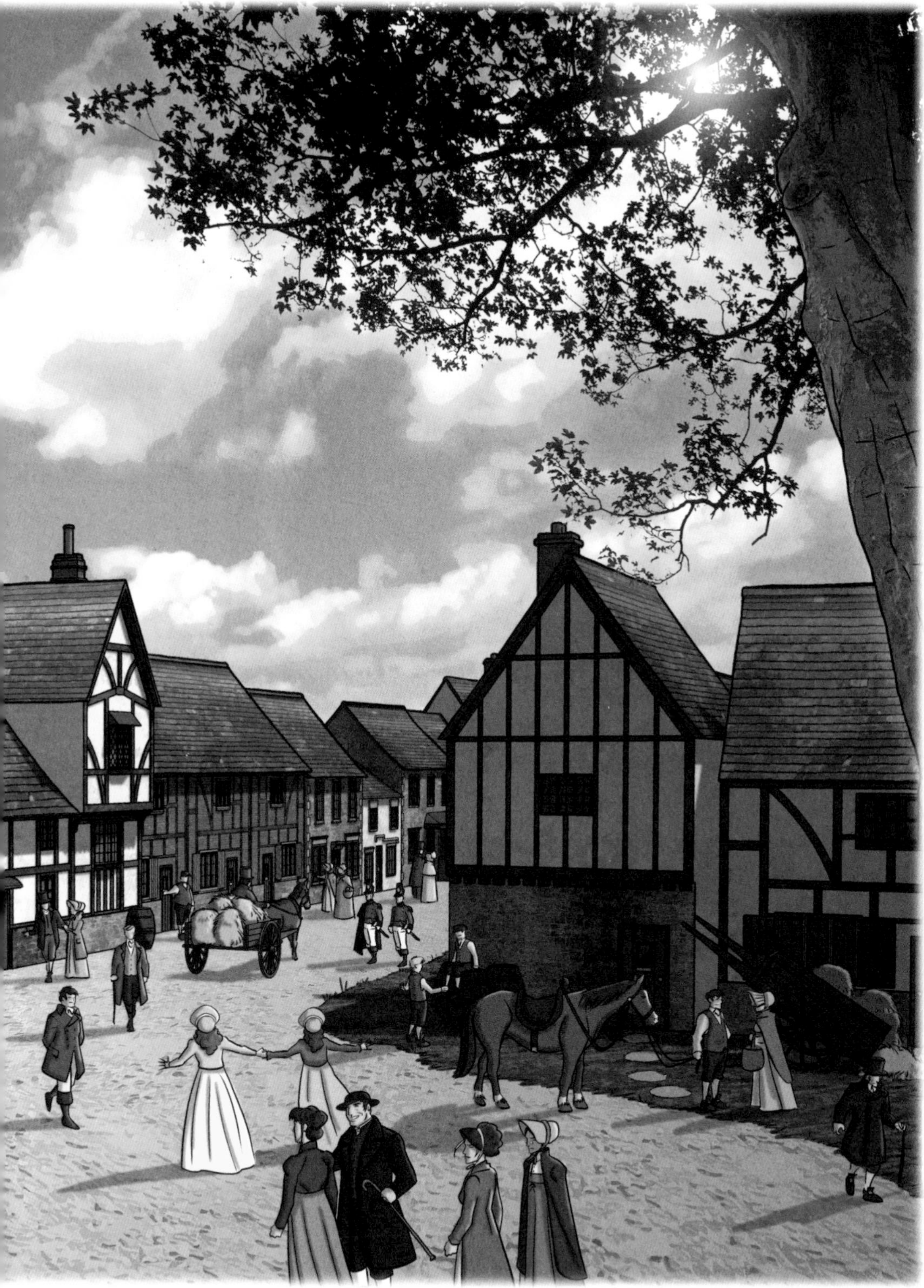

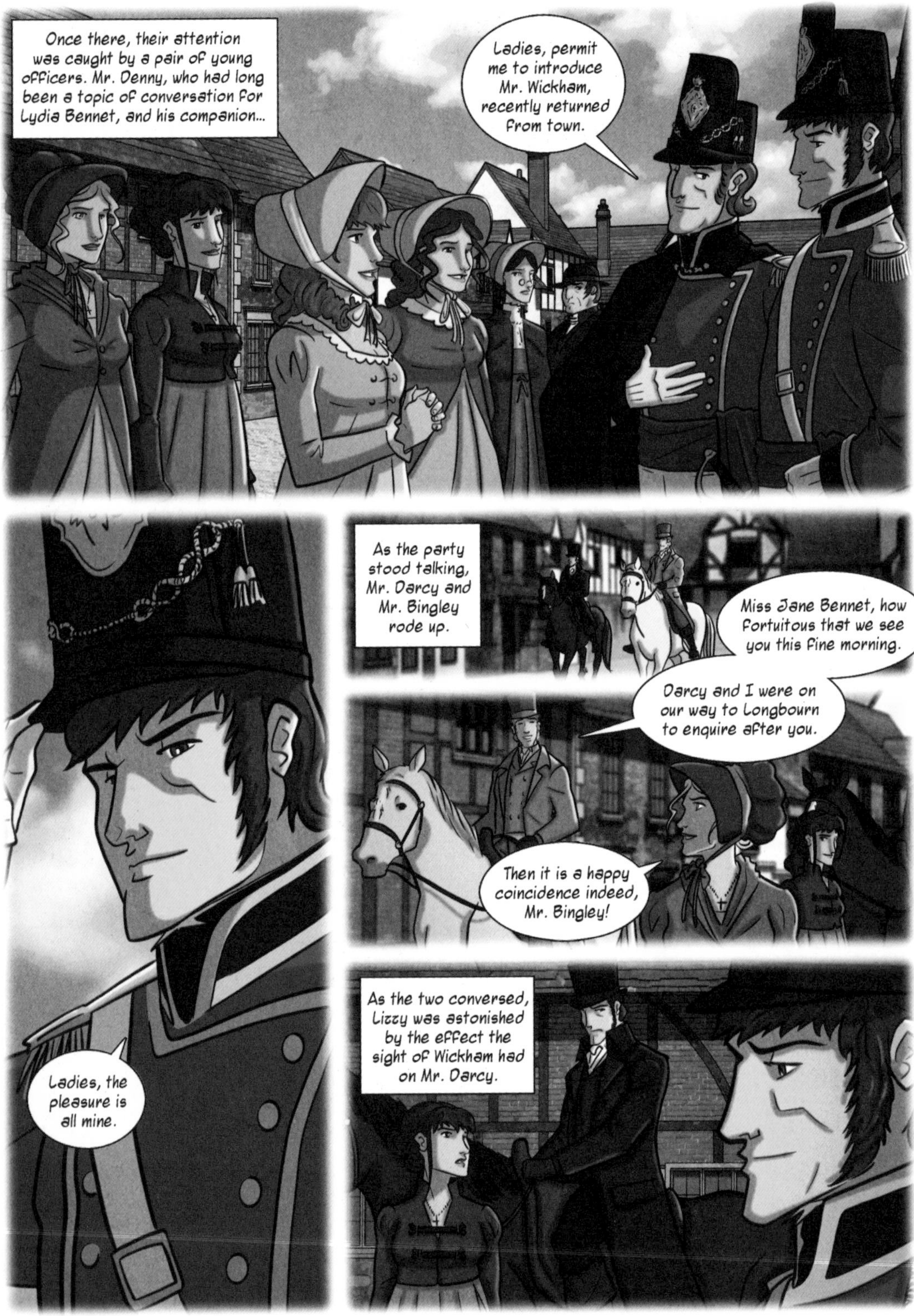
Once there, their attention was caught by a pair of young officers. Mr. Denny, who had long been a topic of conversation for Lydia Bennet, and his companion...
Ladies, permit me to introduce Mr. Wickham, recently returned from town.
Ladies, the pleasure is all mine.
As the party stood talking, Mr. Darcy and Mr. Bingley rode up.
Miss Jane Bennet, how fortuitous that we see you this fine morning.
Darcy and I were on our way to Longbourn to enquire after you.
Then it is a happy coincidence indeed, Mr. Bingley!
As the two conversed, Lizzy was astonished by the effect the sight of Wickham had on Mr. Darcy.

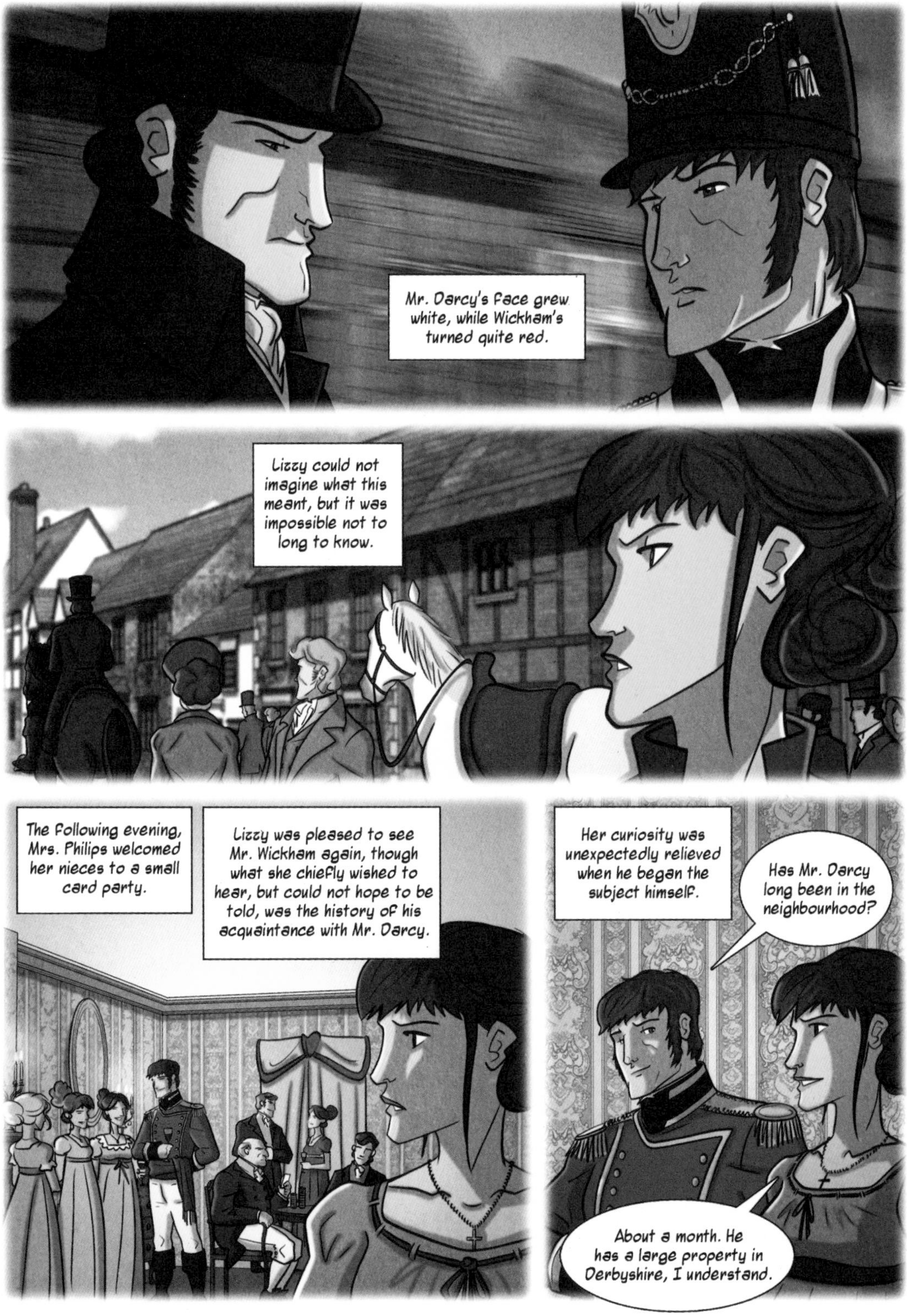
Mr. Darcy's face grew white, while Wickham's turned quite red.
Lizzy could not imagine what this meant, but it was impossible not to long to know.
The following evening, Mrs. Philips welcomed her nieces to a small card party.
Lizzy was pleased to see Mr. Wickham again, though what she chiefly wished to hear, but could not hope to be told, was the history of his acquaintance with Mr. Darcy.
Her curiosity was unexpectedly relieved when he began the subject himself.
Has Mr. Darcy long been in the neighbourhood?
About a month. He has a large property in Derbyshire, I understand.

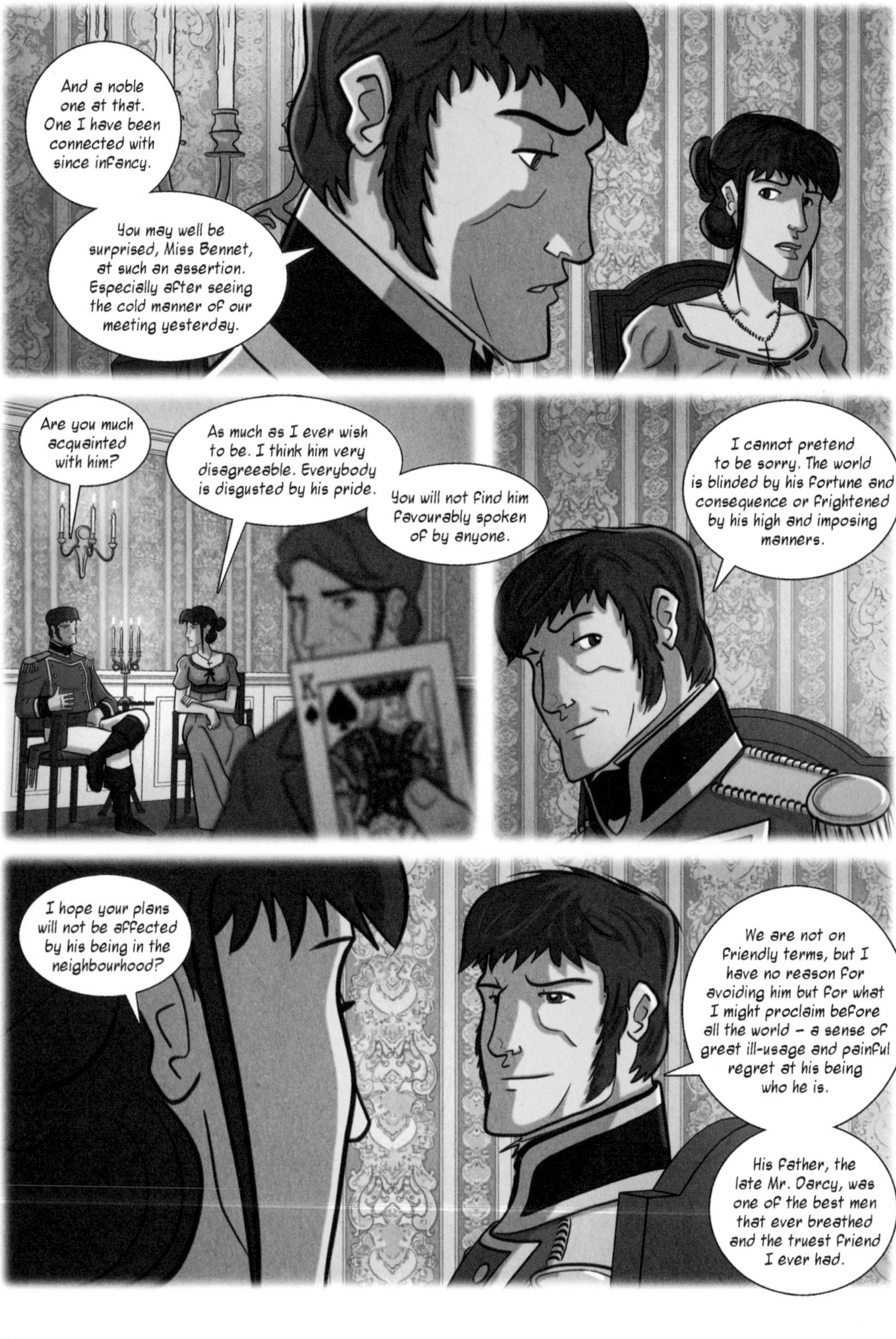
And a noble one at that. One I have been connected with since infancy.
You may well be surprised, Miss Bennet, at such an assertion. Especially after seeing the cold manner of our meeting yesterday.
Are you much acquainted with him?
As much as I ever wish to be. I think him very disagreeable. Everybody is disgusted by his pride.
You will not find him favourably spoken of by anyone.
I cannot pretend to be sorry. The world is blinded by his fortune and consequence or frightened by his high and imposing manners.
I hope your plans will not be affected by his being in the neighbourhood?
We are not on friendly terms, but I have no reason for avoiding him but for what I might proclaim before all the world – a sense of great ill-usage and painful regret at his being who he is.
His father, the late Mr. Darcy, was one of the best men that ever breathed and the truest friend I ever had.

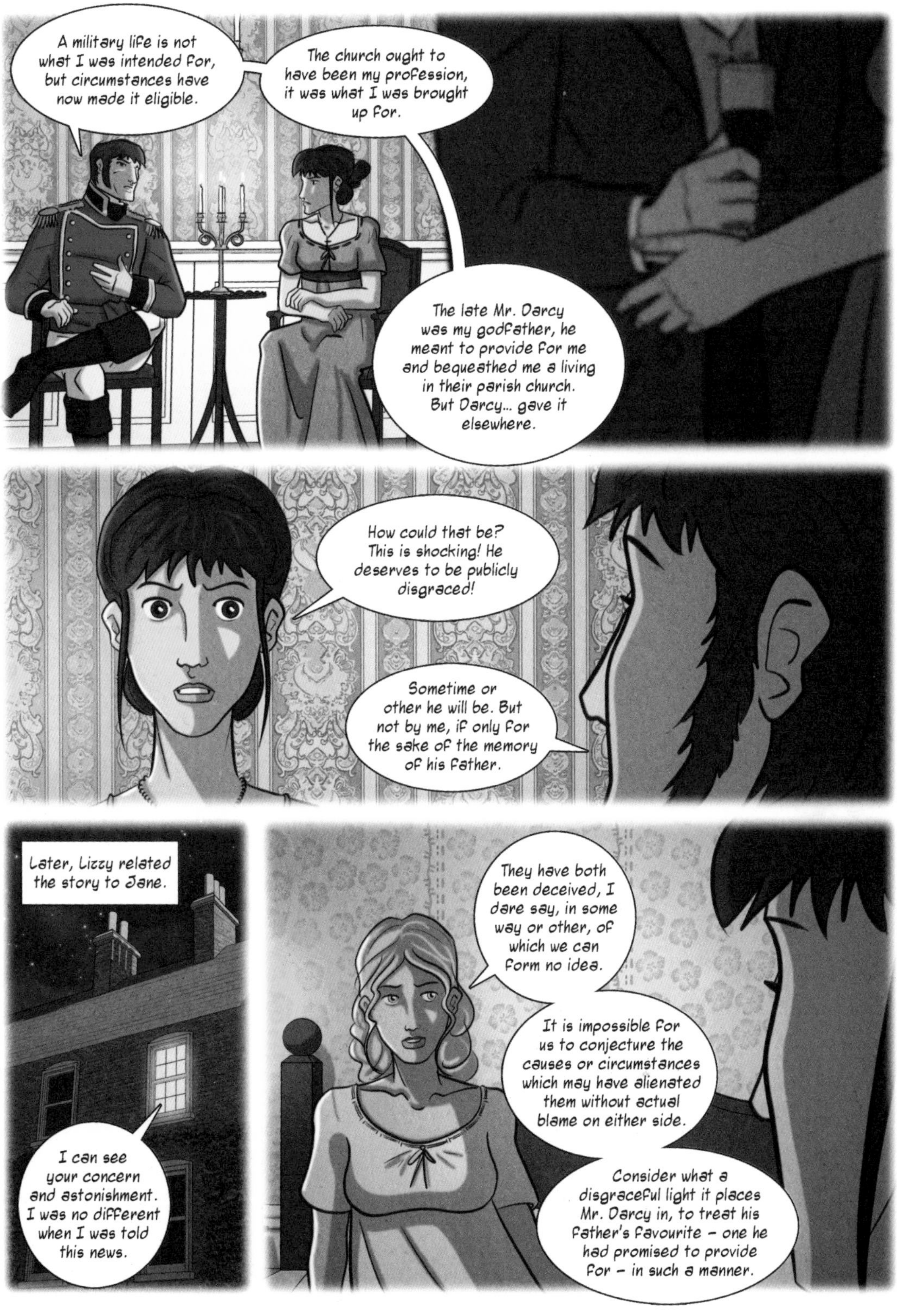
A military life is not what I was intended for, but circumstances have now made it eligible.
The church ought to have been my profession, it was what I was brought up for.
The late Mr. Darcy was my godfather, he meant to provide for me and bequeathed me a living in their parish church. But Darcy... gave it elsewhere.
How could that be? This is shocking! He deserves to be publicly disgraced!
Sometime or other he will be. But not by me, if only for the sake of the memory of his father.
Later, Lizzy related the story to Jane.
I can see your concern and astonishment. I was no different when I was told this news.
They have both been deceived, I dare say, in some way or other, of which we can form no idea.
It is impossible for us to conjecture the causes or circumstances which may have alienated them without actual blame on either side.
Consider what a disgraceful light it places Mr. Darcy in, to treat his father's favourite – one he had promised to provide for – in such a manner.

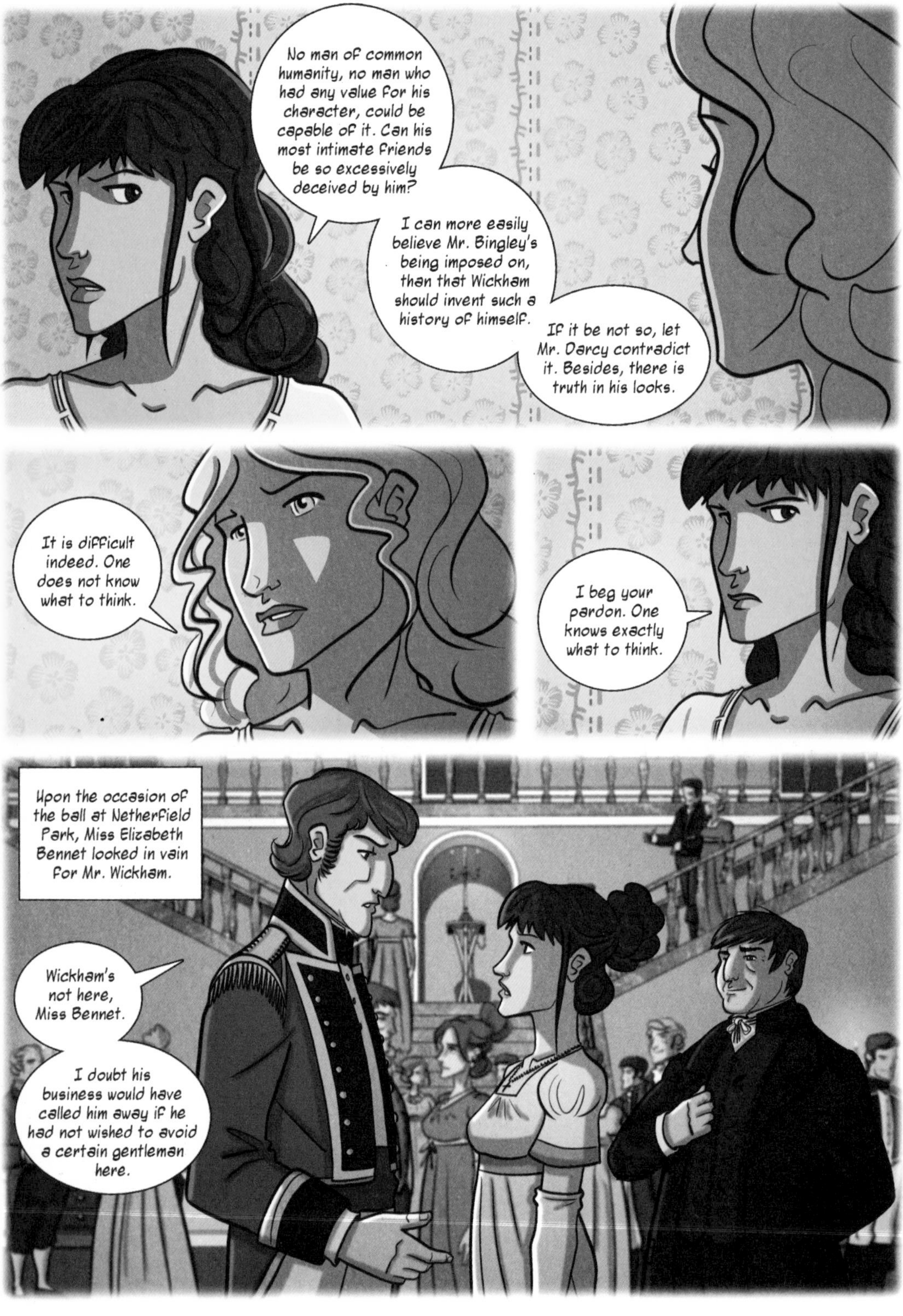
No man of common humanity, no man who had any value for his character, could be capable of it. Can his most intimate friends be so excessively deceived by him?
I can more easily believe Mr. Bingley's being imposed on, than that Wickham should invent such a history of himself.
If it be not so, let Mr. Darcy contradict it. Besides, there is truth in his looks.
It is difficult indeed. One does not know what to think.
I beg your pardon. One knows exactly what to think.
Upon the occasion of the ball at Netherfield Park, Miss Elizabeth Bennet looked in vain for Mr. Wickham.
Wickham's not here, Miss Bennet.
I doubt his business would have called him away if he had not wished to avoid a certain gentleman here.

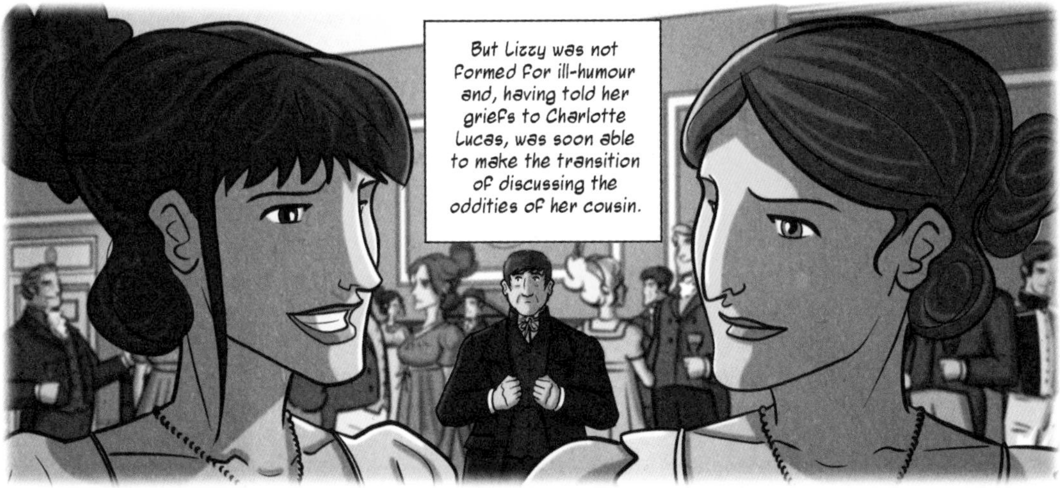
But Lizzy was not formed for ill-humour and, having told her griefs to Charlotte Lucas, was soon able to make the transition of discussing the oddities of her cousin.

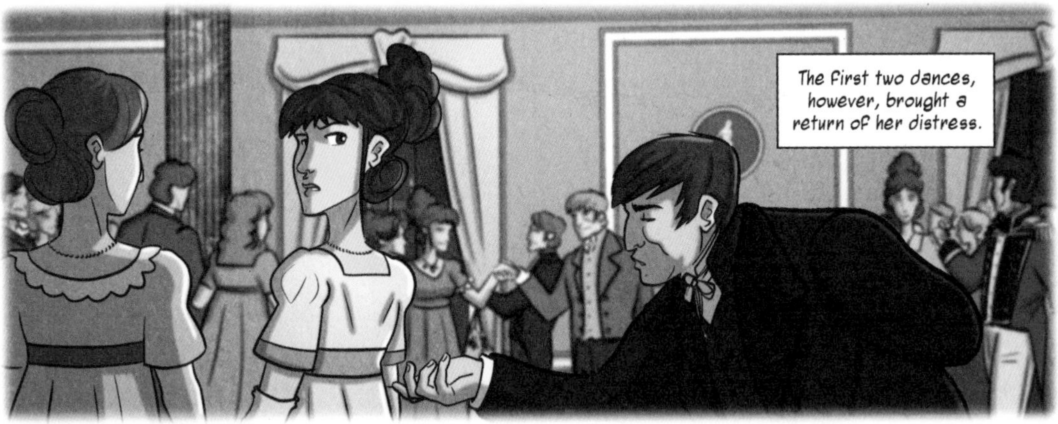
The first two dances, however, brought a return of her distress.

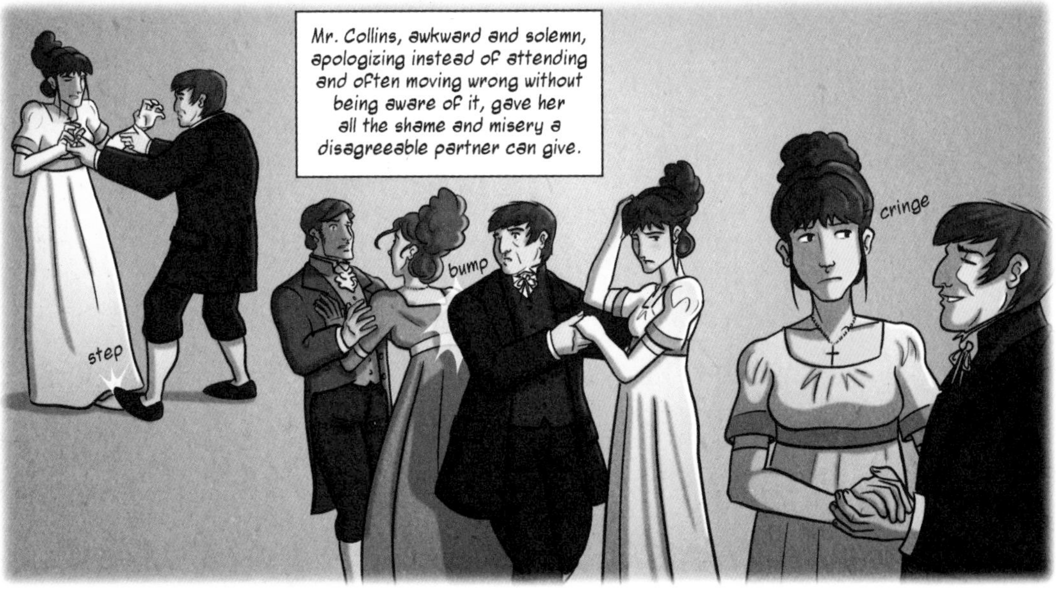
Mr. Collins, awkward and solemn, apologizing instead of attending and often moving wrong without being aware of it, gave her all the shame and misery a disagreeable partner can give.
cringe
bump
step

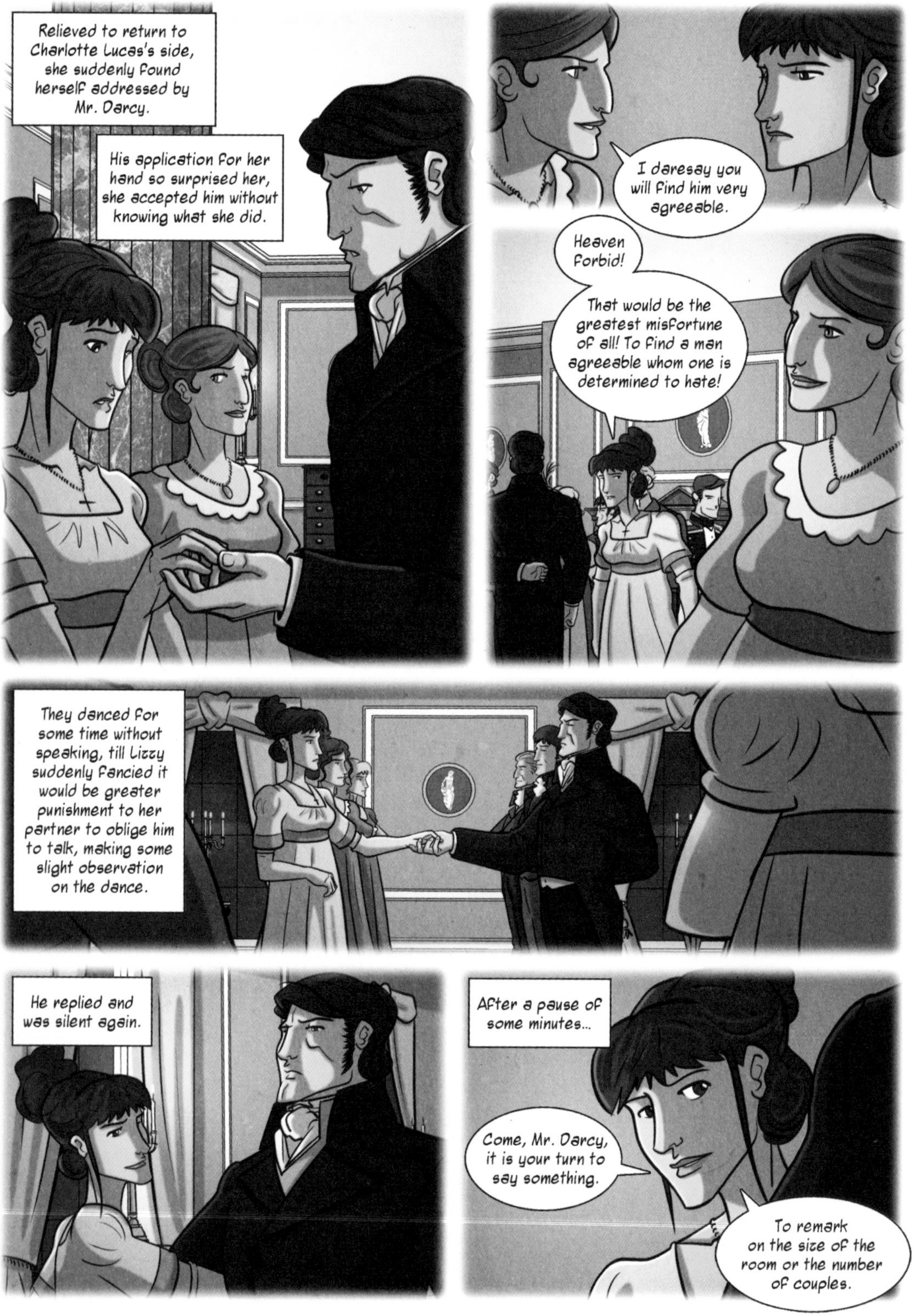
Relieved to return to Charlotte Lucas's side, she suddenly found herself addressed by Mr. Darcy.
His application for her hand so surprised her, she accepted him without knowing what she did.
I daresay you will find him very agreeable.
Heaven forbid!
That would be the greatest misfortune of all! To find a man agreeable whom one is determined to hate!
They danced for some time without speaking, till Lizzy suddenly fancied it would be greater punishment to her partner to oblige him to talk, making some slight observation on the dance.
He replied and was silent again.
After a pause of some minutes...
Come, Mr. Darcy, it is your turn to say something.
To remark on the size of the room or the number of couples.

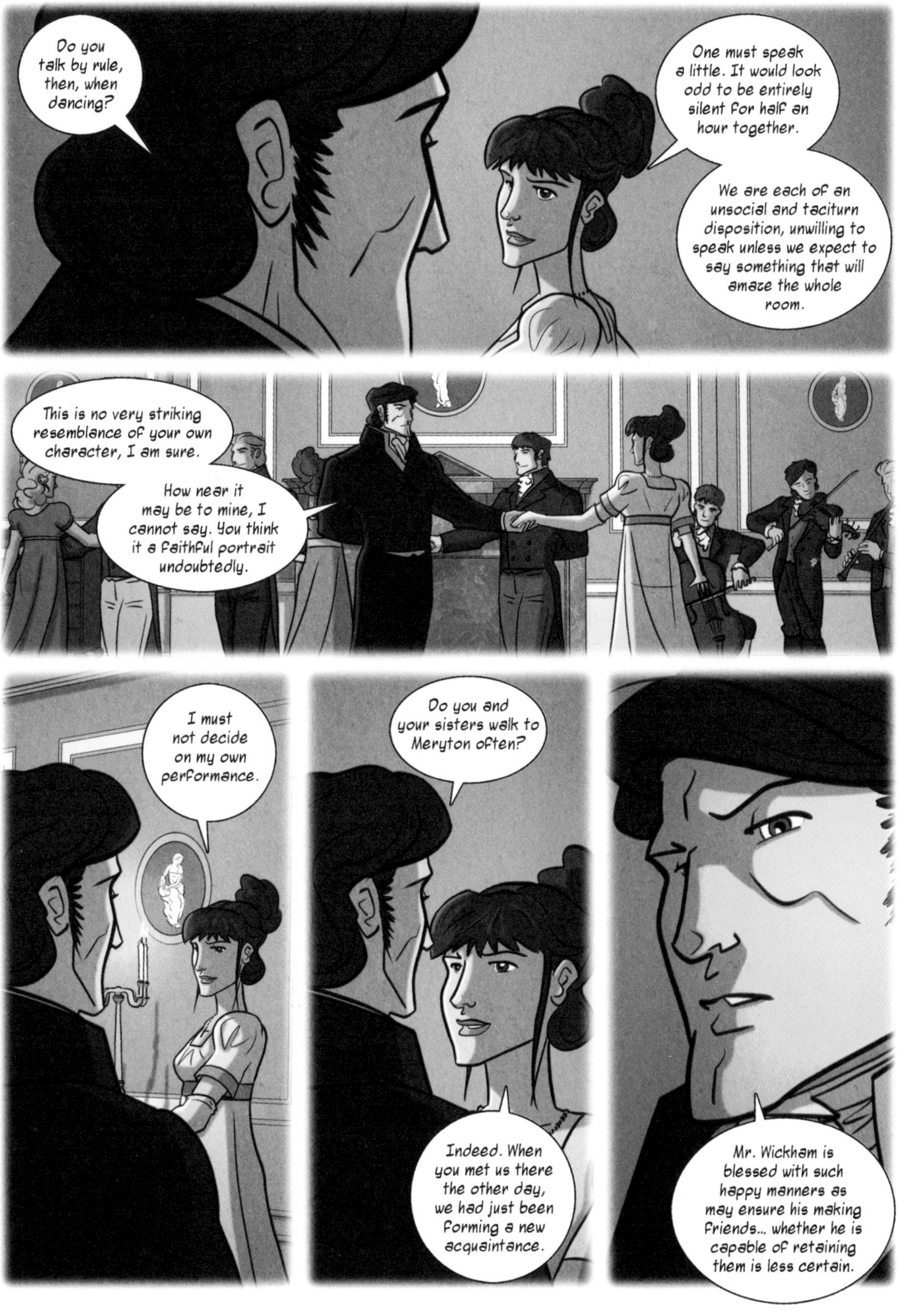
Do you talk by rule, then, when dancing?
One must speak a little. It would look odd to be entirely silent for half an hour together.
We are each of an unsocial and taciturn disposition, unwilling to speak unless we expect to say something that will amaze the whole room.
This is no very striking resemblance of your own character, I am sure.
How near it may be to mine, I cannot say. You think it a faithful portrait undoubtedly.
I must not decide on my own performance.
Do you and your sisters walk to Meryton often?
Indeed. When you met us there the other day, we had just been forming a new acquaintance.
Mr. Wickham is blessed with such happy manners as may ensure his making friends... whether he is capable of retaining them is less certain.

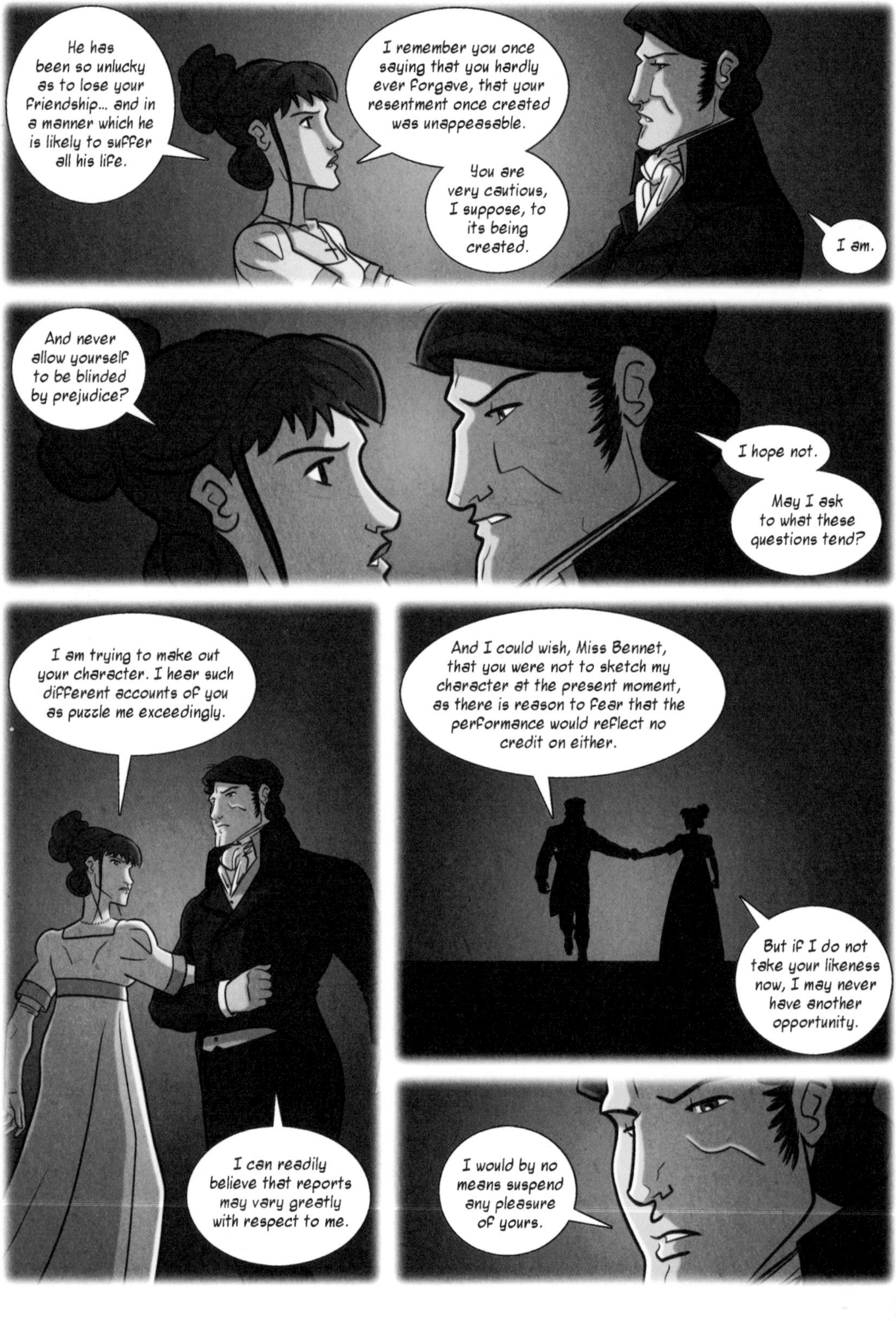
He has been so unlucky as to lose your friendship... and in a manner which he is likely to suffer all his life.
I remember you once saying that you hardly ever forgave, that your resentment once created was unappeasable.
You are very cautious, I suppose, to its being created.
I am.
And never allow yourself to be blinded by prejudice?
I hope not.
May I ask to what these questions tend?
I am trying to make out your character. I hear such different accounts of you as puzzle me exceedingly.
I can readily believe that reports may vary greatly with respect to me.
And I could wish, Miss Bennet, that you were not to sketch my character at the present moment, as there is reason to fear that the performance would reflect no credit on either.
But if I do not take your likeness now, I may never have another opportunity.
I would by no means suspend any pleasure of yours.

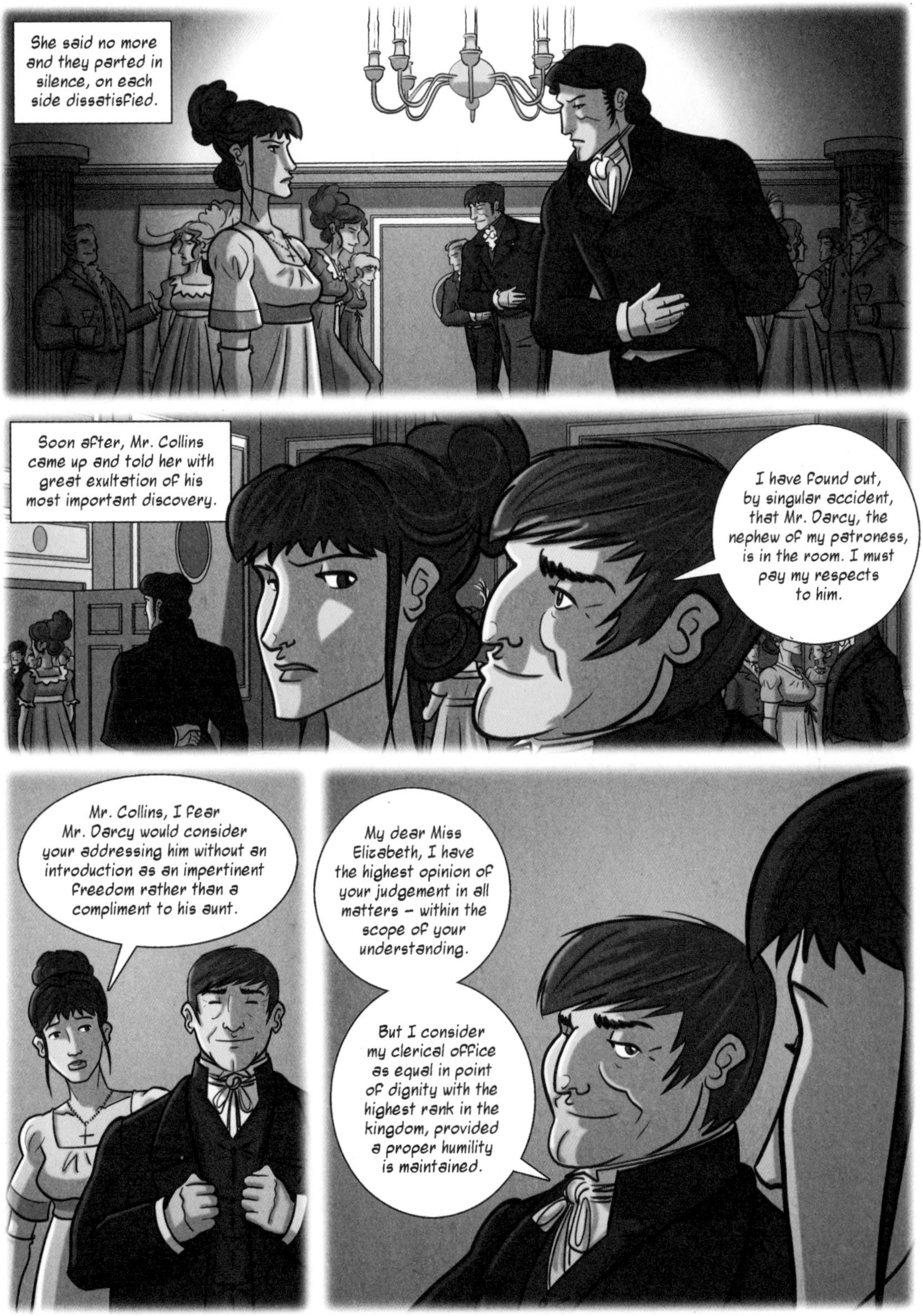
She said no more and they parted in silence, on each side dissatisfied.
Soon after, Mr. Collins came up and told her with great exultation of his most important discovery.
I have found out, by singular accident, that Mr. Darcy, the nephew of my patroness, is in the room. I must pay my respects to him.
Mr. Collins, I fear Mr. Darcy would consider your addressing him without an introduction as an impertinent freedom rather than a compliment to his aunt.
My dear Miss Elizabeth, I have the highest opinion of your judgement in all matters – within the scope of your understanding.
But I consider my clerical office as equal in point of dignity with the highest rank in the kingdom, provided a proper humility is maintained.

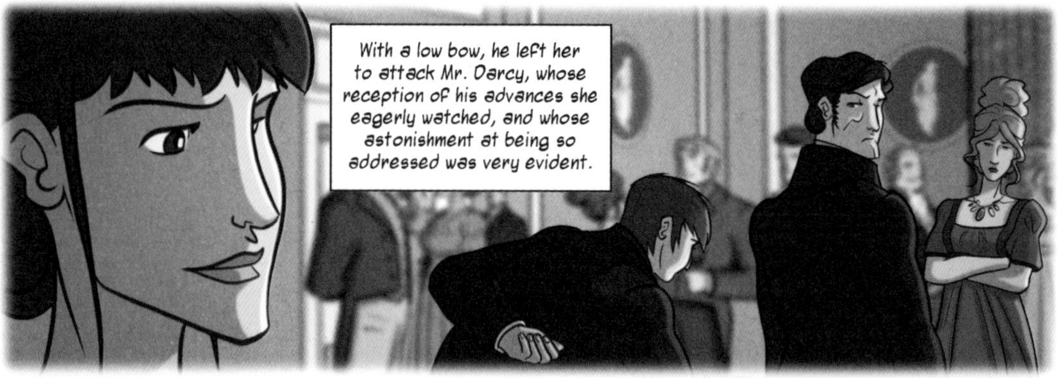
With a low bow, he left her to attack Mr. Darcy, whose reception of his advances she eagerly watched, and whose astonishment at being so addressed was very evident.

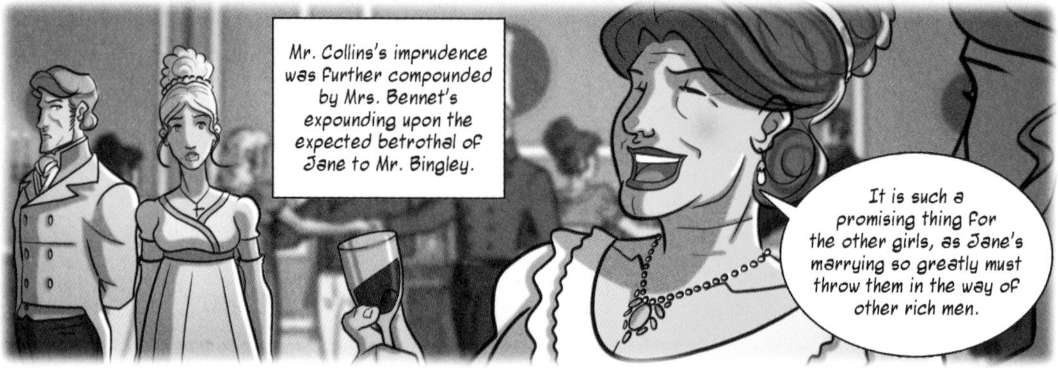
Mr. Collins's imprudence was further compounded by Mrs. Bennet's expounding upon the expected betrothal of Jane to Mr. Bingley.
It is such a promising thing for the other girls, as Jane's marrying so greatly must throw them in the way of other rich men.

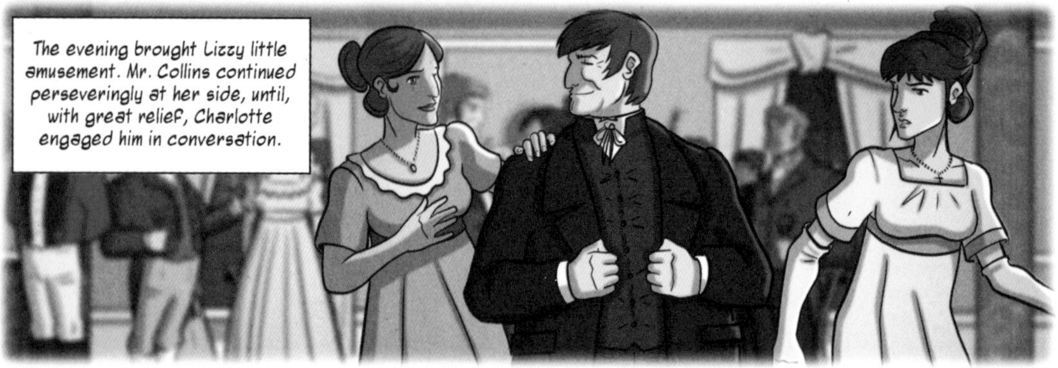
The evening brought Lizzy little amusement. Mr. Collins continued perseveringly at her side, until, with great relief, Charlotte engaged him in conversation.

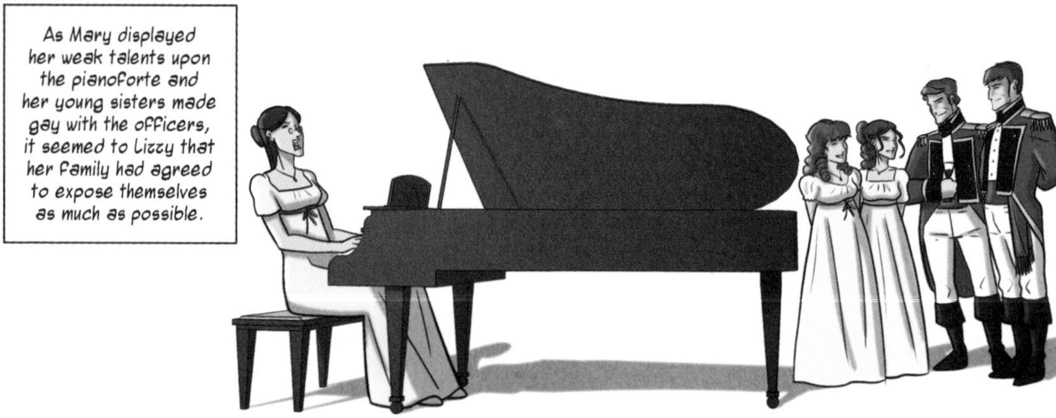
As Mary displayed her weak talents upon the pianoforte and her young sisters made gay with the officers, it seemed to Lizzy that her family had agreed to expose themselves as much as possible.

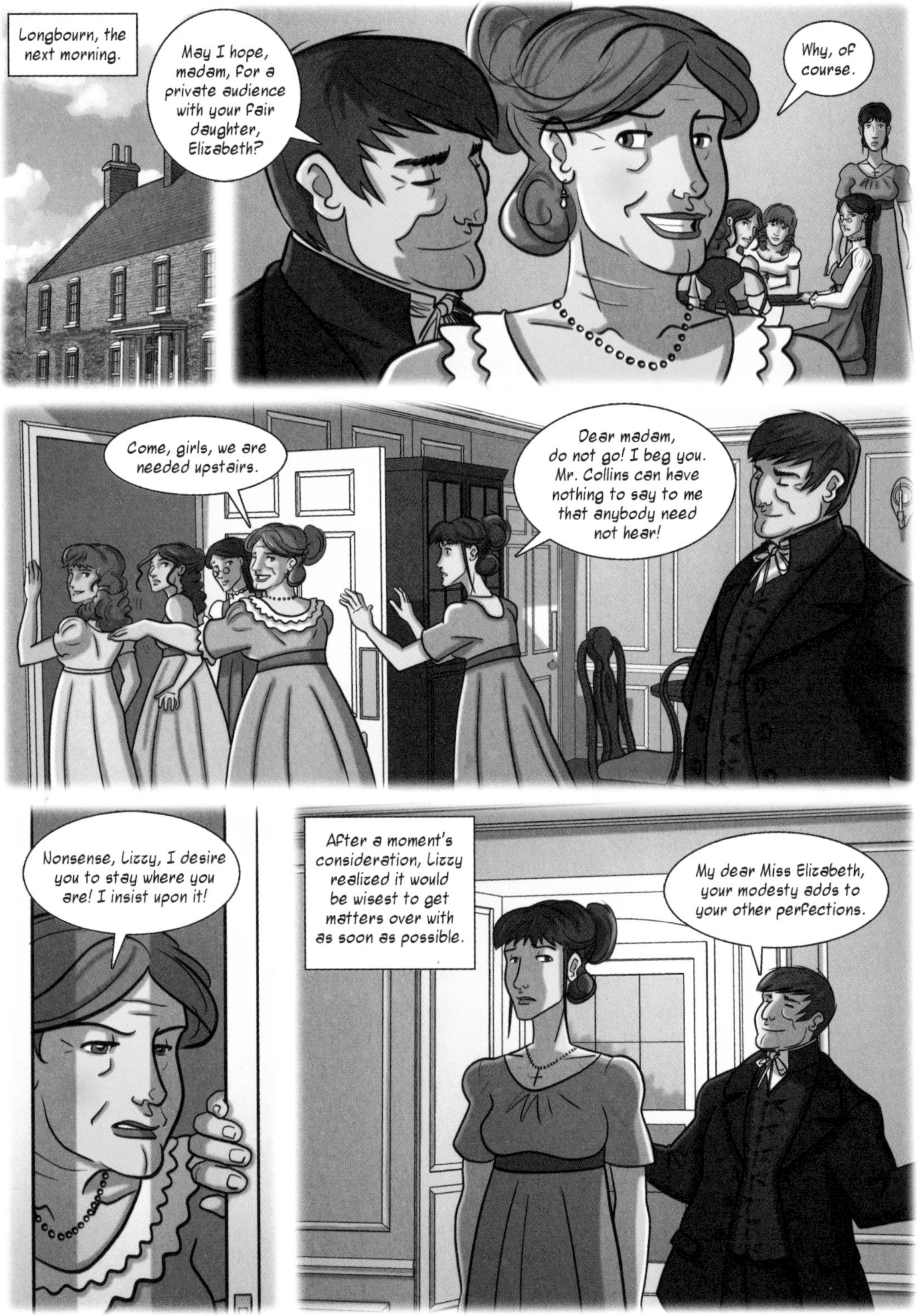
Longbourn, the next morning.
May I hope, madam, for a private audience with your fair daughter, Elizabeth?
Why, of course.
Come, girls, we are needed upstairs.
Dear madam, do not go! I beg you. Mr. Collins can have nothing to say to me that anybody need not hear!
Nonsense, Lizzy, I desire you to stay where you are! I insist upon it!
After a moment's consideration, Lizzy realized it would be wisest to get matters over with as soon as possible.
My dear Miss Elizabeth, your modesty adds to your other perfections.

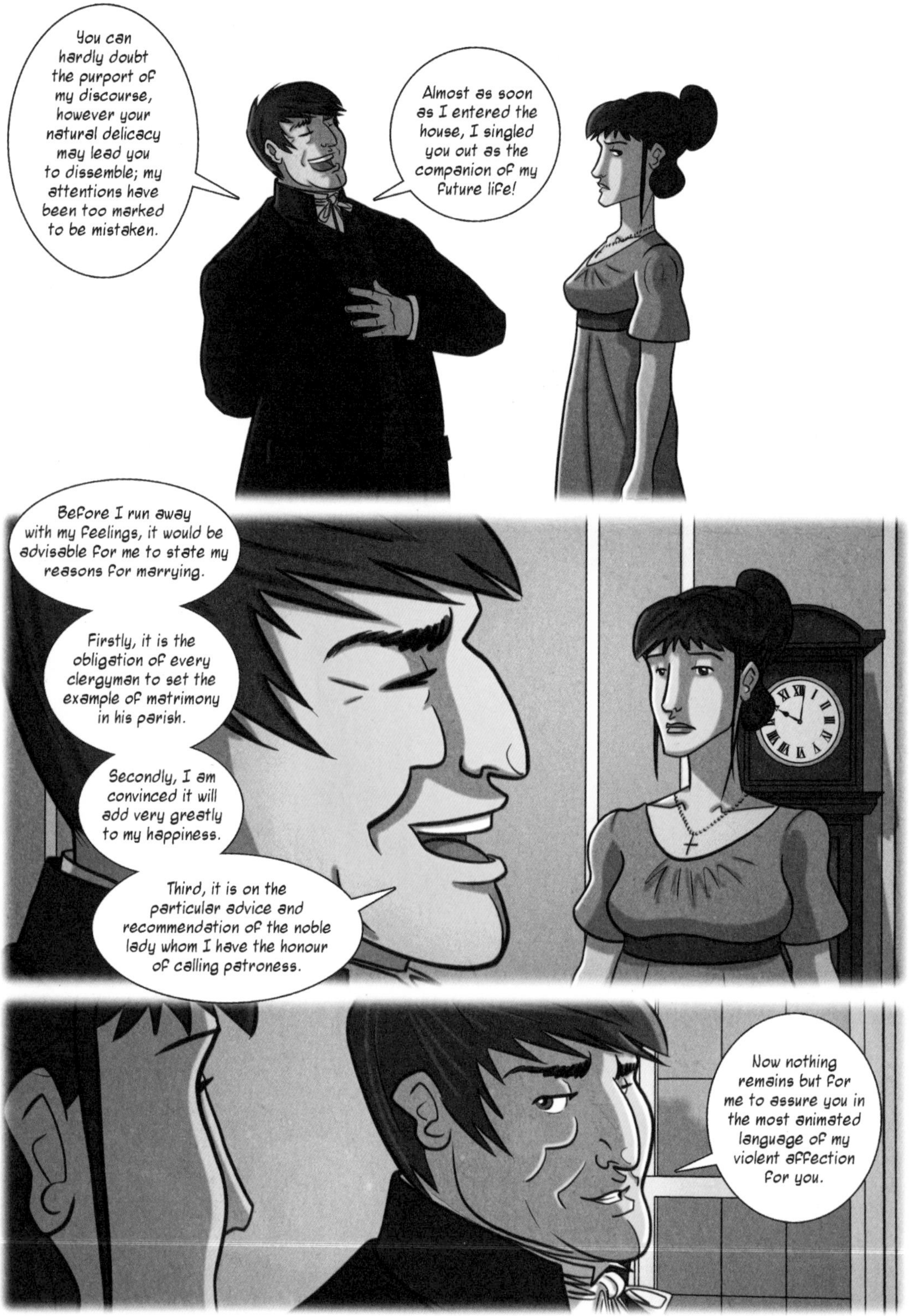
You can hardly doubt the purport of my discourse, however your natural delicacy may lead you to dissemble; my attentions have been too marked to be mistaken.
Almost as soon as I entered the house, I singled you out as the companion of my future life!
Before I run away with my feelings, it would be advisable for me to state my reasons for marrying.
Firstly, it is the obligation of every clergyman to set the example of matrimony in his parish.
Secondly, I am convinced it will add very greatly to my happiness.
Third, it is on the particular advice and recommendation of the noble lady whom I have the honour of calling patroness.
Now nothing remains but for me to assure you in the most animated language of my violent affection for you.

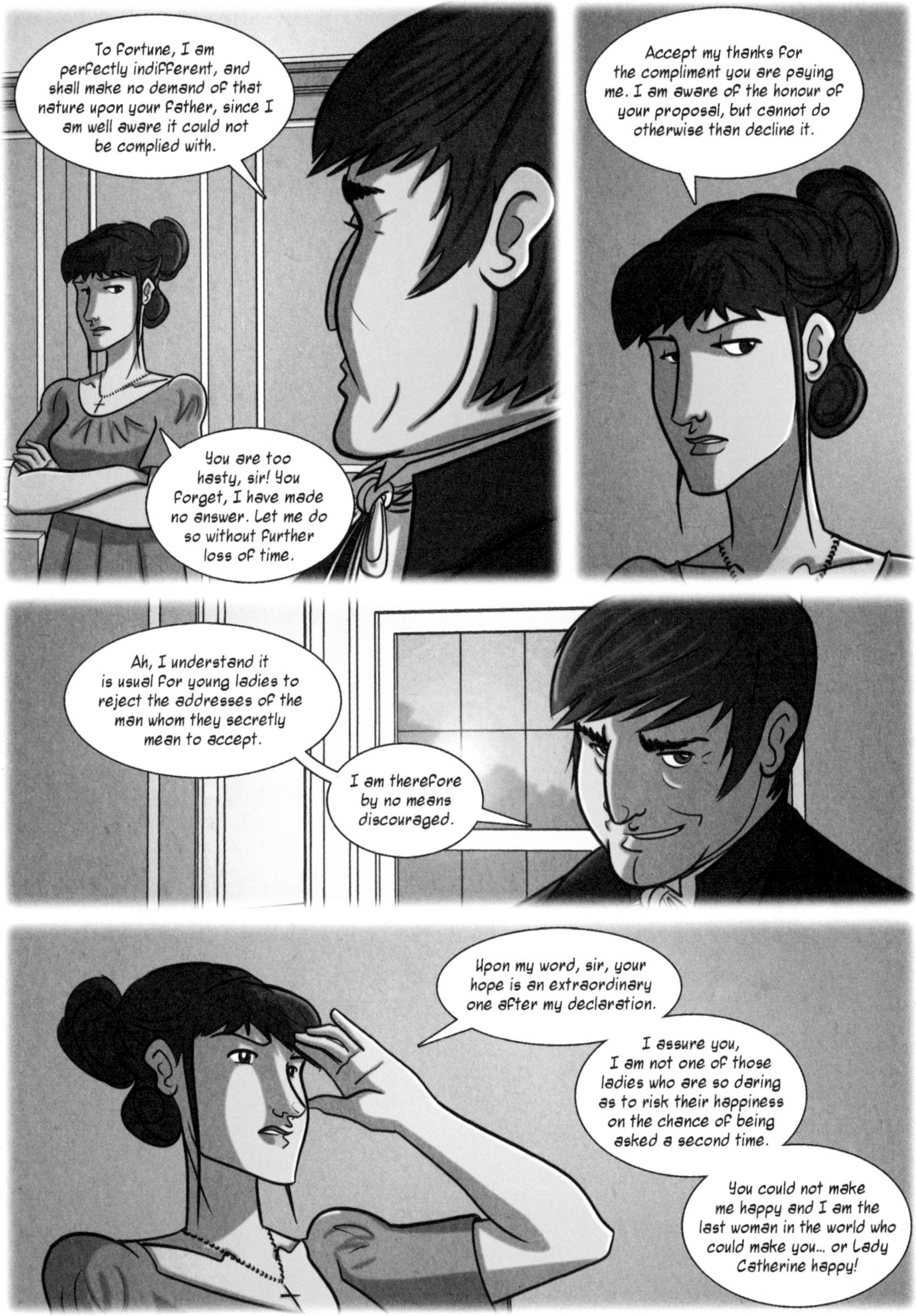
To fortune, I am perfectly indifferent, and shall make no demand of that nature upon your father, since I am well aware it could not be complied with.
You are too hasty, sir! You forget, I have made no answer. Let me do so without further loss of time.
Accept my thanks for the compliment you are paying me. I am aware of the honour of your proposal, but cannot do otherwise than decline it.
Ah, I understand it is usual for young ladies to reject the addresses of the man whom they secretly mean to accept.
I am therefore by no means discouraged.
Upon my word, sir, your hope is an extraordinary one after my declaration.
I assure you, I am not one of those ladies who are so daring as to risk their happiness on the chance of being asked a second time.
You could not make me happy and I am the last woman in the world who could make you... or Lady Catherine happy!

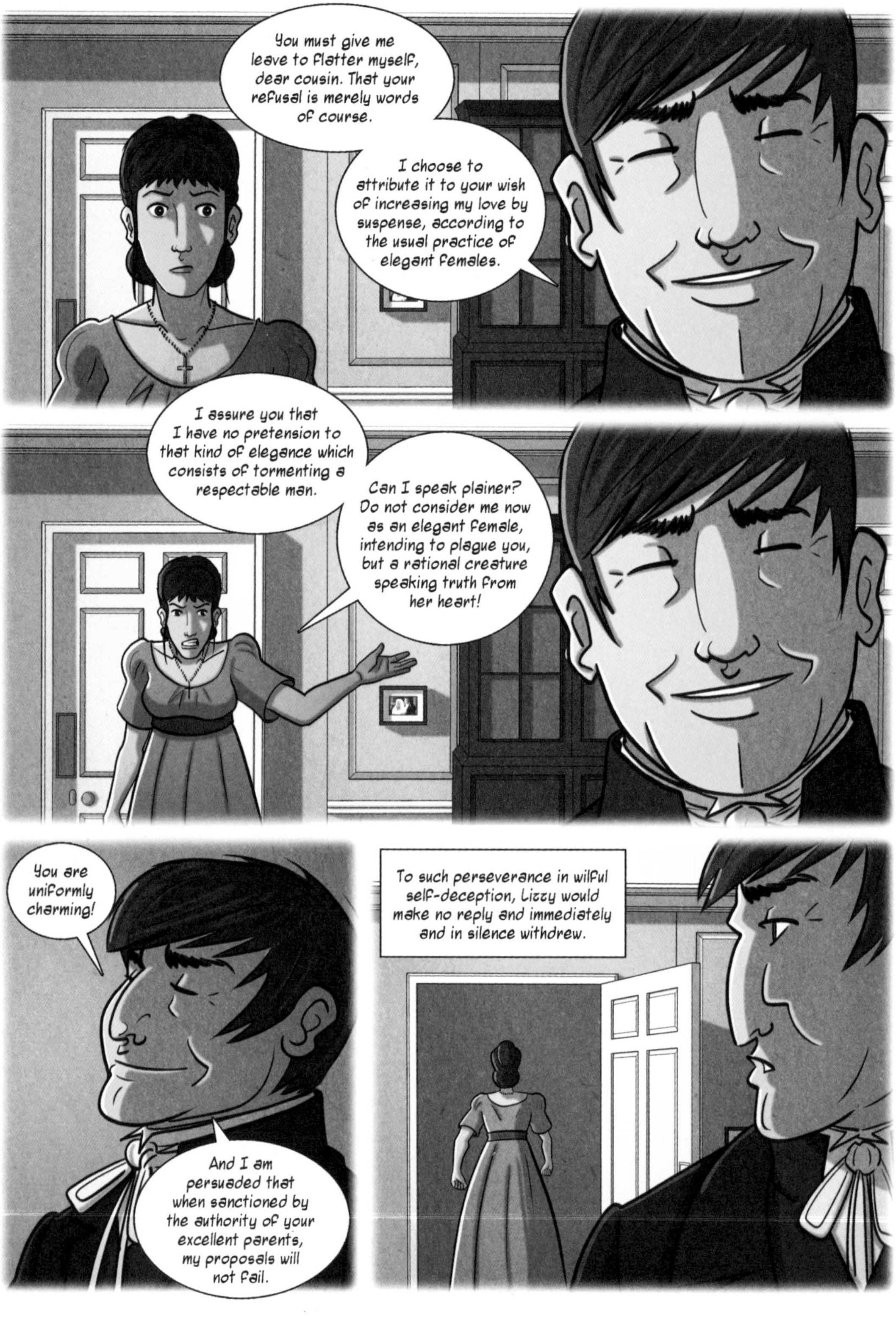
You must give me leave to flatter myself, dear cousin. That your refusal is merely words of course.
I choose to attribute it to your wish of increasing my love by suspense, according to the usual practice of elegant females.
I assure you that I have no pretension to that kind of elegance which consists of tormenting a respectable man.
Can I speak plainer? Do not consider me now as an elegant female, intending to plague you, but a rational creature speaking truth from her heart!
You are uniformly charming!
And I am persuaded that when sanctioned by the authority of your excellent parents, my proposals will not fail.
To such perseverance in wilful self-deception, Lizzy would make no reply and immediately and in silence withdrew.

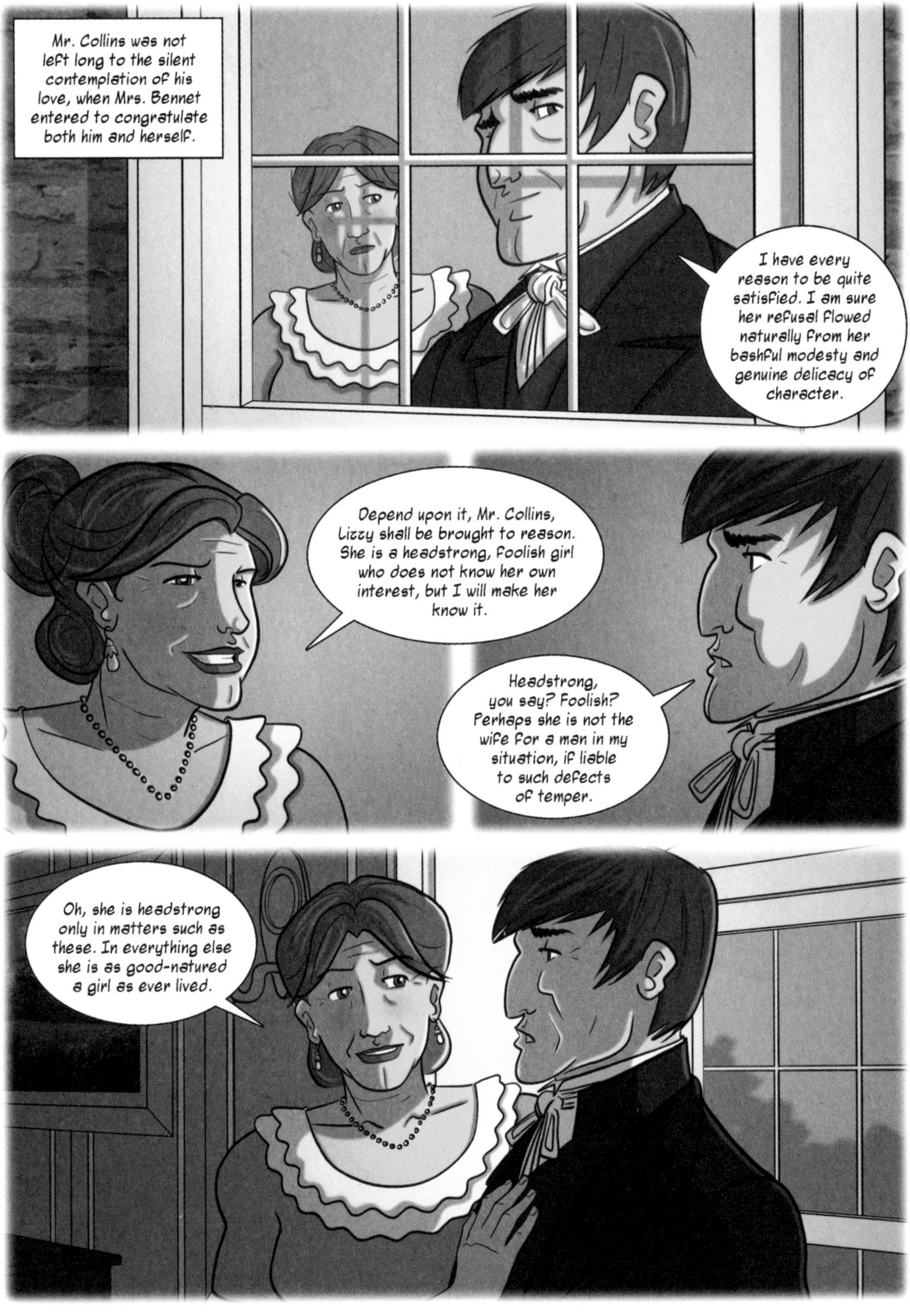
Mr. Collins was not left long to the silent contemplation of his love, when Mrs. Bennet entered to congratulate both him and herself.
I have every reason to be quite satisfied. I am sure her refusal flowed naturally from her bashful modesty and genuine delicacy of character.
Depend upon it, Mr. Collins, Lizzy shall be brought to reason. She is a headstrong, foolish girl who does not know her own interest, but I will make her know it.
Headstrong, you say? Foolish? Perhaps she is not the wife for a man in my situation, if liable to such defects of temper.
Oh, she is headstrong only in matters such as these. In everything else she is as good-natured a girl as ever lived.

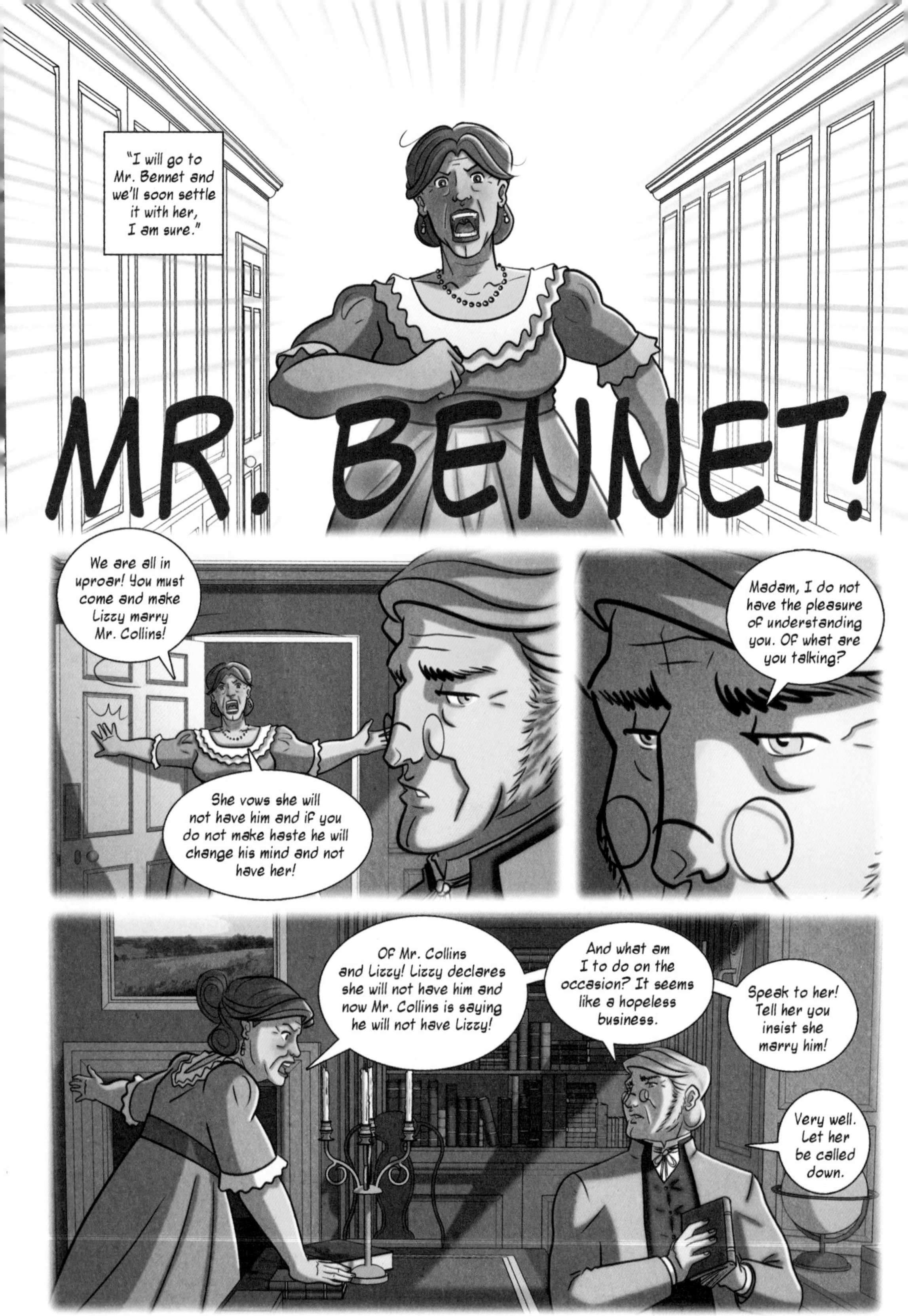
"I will go to Mr. Bennet and we'll soon settle it with her, I am sure."
MR. BENNET!
We are all in uproar! You must come and make Lizzy marry Mr. Collins!
She vows she will not have him and if you do not make haste he will change his mind and not have her!
Madam, I do not have the pleasure of understanding you. Of what are you talking?
Of Mr. Collins and Lizzy! Lizzy declares she will not have him and now Mr. Collins is saying he will not have Lizzy!
And what am I to do on the occasion? It seems like a hopeless business.
Speak to her! Tell her you insist she marry him!
Very well. Let her be called down.

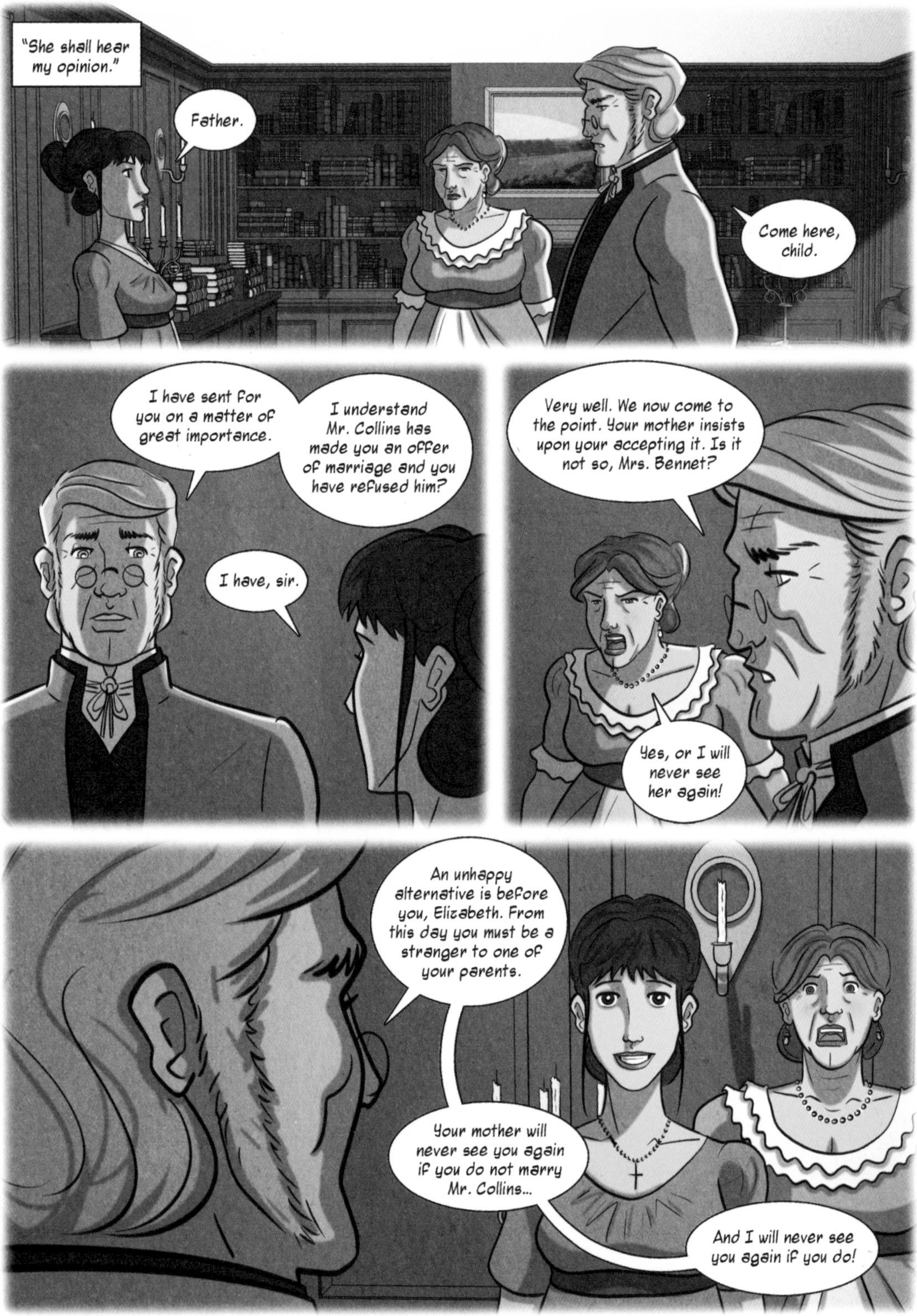
"She shall hear my opinion."
Father.
Come here, child.
I have sent for you on a matter of great importance.
I understand Mr. Collins has made you an offer of marriage and you have refused him?
I have, sir.
Very well. We now come to the point. Your mother insists upon your accepting it. Is it not so, Mrs. Bennet?
Yes, or I will never see her again!
An unhappy alternative is before you, Elizabeth. From this day you must be a stranger to one of your parents.
Your mother will never see you again if you do not marry Mr. Collins...
And I will never see you again if you do!

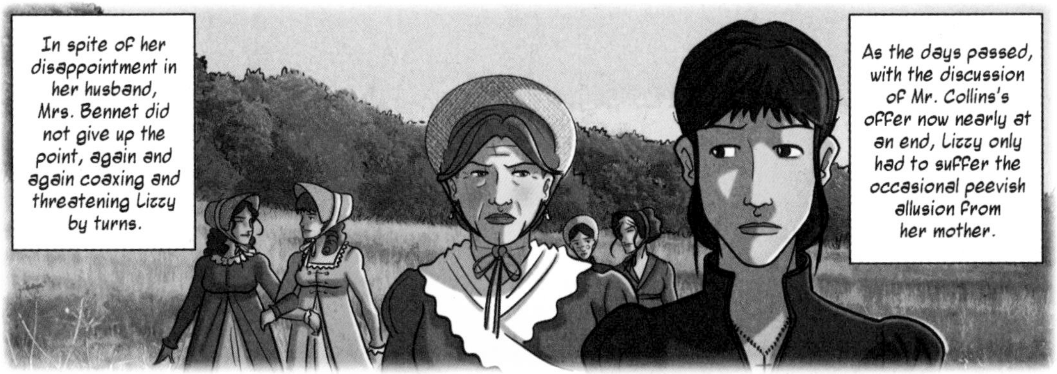
In spite of her disappointment in her husband, Mrs. Bennet did not give up the point, again and again coaxing and threatening Lizzy by turns.
As the days passed, with the discussion of Mr. Collins's offer now nearly at an end, Lizzy only had to suffer the occasional peevish allusion from her mother.

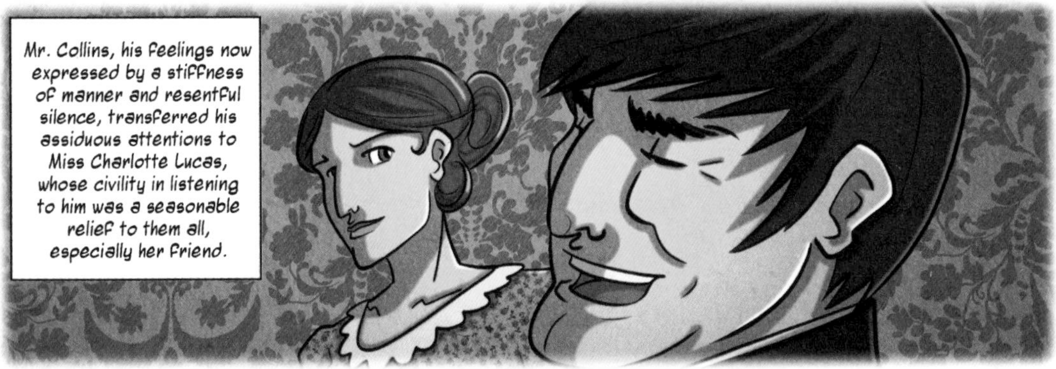
Mr. Collins, his feelings now expressed by a stiffness of manner and resentful silence, transferred his assiduous attentions to Miss Charlotte Lucas, whose civility in listening to him was a seasonable relief to them all, especially her friend.

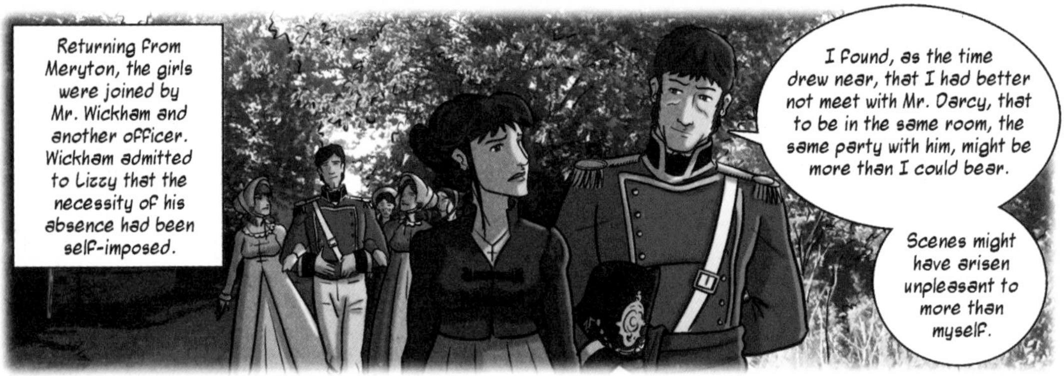
Returning from Meryton, the girls were joined by Mr. Wickham and another officer. Wickham admitted to Lizzy that the necessity of his absence had been self-imposed.
I found, as the time drew near, that I had better not meet with Mr. Darcy, that to be in the same room, the same party with him, might be more than I could bear.
Scenes might have arisen unpleasant to more than myself.

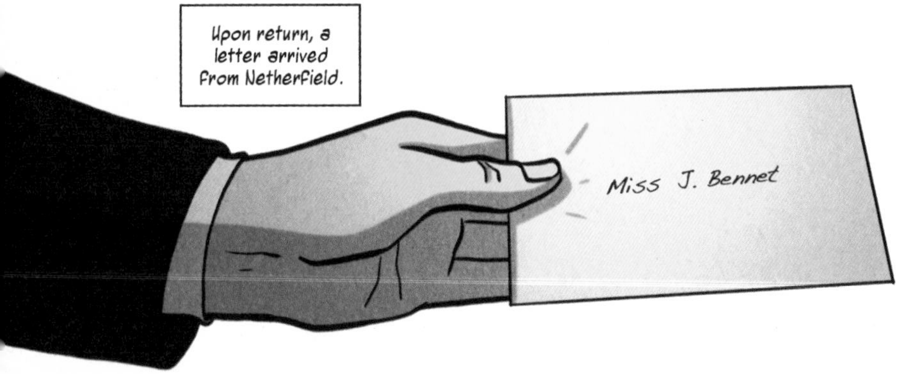
Upon return, a letter arrived from Netherfield.
Miss J. Bennet

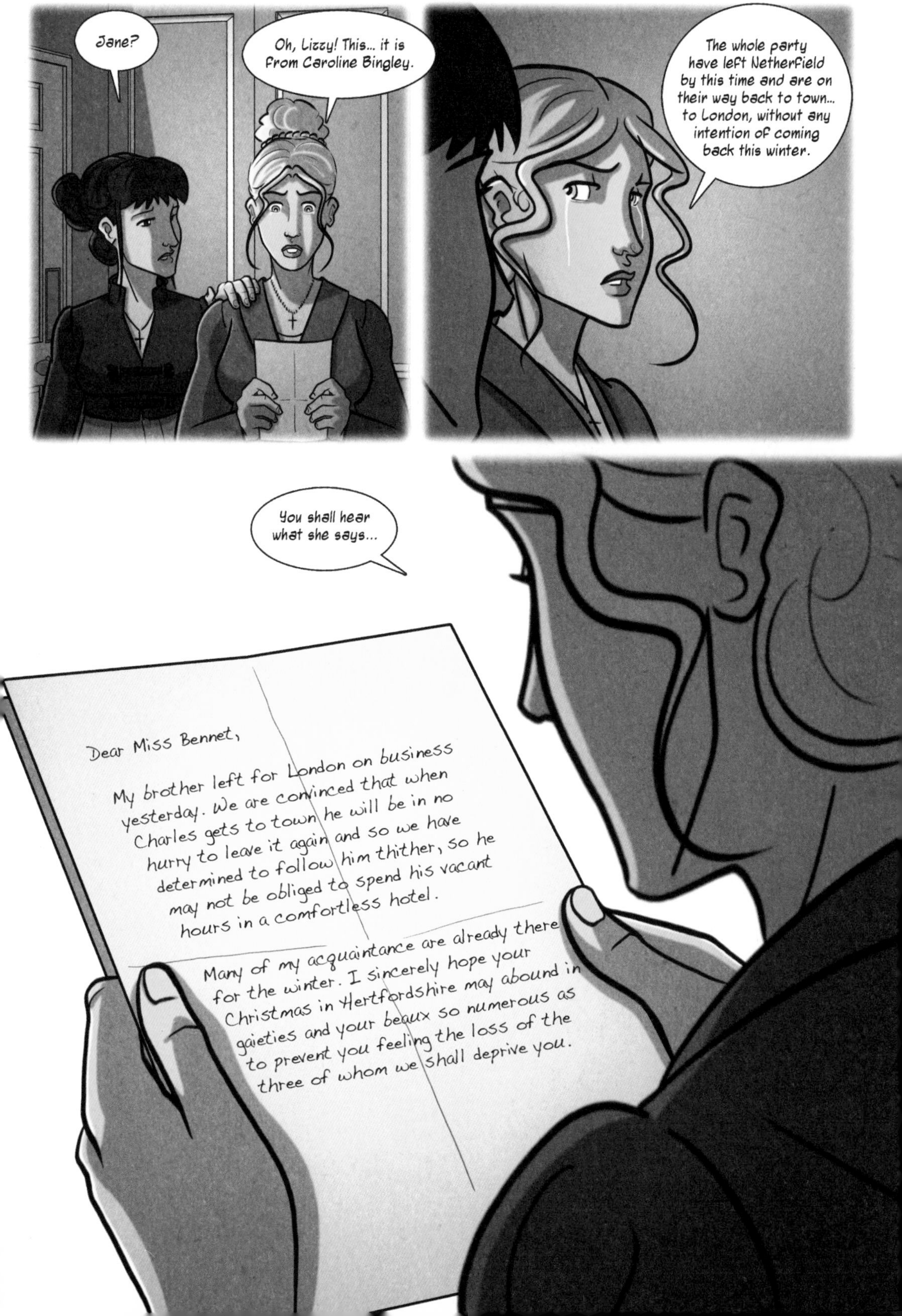
Jane?
Oh, Lizzy! This... it is from Caroline Bingley.
The whole party have left Netherfield by this time and are on their way back to town... to London, without any intention of coming back this winter.
You shall hear what she says...
Dear Miss Bennet,
My brother left for London on business yesterday. We are convinced that when Charles gets to town he will be in no hurry to leave it again and so we have determined to follow him thither, so he may not be obliged to spend his vacant hours in a comfortless hotel.
Many of my acquaintance are already there for the winter. I sincerely hope your Christmas in Hertfordshire may abound in gaieties and your beaux so numerous as to prevent you feeling the loss of the three of whom we shall deprive you.

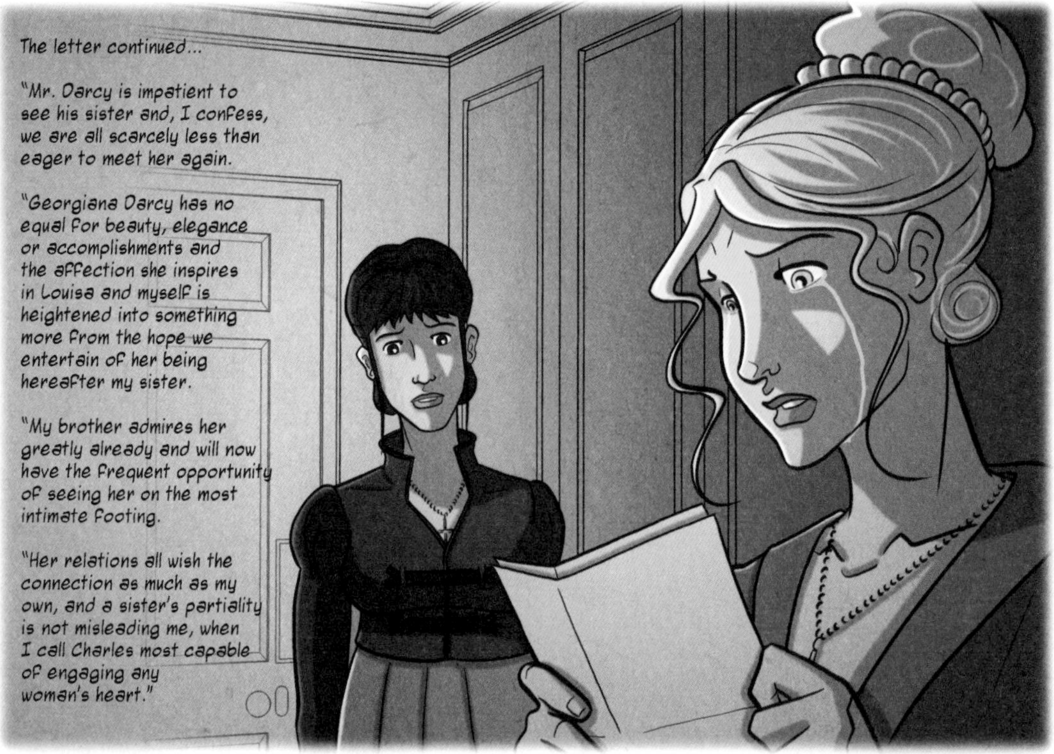
The letter continued...
"Mr. Darcy is impatient to see his sister and, I confess, we are all scarcely less than eager to meet her again.
"Georgiana Darcy has no equal for beauty, elegance or accomplishments and the affection she inspires in Louisa and myself is heightened into something more from the hope we entertain of her being hereafter my sister.
"My brother admires her greatly already and will now have the frequent opportunity of seeing her on the most intimate footing.
"Her relations all wish the connection as much as my own, and a sister's partiality is not misleading me, when I call Charles most capable of engaging any woman's heart."

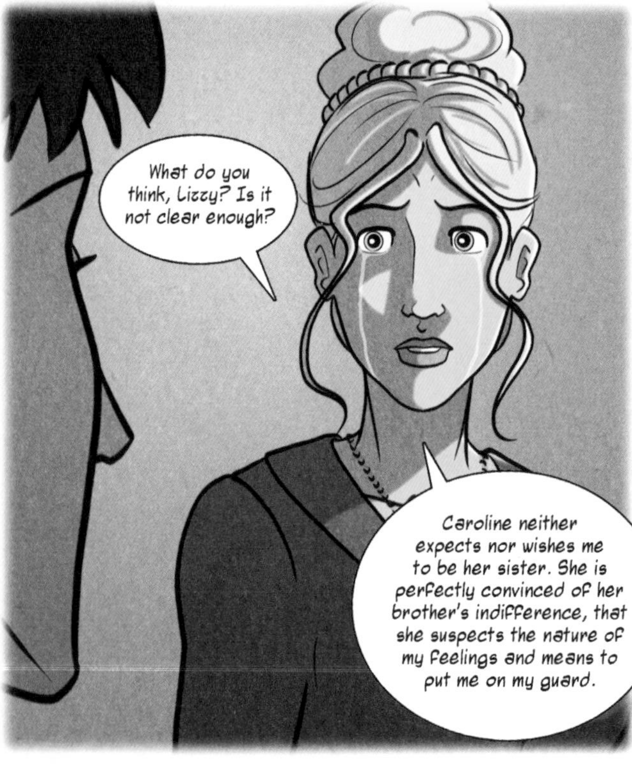
What do you think, Lizzy? Is it not clear enough?
Caroline neither expects nor wishes me to be her sister. She is perfectly convinced of her brother's indifference, that she suspects the nature of my feelings and means to put me on my guard.

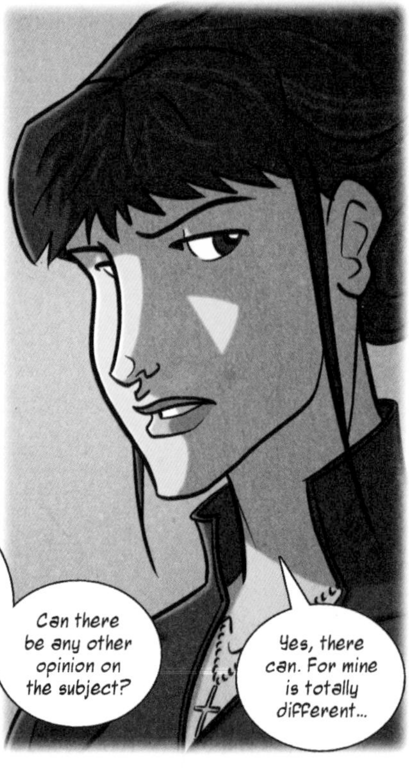
Can there be any other opinion on the subject?
Yes, there can. For mine is totally different...

Miss Bingley sees that her brother is in love with you and wants him to marry Miss Darcy.

She follows him to town in the hope of keeping him there, and tries to persuade you that he does not care about you.

Perhaps she is right?

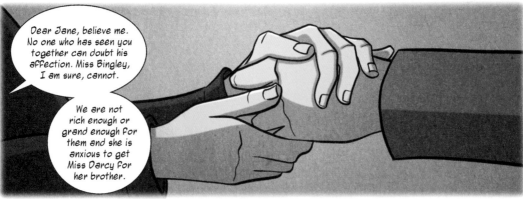

Dear Jane, believe me. No one who has seen you together can doubt his affection. Miss Bingley, I am sure, cannot.

We are not rich enough or grand enough for them and she is anxious to get Miss Darcy for her brother.

I cannot believe Caroline is capable of wilfully deceiving anyone. I can only hope in this case she is deceived herself.

But how can I be happy, in accepting a man whose sisters and friends are all wishing him to marry elsewhere?

You must decide for yourself if the misery of disobliging his sisters is more than equivalent to the happiness of being his wife.

67

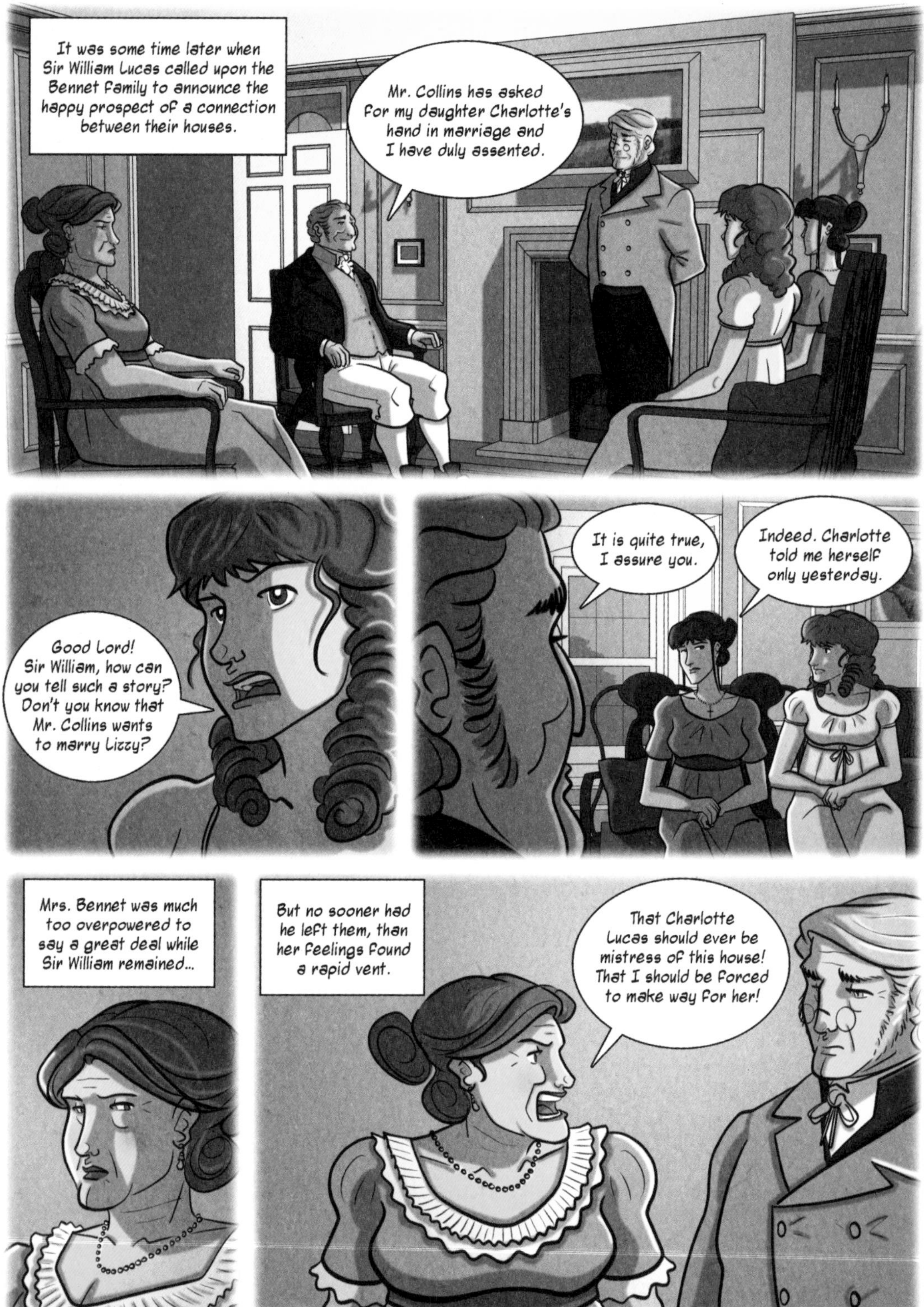
It was some time later when Sir William Lucas called upon the Bennet family to announce the happy prospect of a connection between their houses.
Mr. Collins has asked for my daughter Charlotte's hand in marriage and I have duly assented.
Good Lord! Sir William, how can you tell such a story? Don't you know that Mr. Collins wants to marry Lizzy?
It is quite true, I assure you.
Indeed. Charlotte told me herself only yesterday.
Mrs. Bennet was much too overpowered to say a great deal while Sir William remained...
But no sooner had he left them, than her feelings found a rapid vent.
That Charlotte Lucas should ever be mistress of this house! That I should be forced to make way for her!

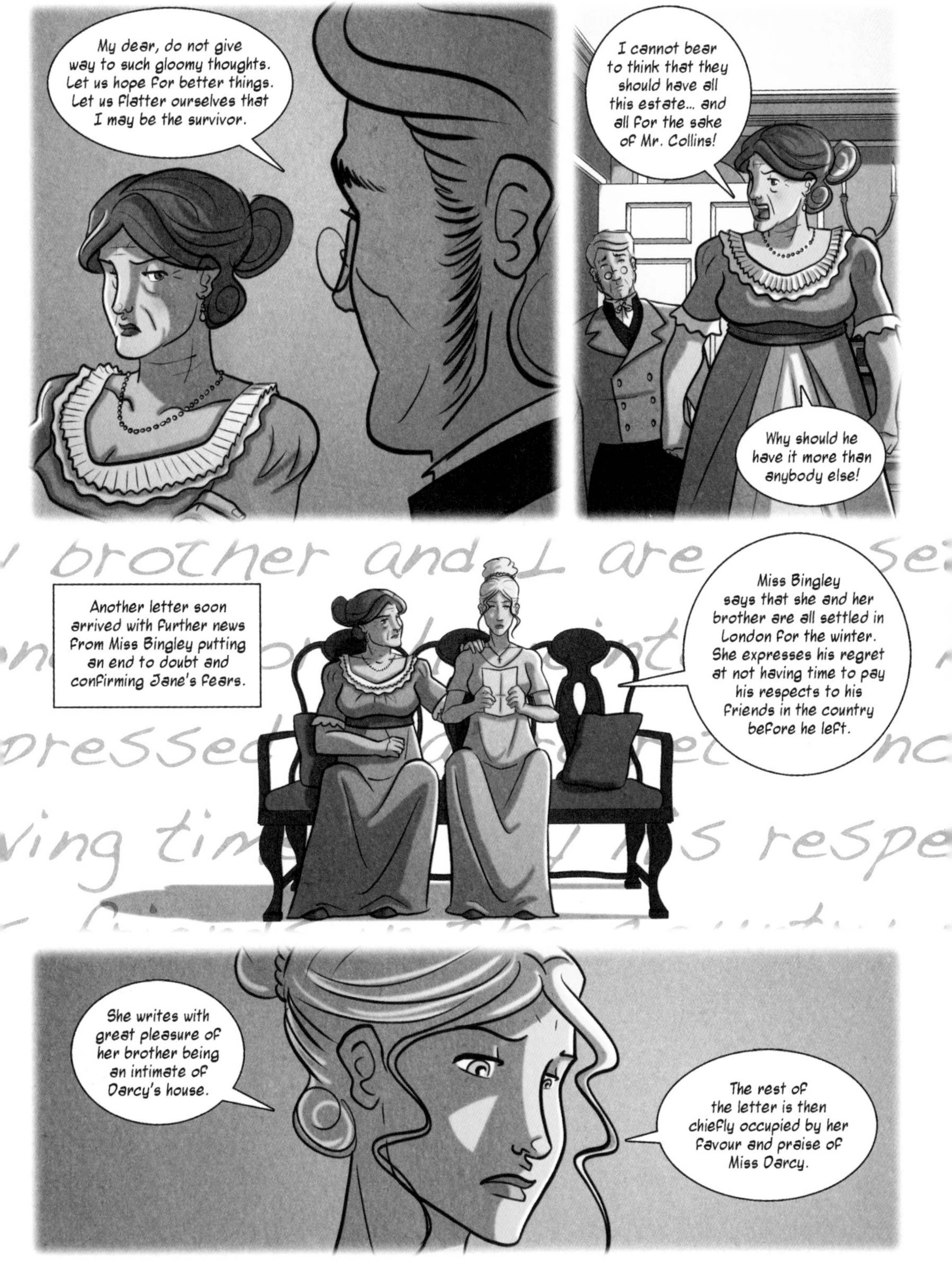
My dear, do not give way to such gloomy thoughts. Let us hope for better things. Let us flatter ourselves that I may be the survivor.
I cannot bear to think that they should have all this estate... and all for the sake of Mr. Collins!
Why should he have it more than anybody else!
Another letter soon arrived with further news from Miss Bingley putting an end to doubt and confirming Jane's fears.
Miss Bingley says that she and her brother are all settled in London for the winter. She expresses his regret at not having time to pay his respects to his friends in the country before he left.
She writes with great pleasure of her brother being an intimate of Darcy's house.
The rest of the letter is then chiefly occupied by her favour and praise of Miss Darcy.

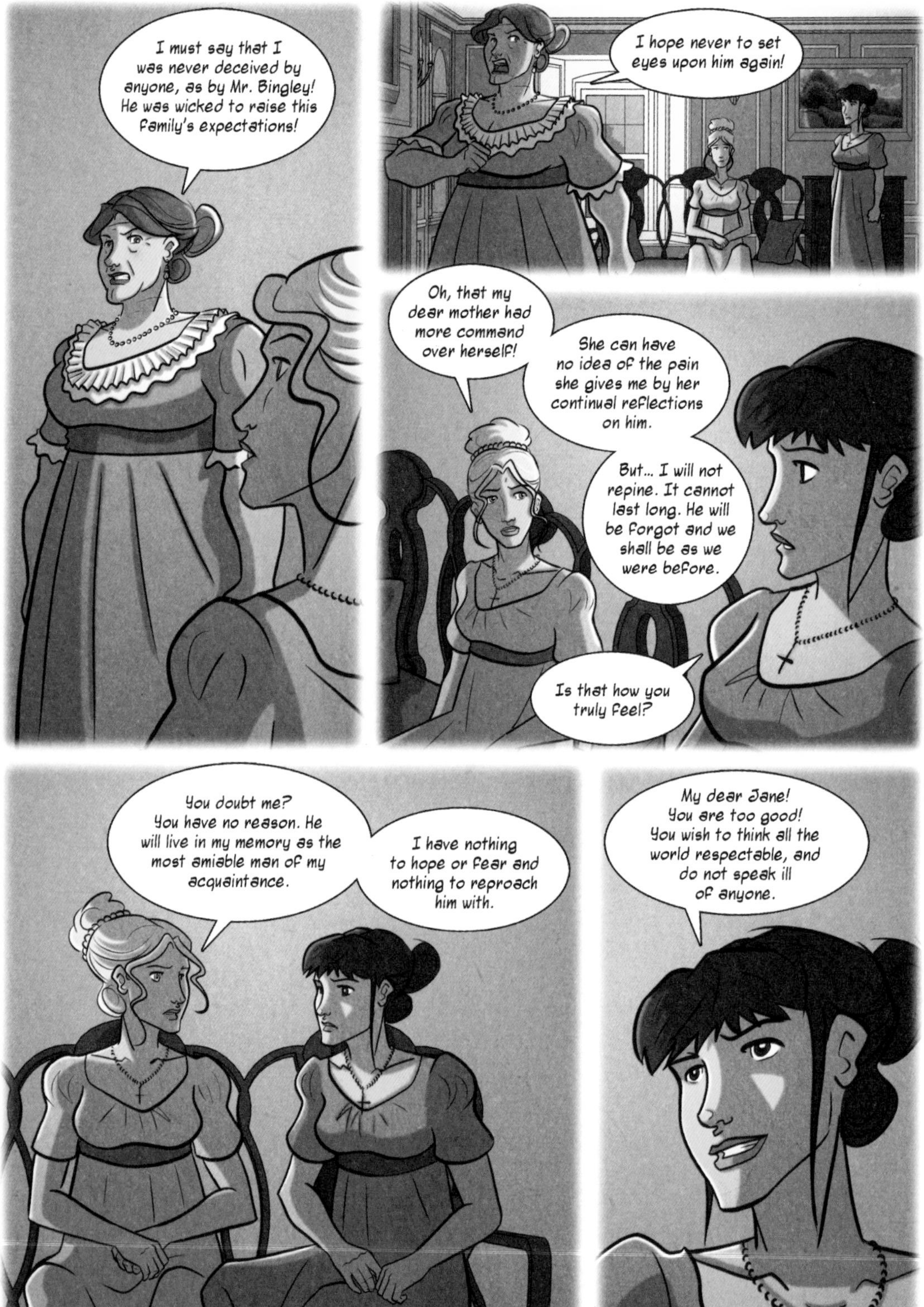
I must say that I was never deceived by anyone, as by Mr. Bingley! He was wicked to raise this family's expectations!
I hope never to set eyes upon him again!
Oh, that my dear mother had more command over herself!
She can have no idea of the pain she gives me by her continual reflections on him.
But... I will not repine. It cannot last long. He will be forgot and we shall be as we were before.
Is that how you truly feel?
You doubt me? You have no reason. He will live in my memory as the most amiable man of my acquaintance.
I have nothing to hope or fear and nothing to reproach him with.
My dear Jane! You are too good! You wish to think all the world respectable, and do not speak ill of anyone.

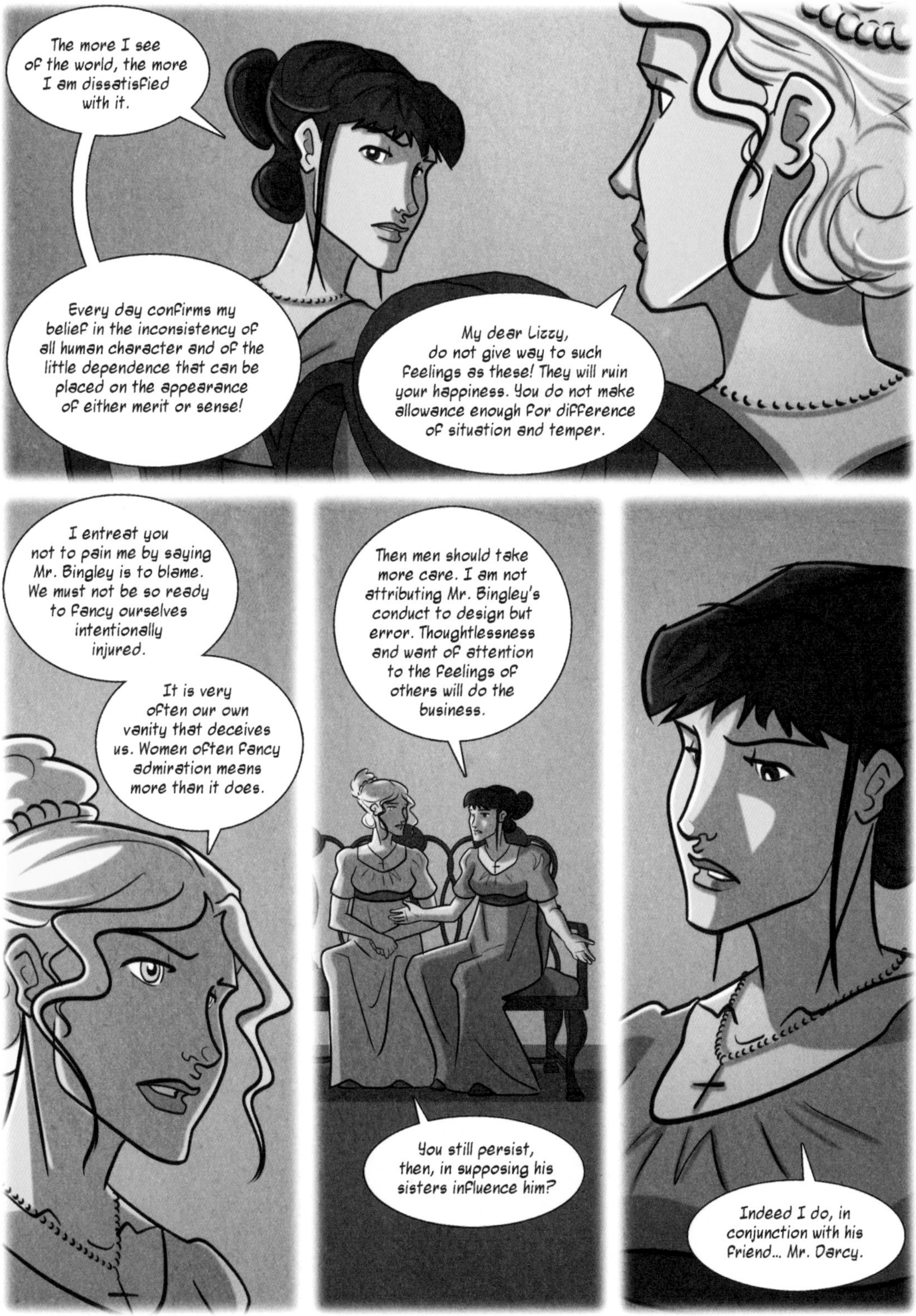
The more I see of the world, the more I am dissatisfied with it.
Every day confirms my belief in the inconsistency of all human character and of the little dependence that can be placed on the appearance of either merit or sense!
My dear Lizzy, do not give way to such feelings as these! They will ruin your happiness. You do not make allowance enough for difference of situation and temper.
I entreat you not to pain me by saying Mr. Bingley is to blame. We must not be so ready to fancy ourselves intentionally injured.
It is very often our own vanity that deceives us. Women often fancy admiration means more than it does.
Then men should take more care. I am not attributing Mr. Bingley's conduct to design but error. Thoughtlessness and want of attention to the feelings of others will do the business.
You still persist, then, in supposing his sisters influence him?
Indeed I do, in conjunction with his friend... Mr. Darcy.

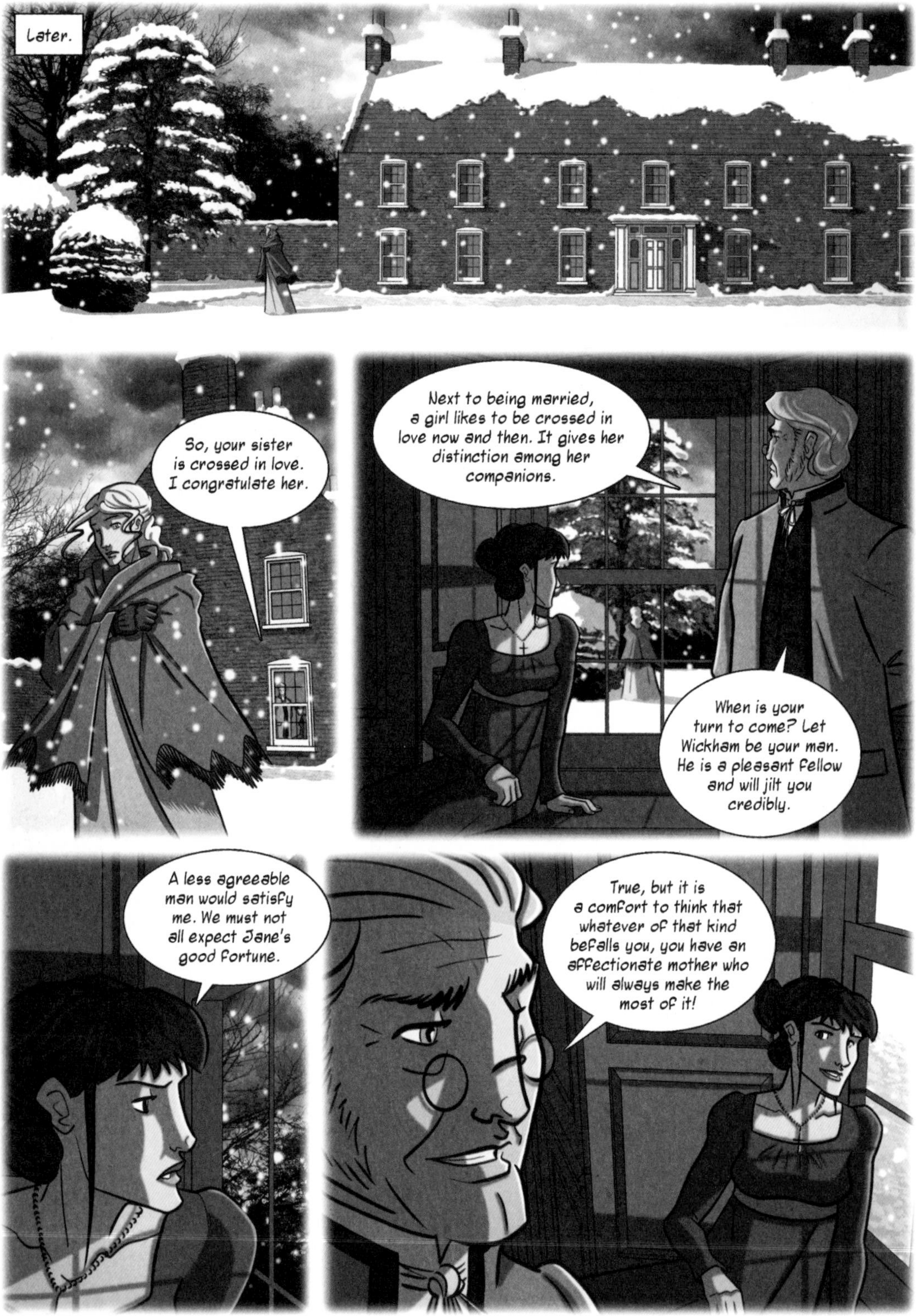
Later.
So, your sister is crossed in love. I congratulate her.
Next to being married, a girl likes to be crossed in love now and then. It gives her distinction among her companions.
When is your turn to come? Let Wickham be your man. He is a pleasant fellow and will jilt you credibly.
A less agreeable man would satisfy me. We must not all expect Jane's good fortune.
True, but it is a comfort to think that whatever of that kind befalls you, you have an affectionate mother who will always make the most of it!

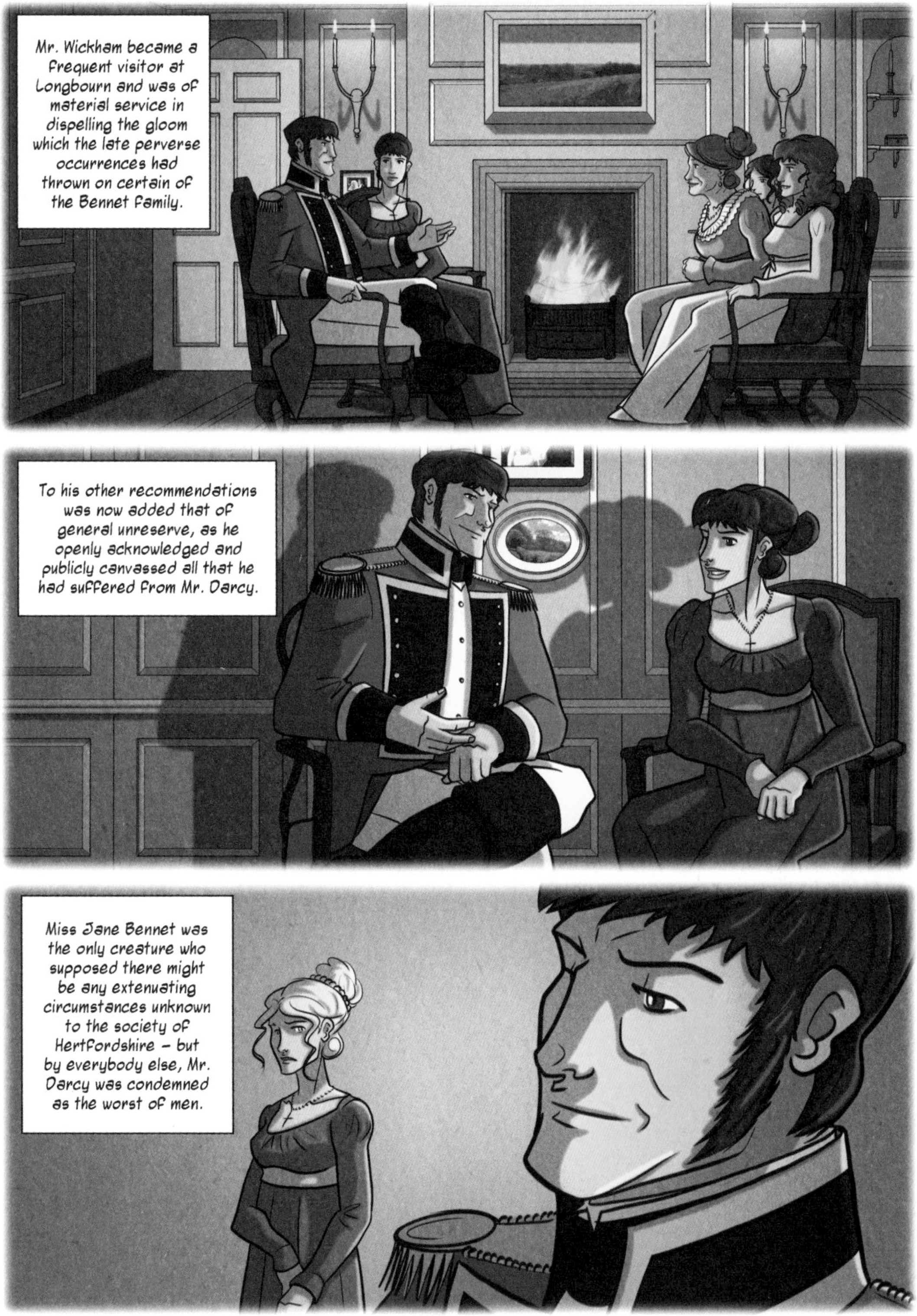
Mr. Wickham became a frequent visitor at Longbourn and was of material service in dispelling the gloom which the late perverse occurrences had thrown on certain of the Bennet family.
To his other recommendations was now added that of general unreserve, as he openly acknowledged and publicly canvassed all that he had suffered from Mr. Darcy.
Miss Jane Bennet was the only creature who supposed there might be any extenuating circumstances unknown to the society of Hertfordshire – but by everybody else, Mr. Darcy was condemned as the worst of men.

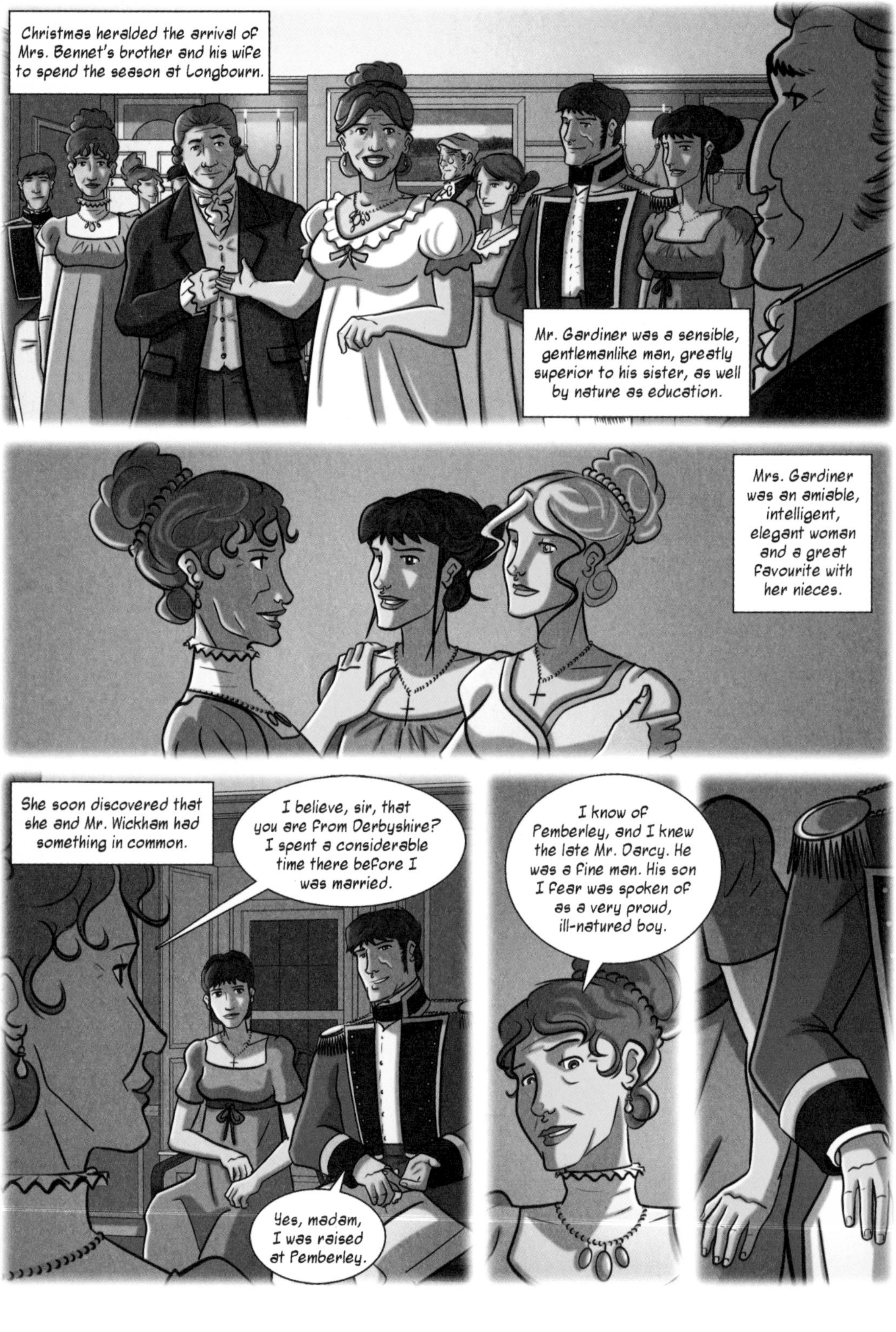
Christmas heralded the arrival of Mrs. Bennet's brother and his wife to spend the season at Longbourn.
Mr. Gardiner was a sensible, gentlemanlike man, greatly superior to his sister, as well by nature as education.
Mrs. Gardiner was an amiable, intelligent, elegant woman and a great favourite with her nieces.
She soon discovered that she and Mr. Wickham had something in common.
I believe, sir, that you are from Derbyshire? I spent a considerable time there before I was married.
Yes, madam, I was raised at Pemberley.
I know of Pemberley, and I knew the late Mr. Darcy. He was a fine man. His son I fear was spoken of as a very proud, ill-natured boy.

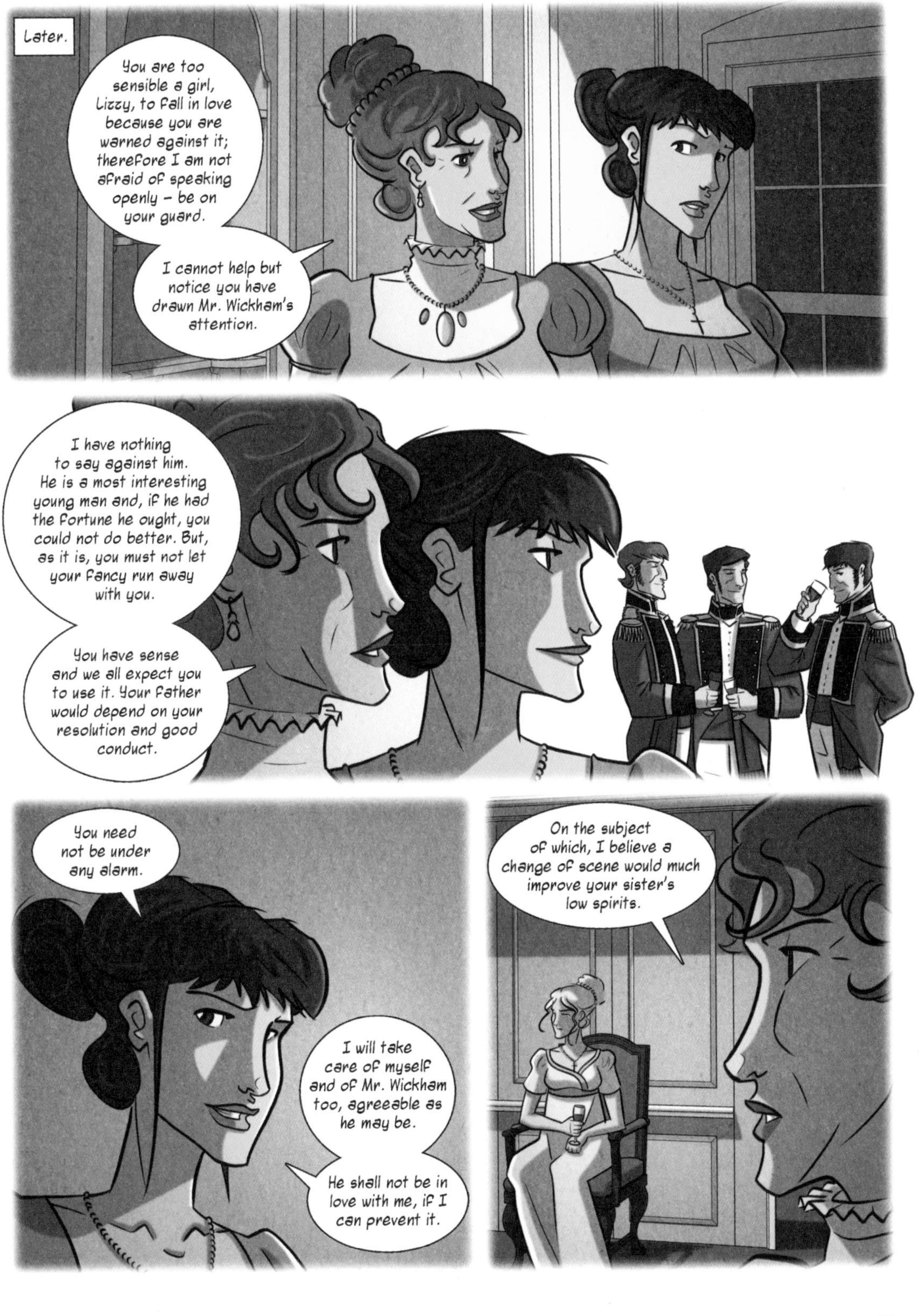
Later.
You are too sensible a girl, Lizzy, to fall in love because you are warned against it; therefore I am not afraid of speaking openly – be on your guard.
I cannot help but notice you have drawn Mr. Wickham's attention.
I have nothing to say against him. He is a most interesting young man and, if he had the fortune he ought, you could not do better. But, as it is, you must not let your fancy run away with you.
You have sense and we all expect you to use it. Your father would depend on your resolution and good conduct.
You need not be under any alarm.
I will take care of myself and of Mr. Wickham too, agreeable as he may be.
He shall not be in love with me, if I can prevent it.
On the subject of which, I believe a change of scene would much improve your sister's low spirits.

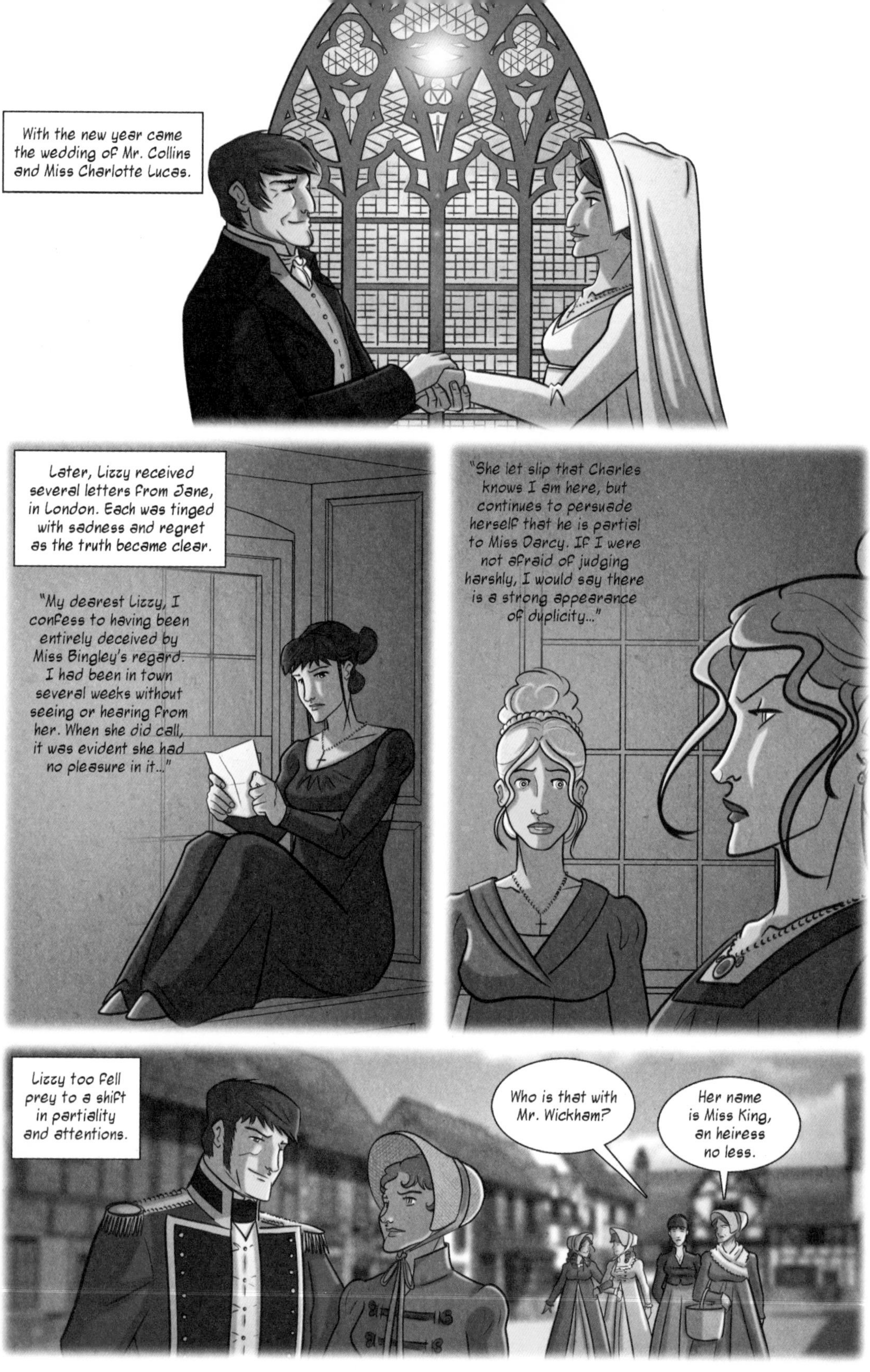
With the new year came the wedding of Mr. Collins and Miss Charlotte Lucas.
Later, Lizzy received several letters from Jane, in London. Each was tinged with sadness and regret as the truth became clear.
"My dearest Lizzy, I confess to having been entirely deceived by Miss Bingley's regard. I had been in town several weeks without seeing or hearing from her. When she did call, it was evident she had no pleasure in it..."
"She let slip that Charles knows I am here, but continues to persuade herself that he is partial to Miss Darcy. If I were not afraid of judging harshly, I would say there is a strong appearance of duplicity..."
Lizzy too fell prey to a shift in partiality and attentions.
Who is that with Mr. Wickham?
Her name is Miss King, an heiress no less.

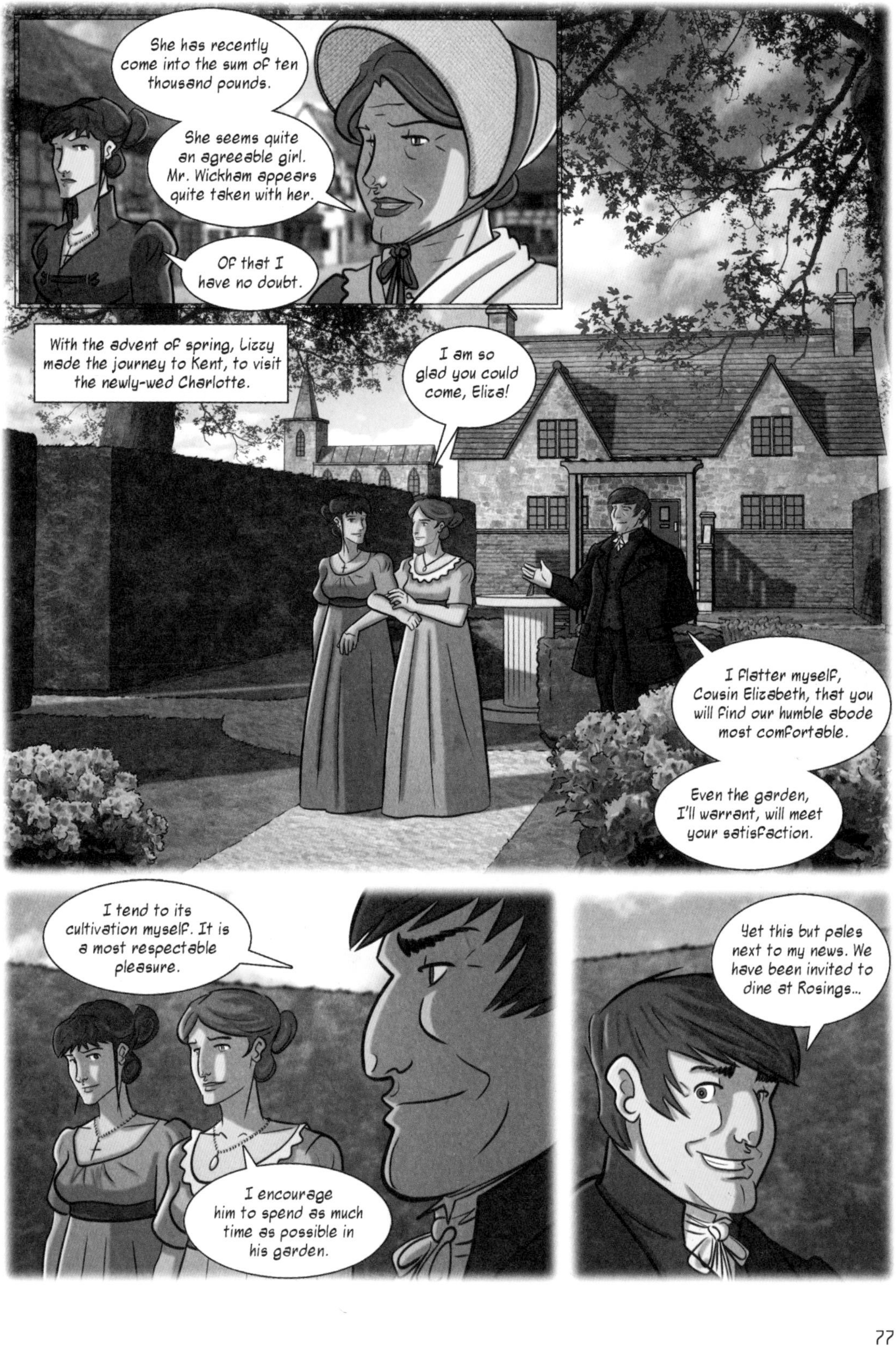

She has recently come into the sum of ten thousand pounds.
She seems quite an agreeable girl. Mr. Wickham appears quite taken with her.
Of that I have no doubt.
With the advent of spring, Lizzy made the journey to Kent, to visit the newly-wed Charlotte.
I am so glad you could come, Eliza!
I flatter myself, Cousin Elizabeth, that you will find our humble abode most comfortable.
Even the garden, I'll warrant, will meet your satisfaction.
I tend to its cultivation myself. It is a most respectable pleasure.
I encourage him to spend as much time as possible in his garden.
Yet this but pales next to my news. We have been invited to dine at Rosings...

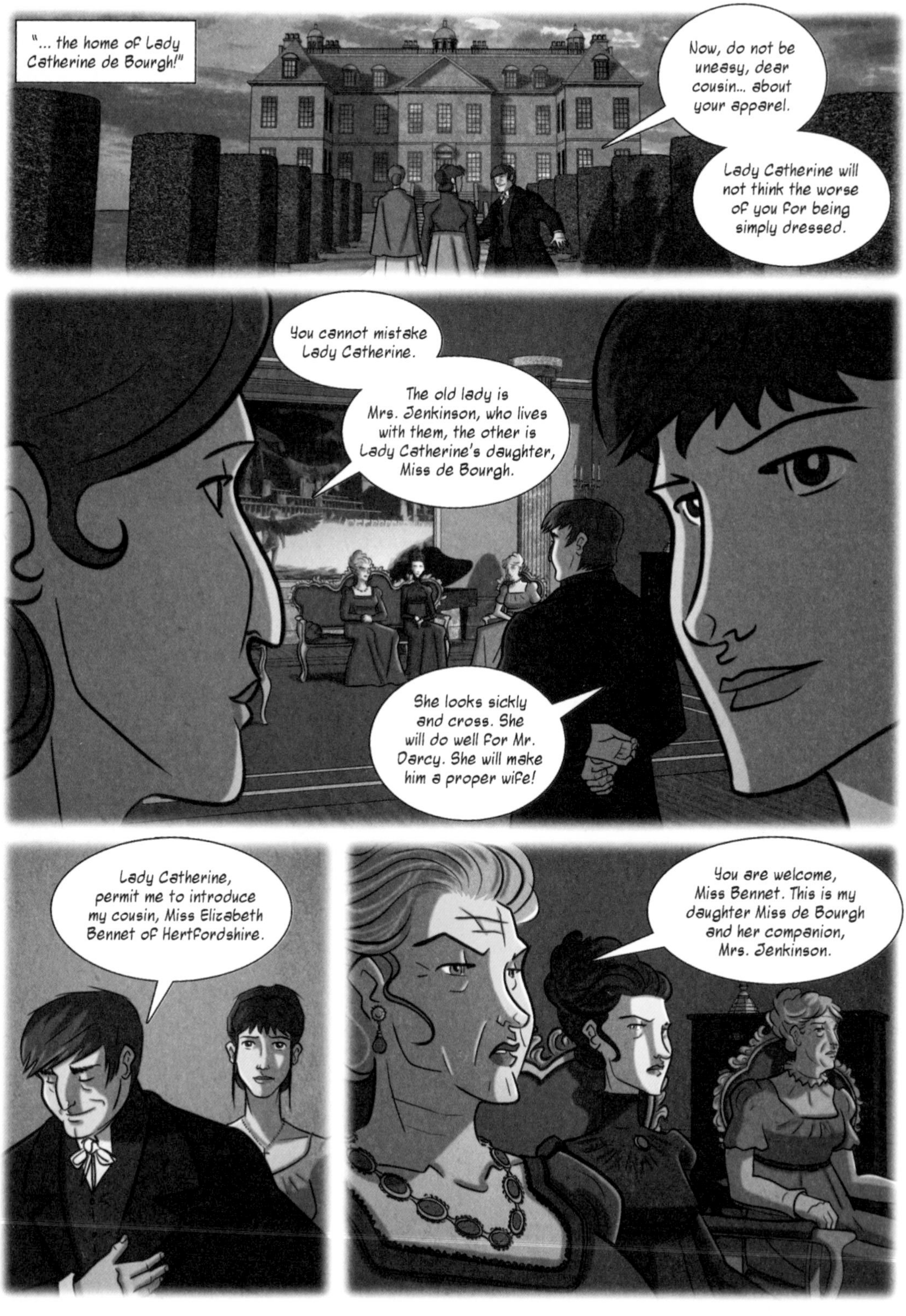
"... the home of Lady Catherine de Bourgh!"
Now, do not be uneasy, dear cousin... about your apparel.
Lady Catherine will not think the worse of you for being simply dressed.
You cannot mistake Lady Catherine.
The old lady is Mrs. Jenkinson, who lives with them, the other is Lady Catherine's daughter, Miss de Bourgh.
She looks sickly and cross. She will do well for Mr. Darcy. She will make him a proper wife!
Lady Catherine, permit me to introduce my cousin, Miss Elizabeth Bennet of Hertfordshire.
You are welcome, Miss Bennet. This is my daughter Miss de Bourgh and her companion, Mrs. Jenkinson.

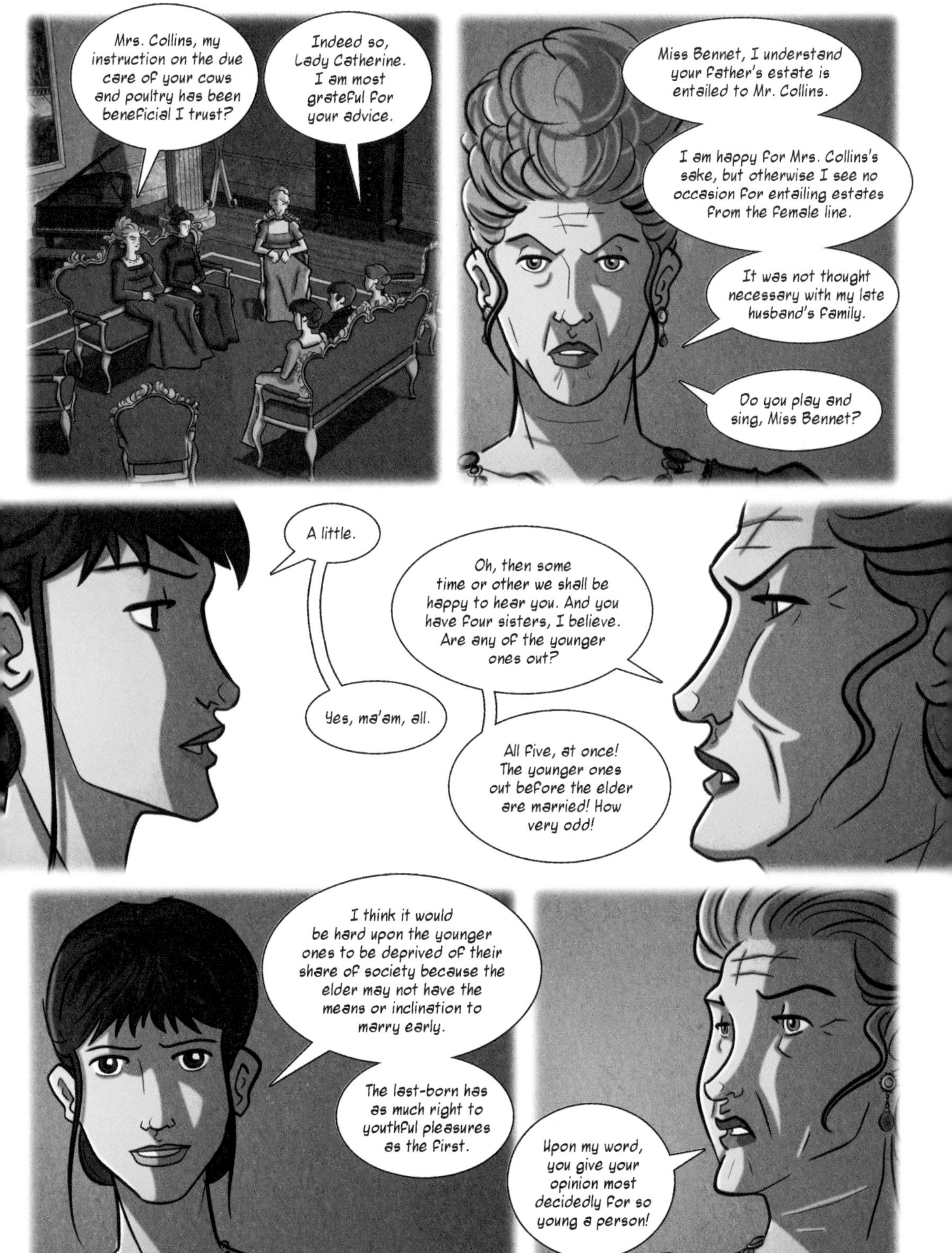
Mrs. Collins, my instruction on the due care of your cows and poultry has been beneficial I trust?
Indeed so, Lady Catherine. I am most grateful for your advice.
Miss Bennet, I understand your father's estate is entailed to Mr. Collins.
I am happy for Mrs. Collins's sake, but otherwise I see no occasion for entailing estates from the female line.
It was not thought necessary with my late husband's family.
Do you play and sing, Miss Bennet?
A little.
Oh, then some time or other we shall be happy to hear you. And you have four sisters, I believe. Are any of the younger ones out?
Yes, ma'am, all.
All five, at once! The younger ones out before the elder are married! How very odd!
I think it would be hard upon the younger ones to be deprived of their share of society because the elder may not have the means or inclination to marry early.
The last-born has as much right to youthful pleasures as the first.
Upon my word, you give your opinion most decidedly for so young a person!

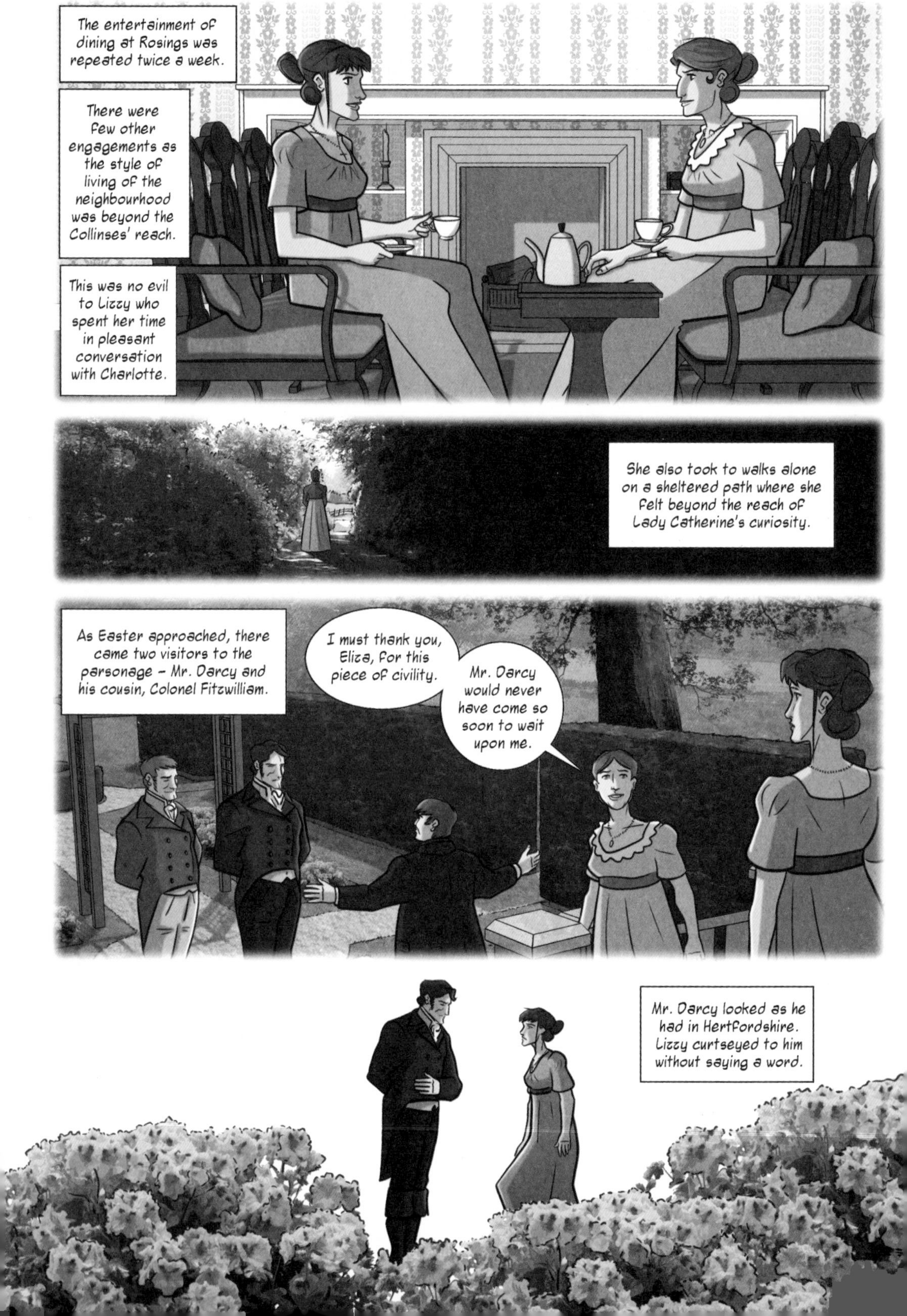
The entertainment of dining at Rosings was repeated twice a week.
There were few other engagements as the style of living of the neighbourhood was beyond the Collinses' reach.
This was no evil to Lizzy who spent her time in pleasant conversation with Charlotte.
She also took to walks alone on a sheltered path where she felt beyond the reach of Lady Catherine's curiosity.
As Easter approached, there came two visitors to the parsonage – Mr. Darcy and his cousin, Colonel Fitzwilliam.
I must thank you, Eliza, for this piece of civility.
Mr. Darcy would never have come so soon to wait upon me.
Mr. Darcy looked as he had in Hertfordshire. Lizzy curtseyed to him without saying a word.

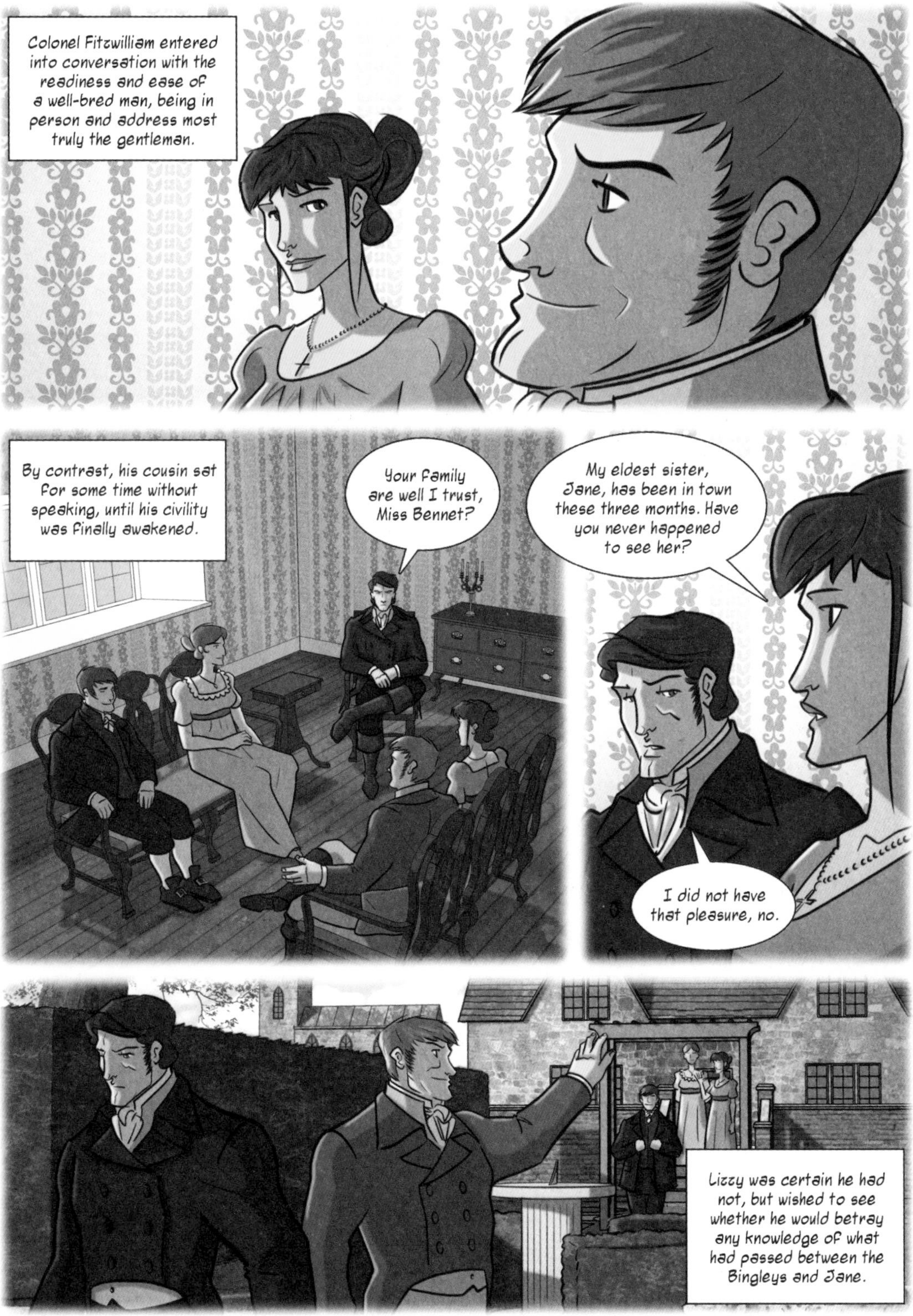
Colonel Fitzwilliam entered into conversation with the readiness and ease of a well-bred man, being in person and address most truly the gentleman.
By contrast, his cousin sat for some time without speaking, until his civility was finally awakened.
Your family are well I trust, Miss Bennet?
My eldest sister, Jane, has been in town these three months. Have you never happened to see her?
I did not have that pleasure, no.
Lizzy was certain he had not, but wished to see whether he would betray any knowledge of what had passed between the Bingleys and Jane.

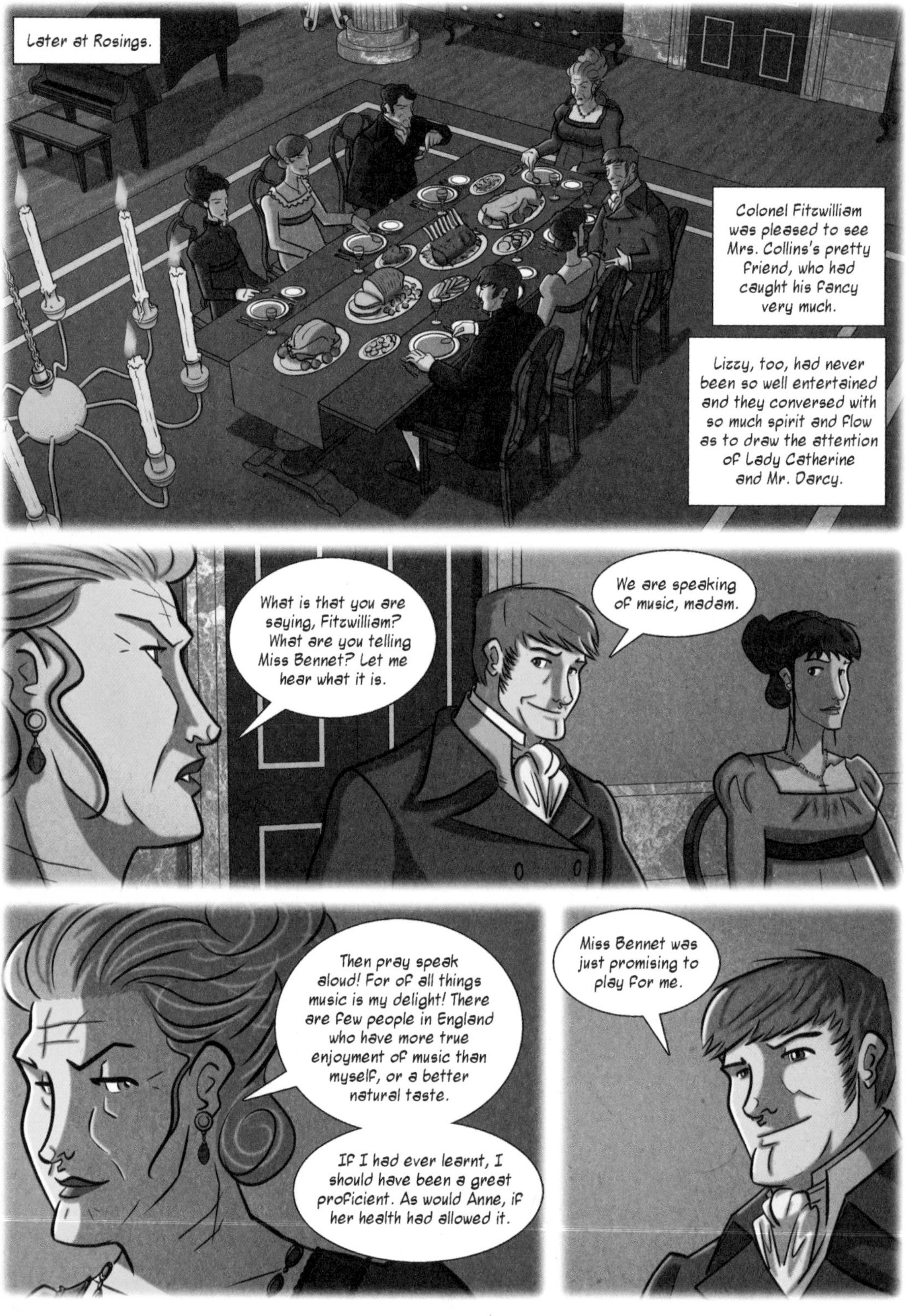
Later at Rosings.
Colonel Fitzwilliam was pleased to see Mrs. Collins's pretty friend, who had caught his fancy very much.
Lizzy, too, had never been so well entertained and they conversed with so much spirit and flow as to draw the attention of Lady Catherine and Mr. Darcy.
What is that you are saying, Fitzwilliam? What are you telling Miss Bennet? Let me hear what it is.
We are speaking of music, madam.
Then pray speak aloud! For of all things music is my delight! There are few people in England who have more true enjoyment of music than myself, or a better natural taste.
If I had ever learnt, I should have been a great proficient. As would Anne, if her health had allowed it.
Miss Bennet was just promising to play for me.

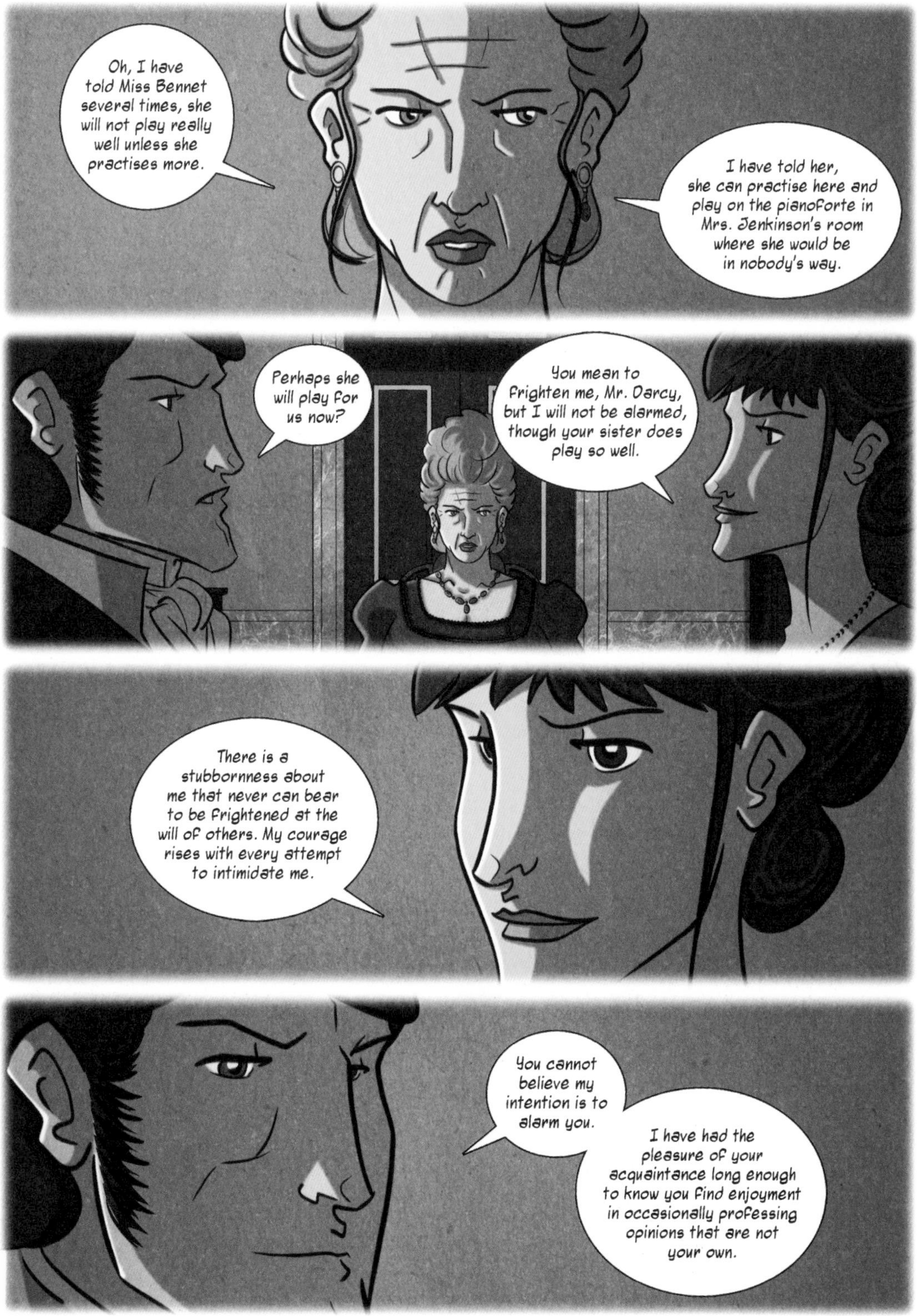
Oh, I have told Miss Bennet several times, she will not play really well unless she practises more.
I have told her, she can practise here and play on the pianoforte in Mrs. Jenkinson's room where she would be in nobody's way.
Perhaps she will play for us now?
You mean to frighten me, Mr. Darcy, but I will not be alarmed, though your sister does play so well.
There is a stubbornness about me that never can bear to be frightened at the will of others. My courage rises with every attempt to intimidate me.
You cannot believe my intention is to alarm you.
I have had the pleasure of your acquaintance long enough to know you find enjoyment in occasionally professing opinions that are not your own.

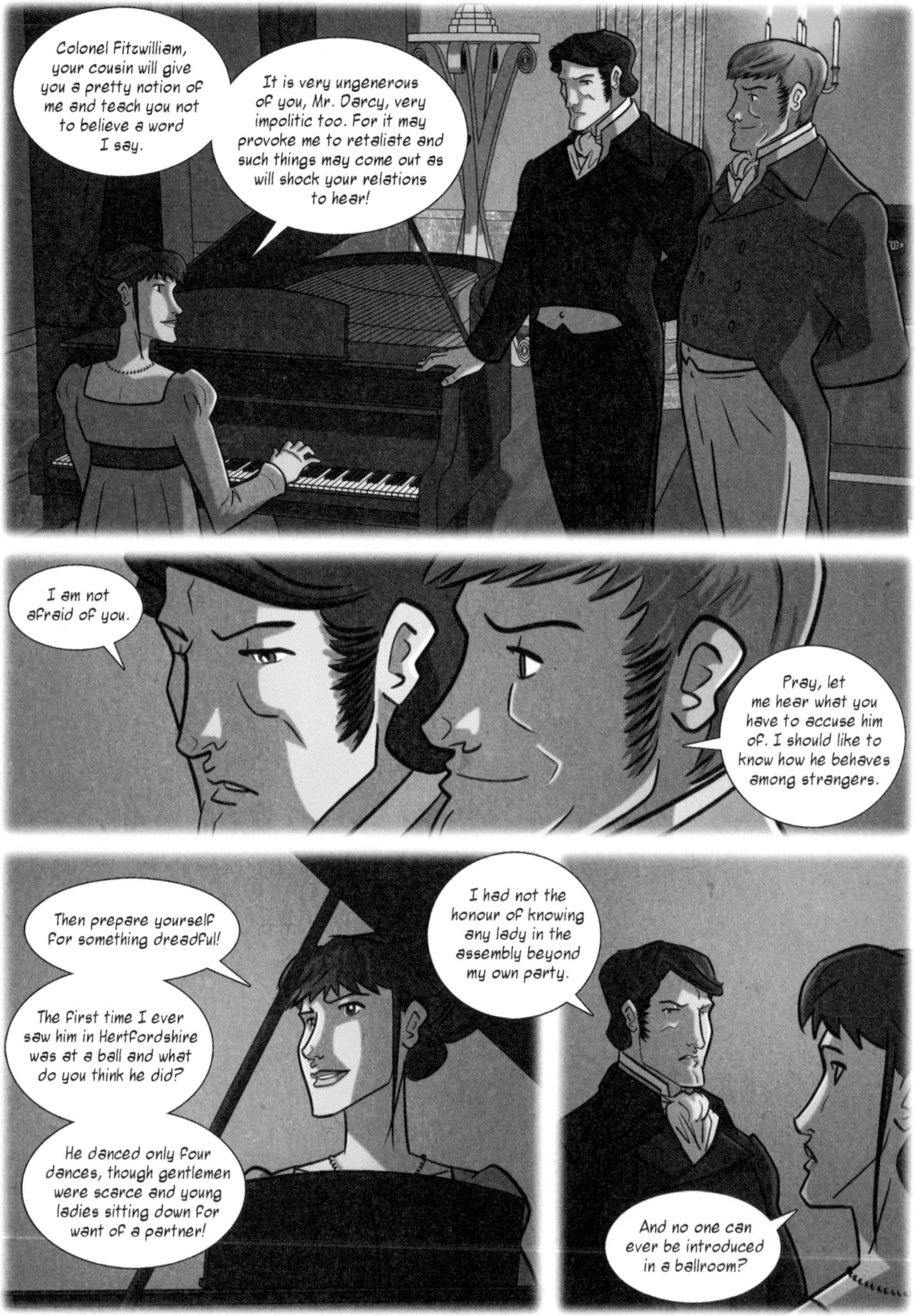
Colonel Fitzwilliam, your cousin will give you a pretty notion of me and teach you not to believe a word I say.
It is very ungenerous of you, Mr. Darcy, very impolitic too. For it may provoke me to retaliate and such things may come out as will shock your relations to hear!
I am not afraid of you.
Pray, let me hear what you have to accuse him of. I should like to know how he behaves among strangers.
Then prepare yourself for something dreadful!
The first time I ever saw him in Hertfordshire was at a ball and what do you think he did?
He danced only four dances, though gentlemen were scarce and young ladies sitting down for want of a partner!
I had not the honour of knowing any lady in the assembly beyond my own party.
And no one can ever be introduced in a ballroom?

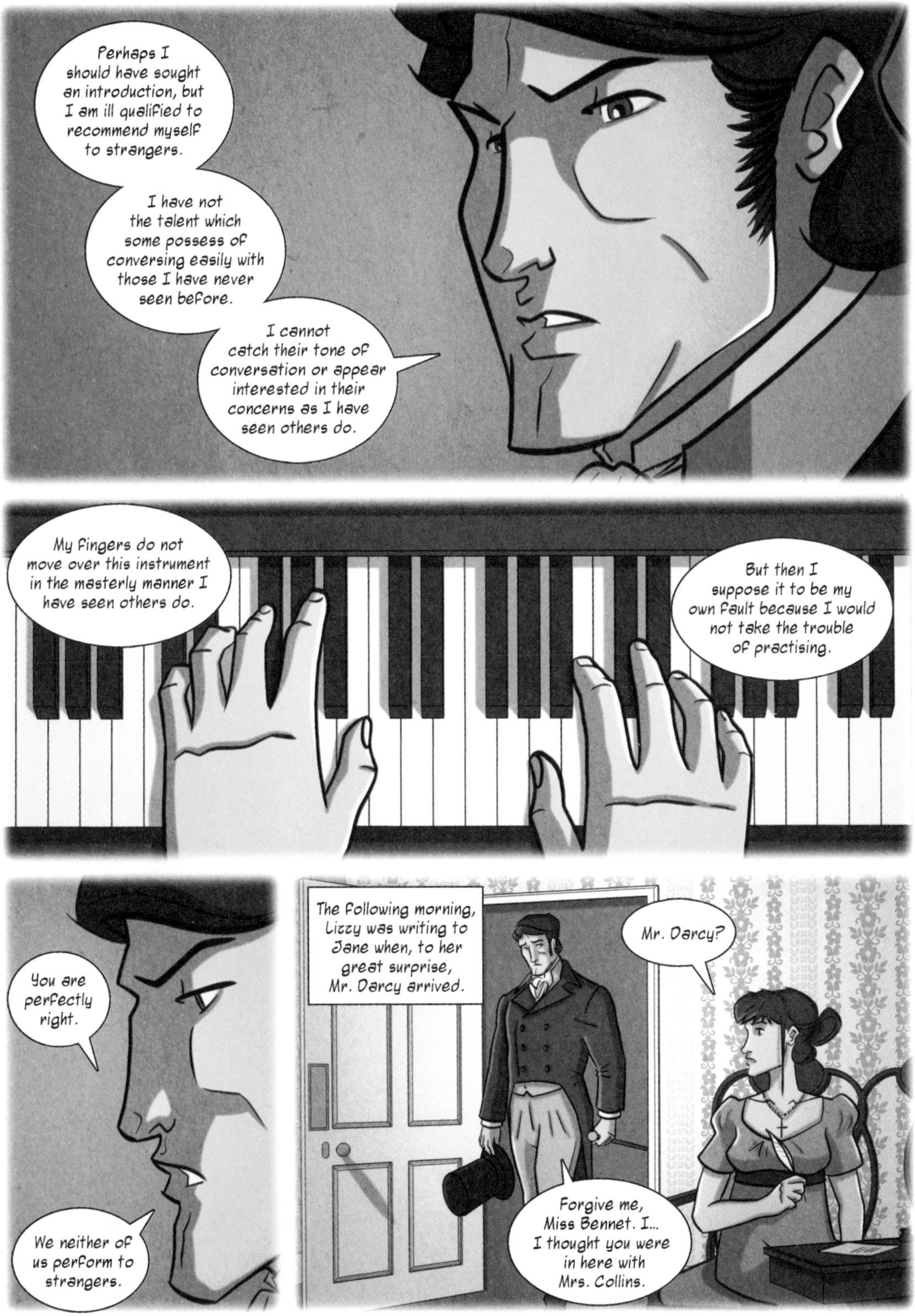
Perhaps I should have sought an introduction, but I am ill qualified to recommend myself to strangers.
I have not the talent which some possess of conversing easily with those I have never seen before.
I cannot catch their tone of conversation or appear interested in their concerns as I have seen others do.
My fingers do not move over this instrument in the masterly manner I have seen others do.
But then I suppose it to be my own fault because I would not take the trouble of practising.
You are perfectly right.
We neither of us perform to strangers.
The following morning, Lizzy was writing to Jane when, to her great surprise, Mr. Darcy arrived.
Mr. Darcy?
Forgive me, Miss Bennet. I... I thought you were in here with Mrs. Collins.

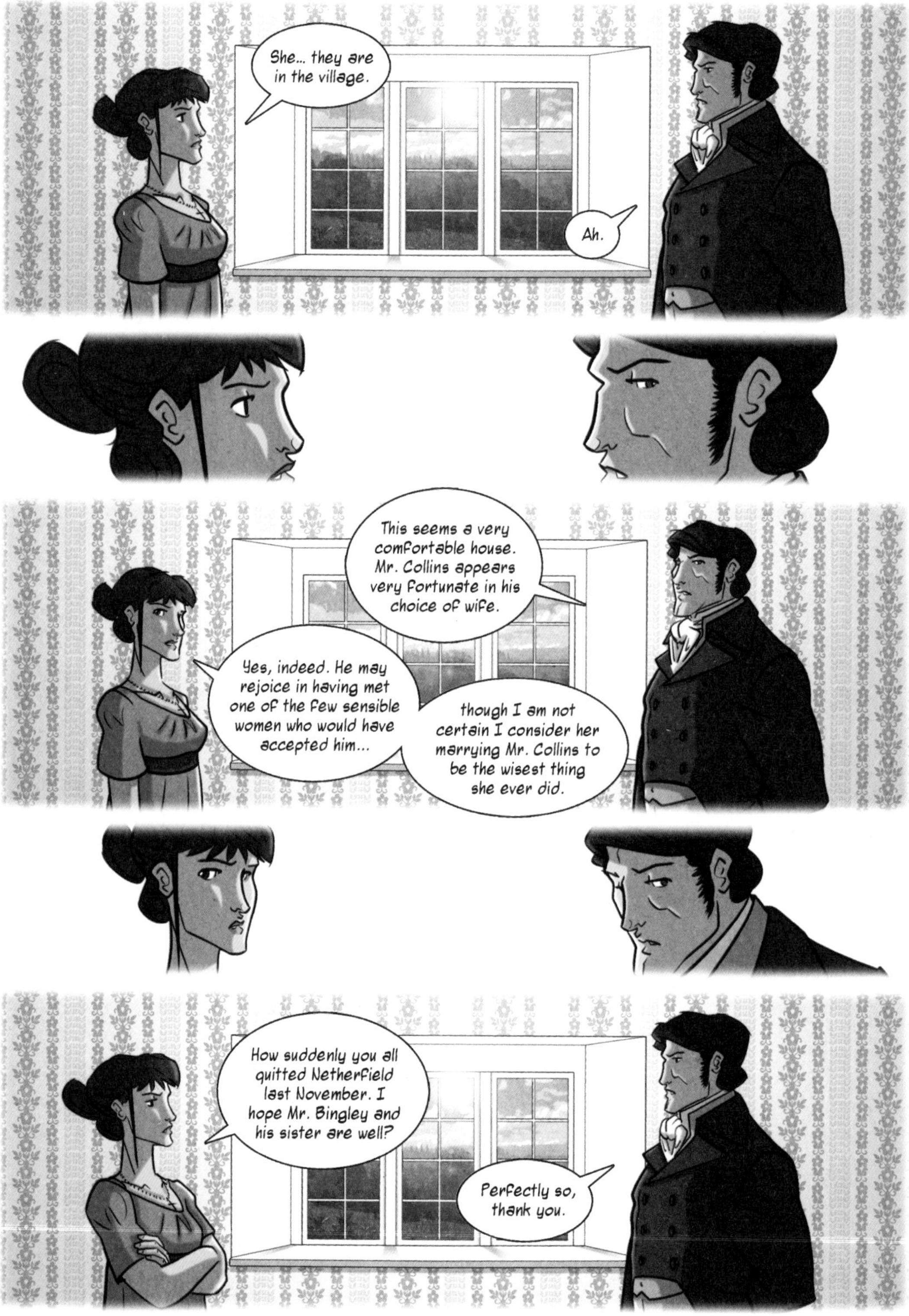
She... they are in the village.
Ah.
This seems a very comfortable house. Mr. Collins appears very fortunate in his choice of wife.
Yes, indeed. He may rejoice in having met one of the few sensible women who would have accepted him...
though I am not certain I consider her marrying Mr. Collins to be the wisest thing she ever did.
How suddenly you all quitted Netherfield last November. I hope Mr. Bingley and his sister are well?
Perfectly so, thank you.

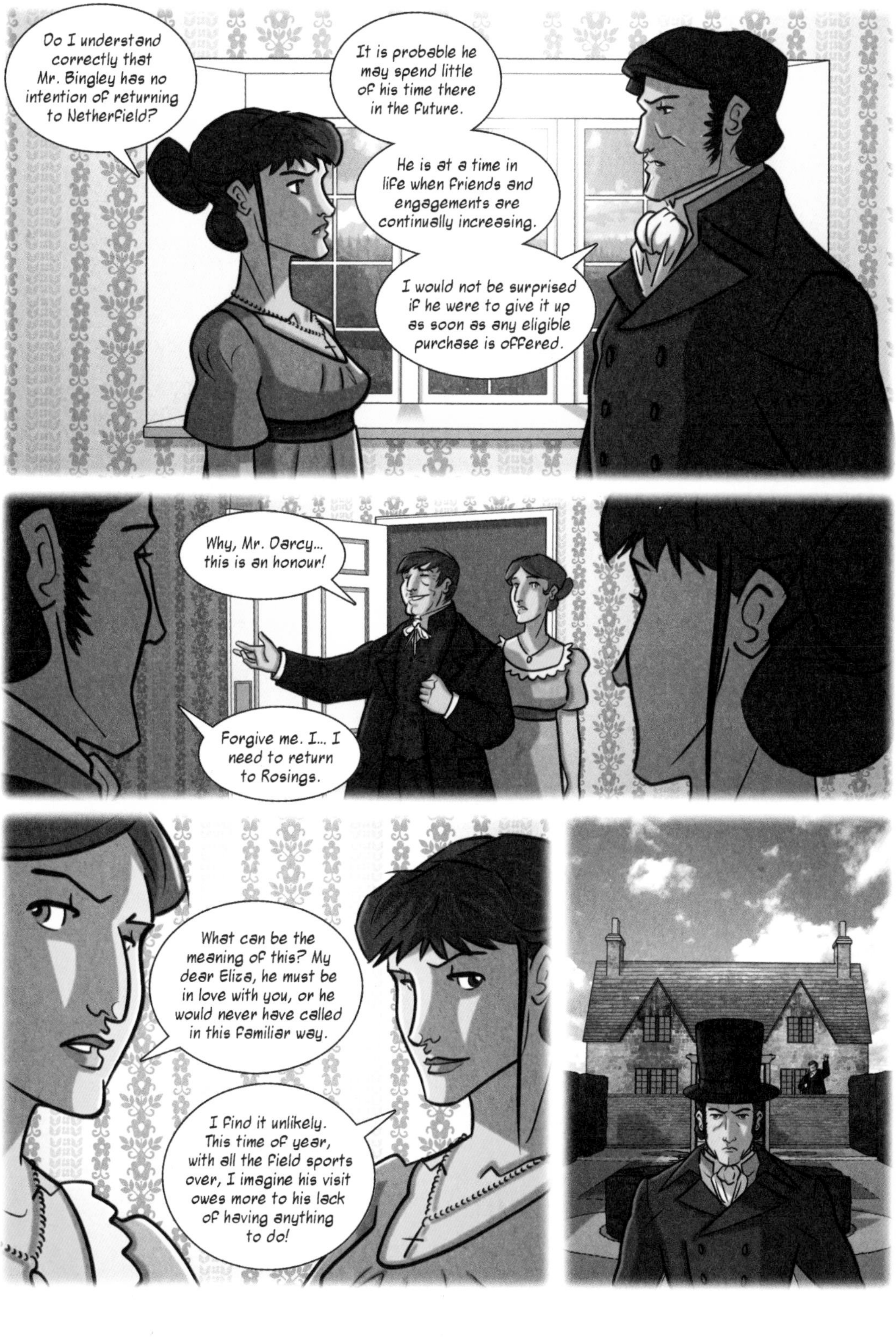
Do I understand correctly that Mr. Bingley has no intention of returning to Netherfield?
It is probable he may spend little of his time there in the future.
He is at a time in life when friends and engagements are continually increasing.
I would not be surprised if he were to give it up as soon as any eligible purchase is offered.
Why, Mr. Darcy... this is an honour!
Forgive me. I... I need to return to Rosings.
What can be the meaning of this? My dear Eliza, he must be in love with you, or he would never have called in this familiar way.
I find it unlikely. This time of year, with all the field sports over, I imagine his visit owes more to his lack of having anything to do!

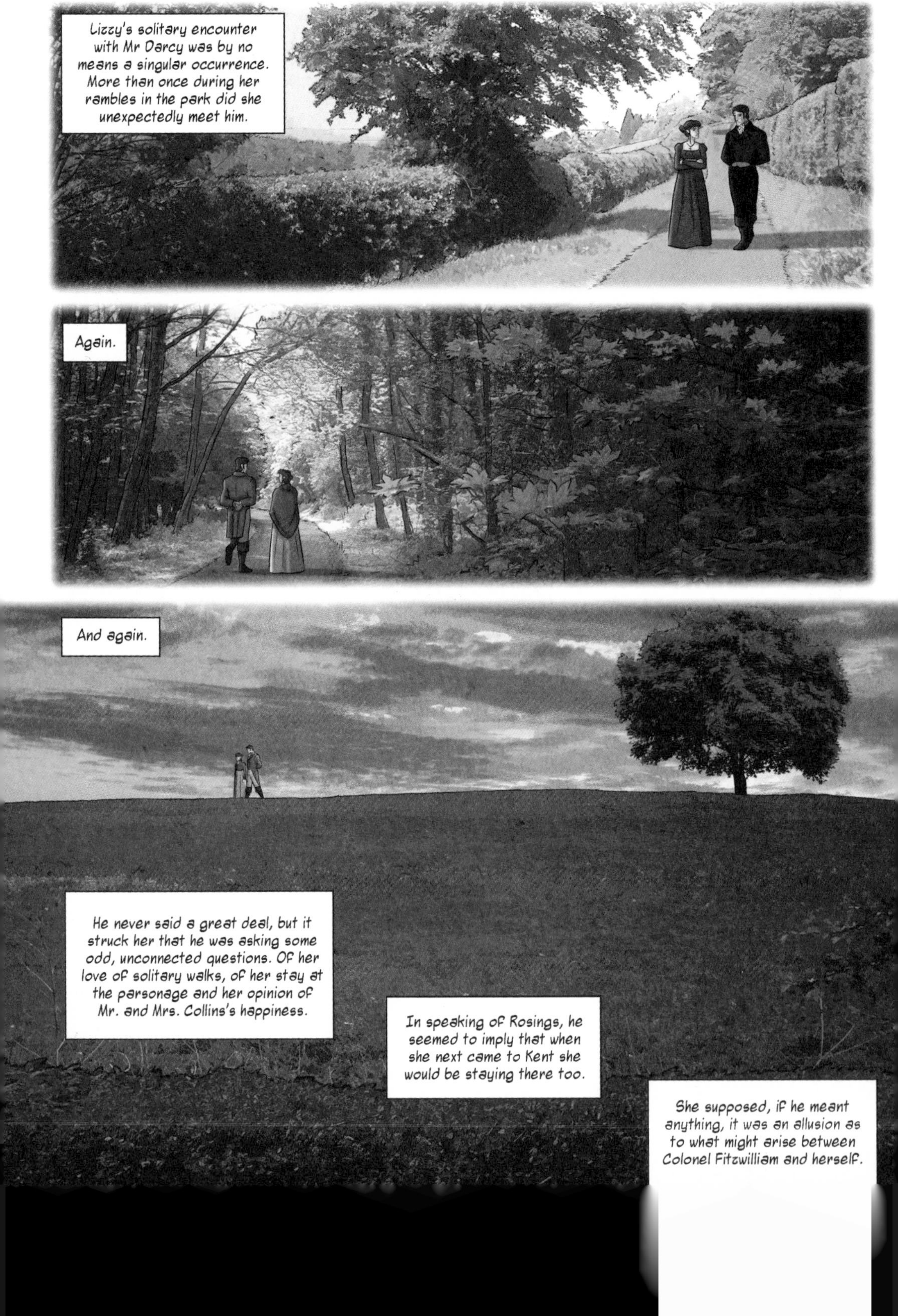
Lizzy's solitary encounter with Mr Darcy was by no means a singular occurrence. More than once during her rambles in the park did she unexpectedly meet him.
Again.
And again.
He never said a great deal, but it struck her that he was asking some odd, unconnected questions. Of her love of solitary walks, of her stay at the parsonage and her opinion of Mr. and Mrs. Collins's happiness.
In speaking of Rosings, he seemed to imply that when she next came to Kent she would be staying there too.
She supposed, if he meant anything, it was an allusion as to what might arise between Colonel Fitzwilliam and herself.

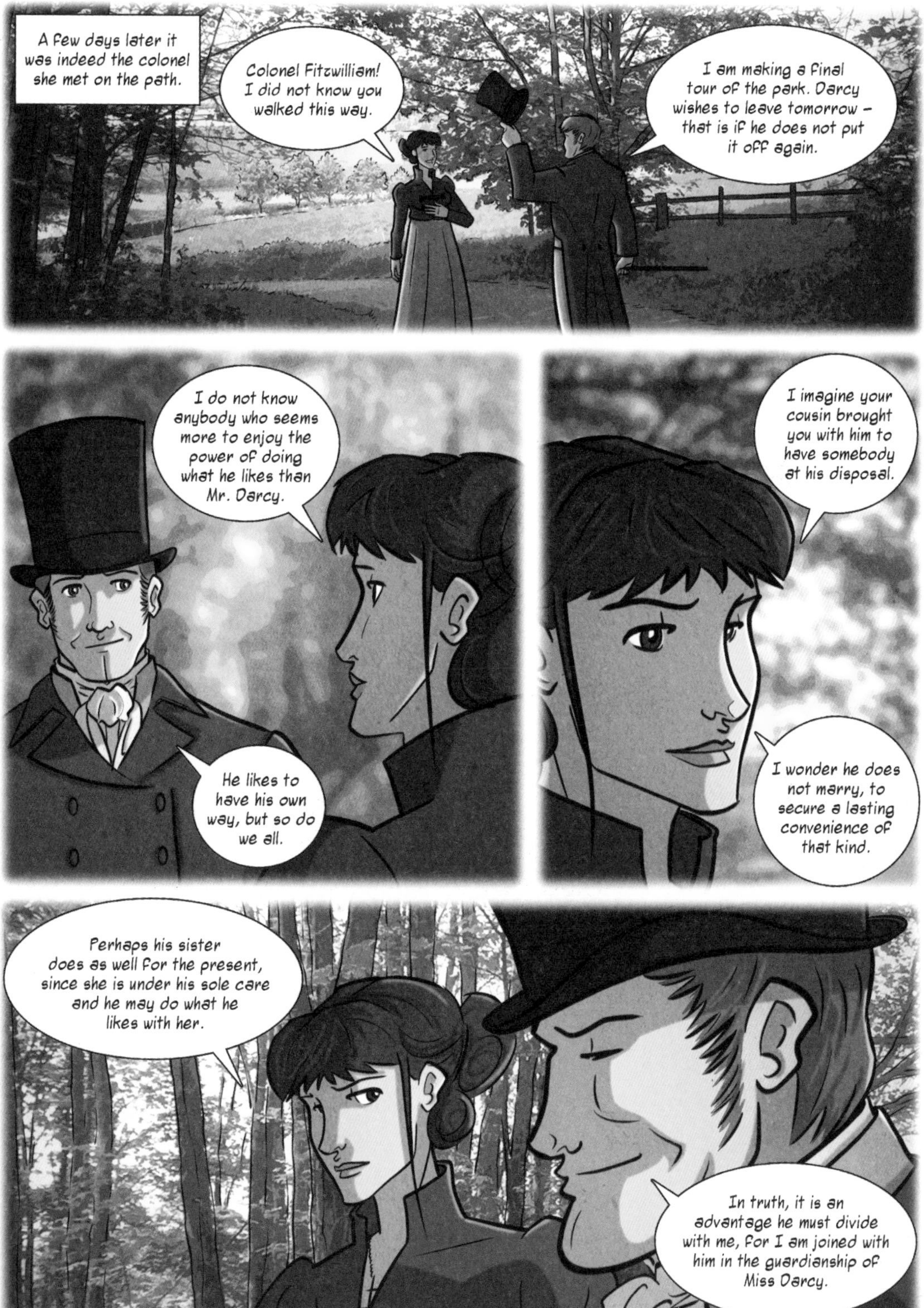
A few days later it was indeed the colonel she met on the path.
Colonel Fitzwilliam! I did not know you walked this way.
I am making a final tour of the park. Darcy wishes to leave tomorrow – that is if he does not put it off again.
I do not know anybody who seems more to enjoy the power of doing what he likes than Mr. Darcy.
He likes to have his own way, but so do we all.
I imagine your cousin brought you with him to have somebody at his disposal.
I wonder he does not marry, to secure a lasting convenience of that kind.
Perhaps his sister does as well for the present, since she is under his sole care and he may do what he likes with her.
In truth, it is an advantage he must divide with me, for I am joined with him in the guardianship of Miss Darcy.

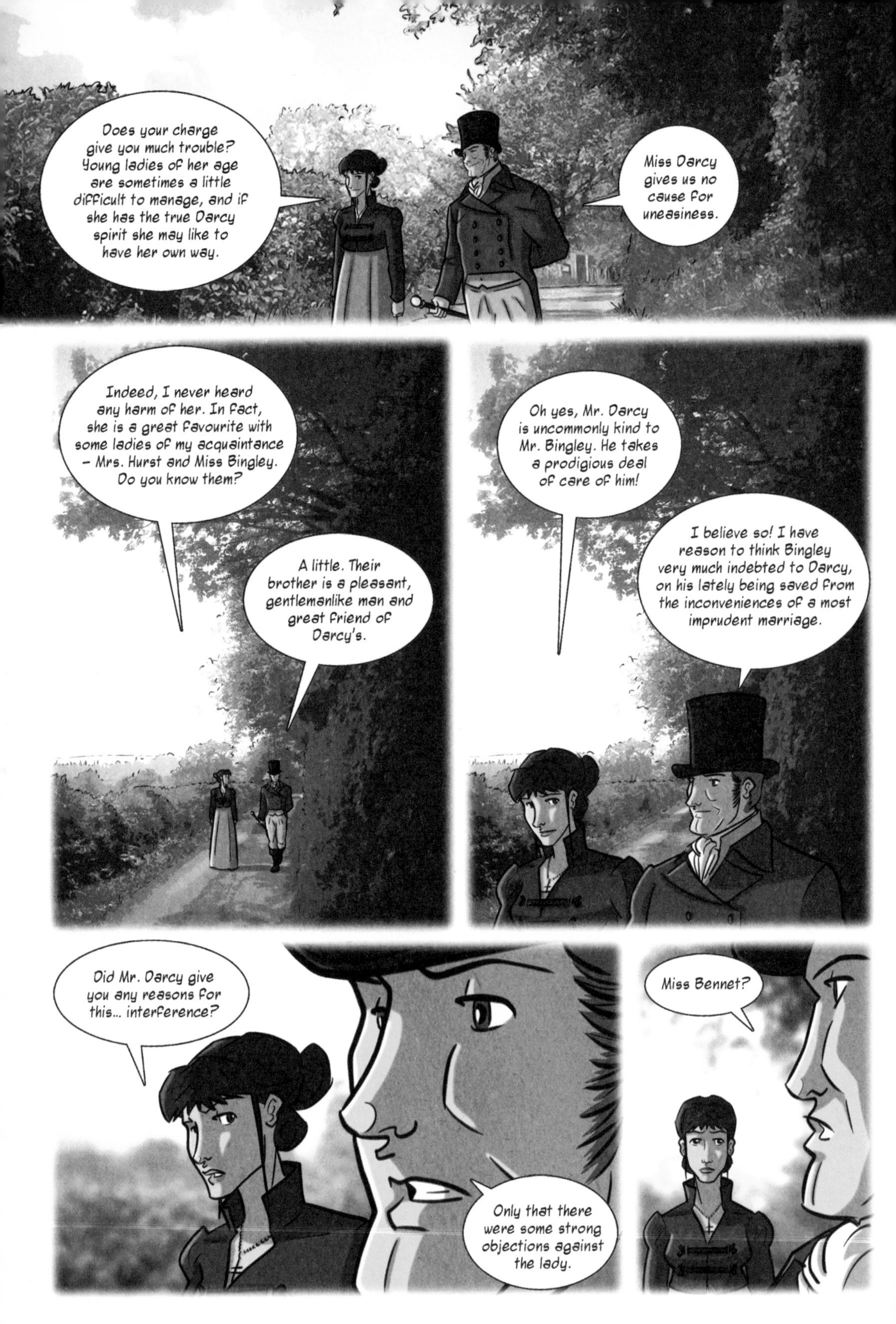
Does your charge give you much trouble? Young ladies of her age are sometimes a little difficult to manage, and if she has the true Darcy spirit she may like to have her own way.
Miss Darcy gives us no cause for uneasiness.
Indeed, I never heard any harm of her. In fact, she is a great favourite with some ladies of my acquaintance – Mrs. Hurst and Miss Bingley. Do you know them?
A little. Their brother is a pleasant, gentlemanlike man and great friend of Darcy's.
Oh yes, Mr. Darcy is uncommonly kind to Mr. Bingley. He takes a prodigious deal of care of him!
I believe so! I have reason to think Bingley very much indebted to Darcy, on his lately being saved from the inconveniences of a most imprudent marriage.
Did Mr. Darcy give you any reasons for this... interference?
Only that there were some strong objections against the lady.
Miss Bennet?

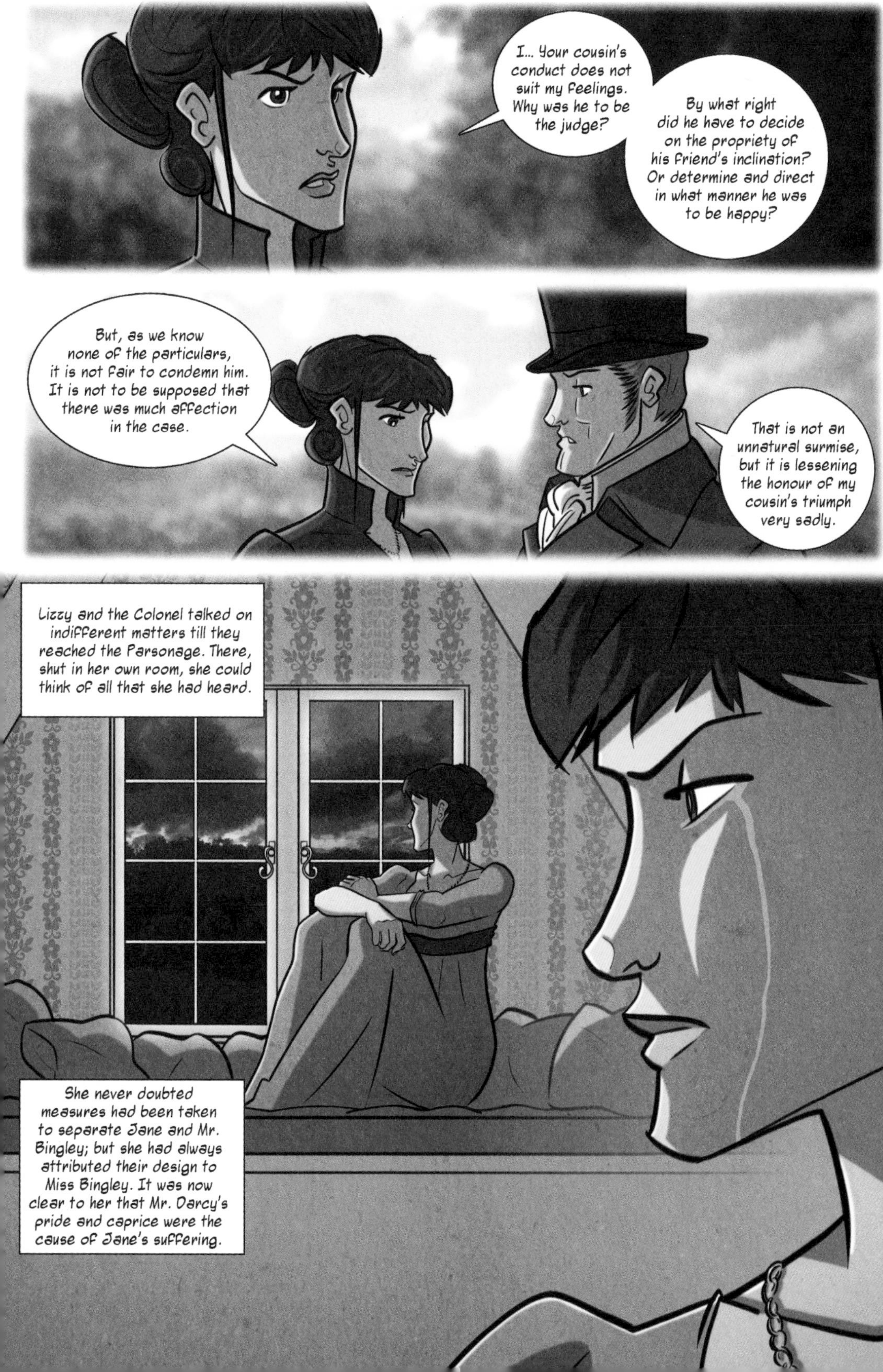
I... Your cousin's conduct does not suit my feelings. Why was he to be the judge?
By what right did he have to decide on the propriety of his friend's inclination? Or determine and direct in what manner he was to be happy?
But, as we know none of the particulars, it is not fair to condemn him. It is not to be supposed that there was much affection in the case.
That is not an unnatural surmise, but it is lessening the honour of my cousin's triumph very sadly.
Lizzy and the Colonel talked on indifferent matters till they reached the Parsonage. There, shut in her own room, she could think of all that she had heard.
She never doubted measures had been taken to separate Jane and Mr. Bingley; but she had always attributed their design to Miss Bingley. It was now clear to her that Mr. Darcy's pride and caprice were the cause of Jane's suffering.

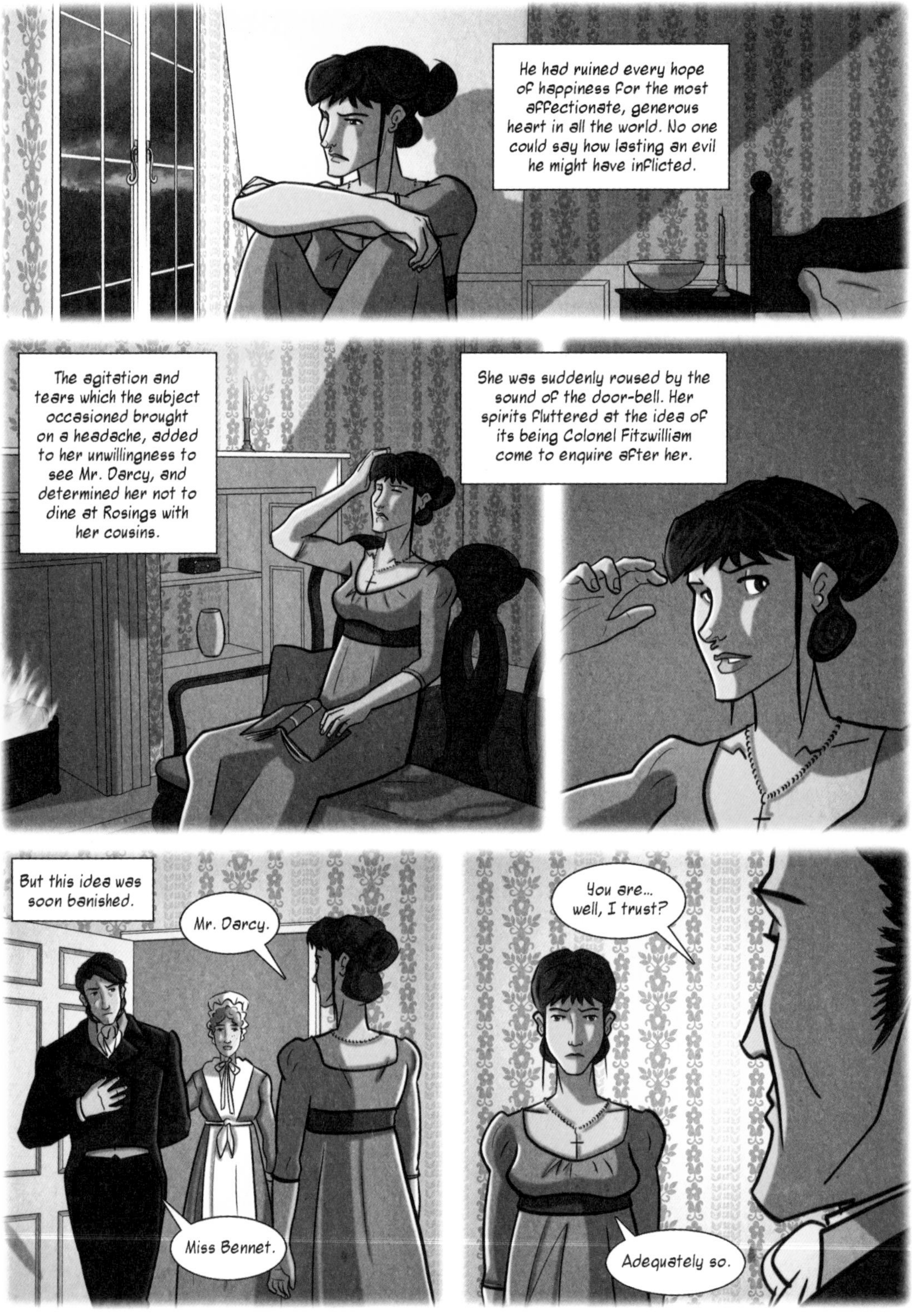
He had ruined every hope of happiness for the most affectionate, generous heart in all the world. No one could say how lasting an evil he might have inflicted.
The agitation and tears which the subject occasioned brought on a headache, added to her unwillingness to see Mr. Darcy, and determined her not to dine at Rosings with her cousins.
She was suddenly roused by the sound of the door-bell. Her spirits fluttered at the idea of its being Colonel Fitzwilliam come to enquire after her.
But this idea was soon banished.
Mr. Darcy.
Miss Bennet.
You are... well, I trust?
Adequately so.

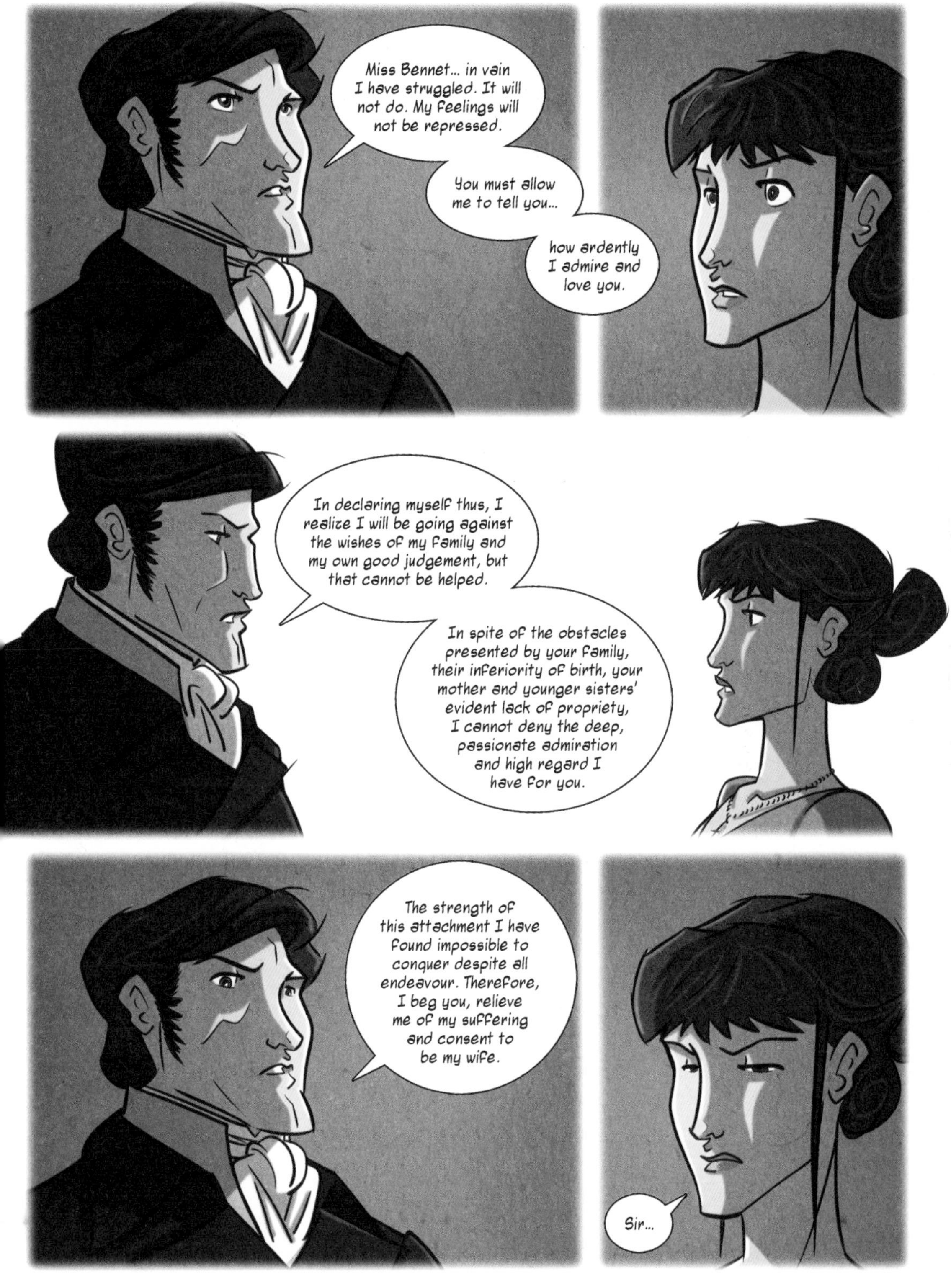
Miss Bennet... in vain I have struggled. It will not do. My feelings will not be repressed.
You must allow me to tell you...
how ardently I admire and love you.
In declaring myself thus, I realize I will be going against the wishes of my family and my own good judgement, but that cannot be helped.
In spite of the obstacles presented by your family, their inferiority of birth, your mother and younger sisters' evident lack of propriety, I cannot deny the deep, passionate admiration and high regard I have for you.
The strength of this attachment I have found impossible to conquer despite all endeavour. Therefore, I beg you, relieve me of my suffering and consent to be my wife.
Sir...

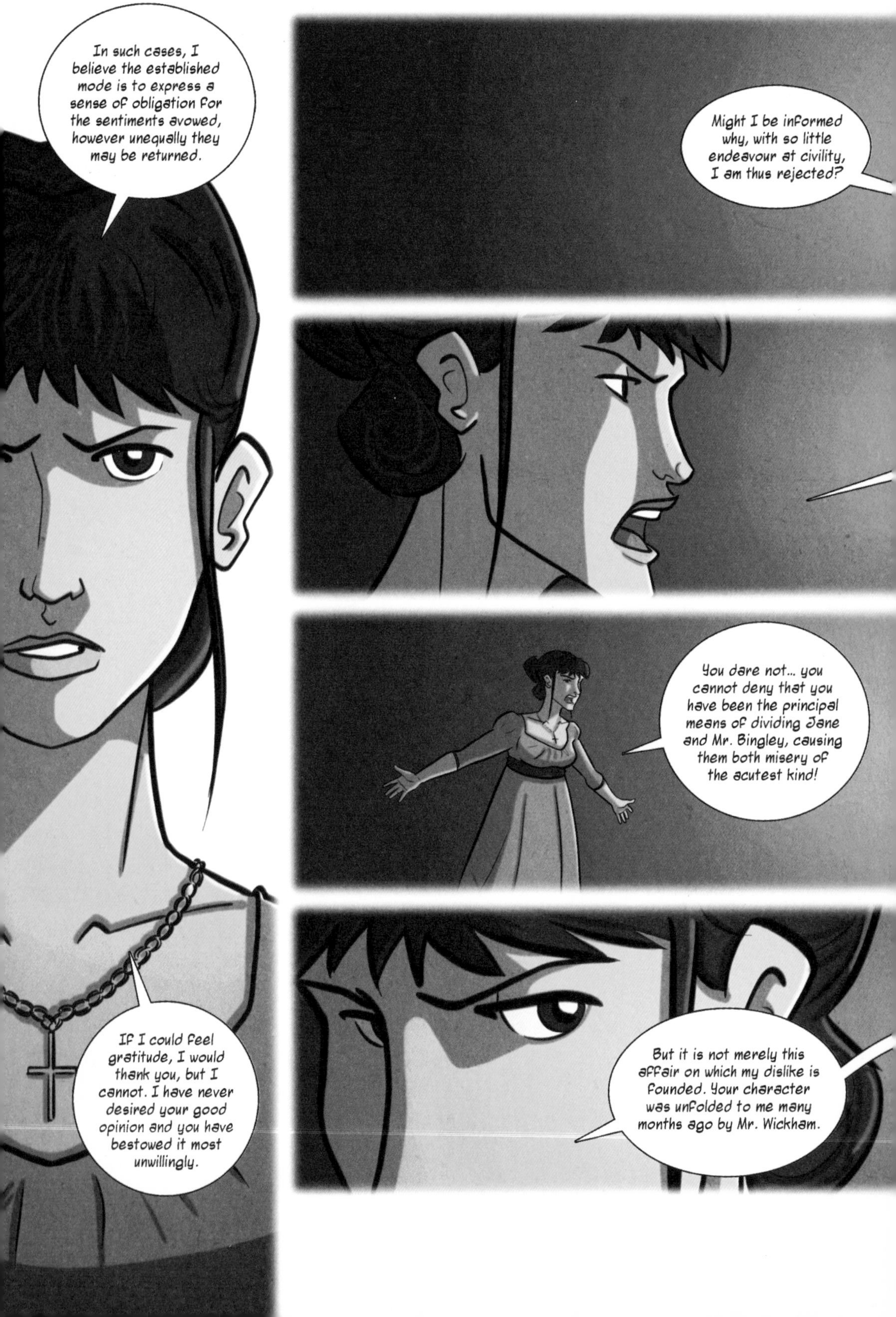
In such cases, I believe the established mode is to express a sense of obligation for the sentiments avowed, however unequally they may be returned.
If I could feel gratitude, I would thank you, but I cannot. I have never desired your good opinion and you have bestowed it most unwillingly.
Might I be informed why, with so little endeavour at civility, I am thus rejected?
You dare not... you cannot deny that you have been the principal means of dividing Jane and Mr. Bingley, causing them both misery of the acutest kind!
But it is not merely this affair on which my dislike is founded. Your character was unfolded to me many months ago by Mr. Wickham.

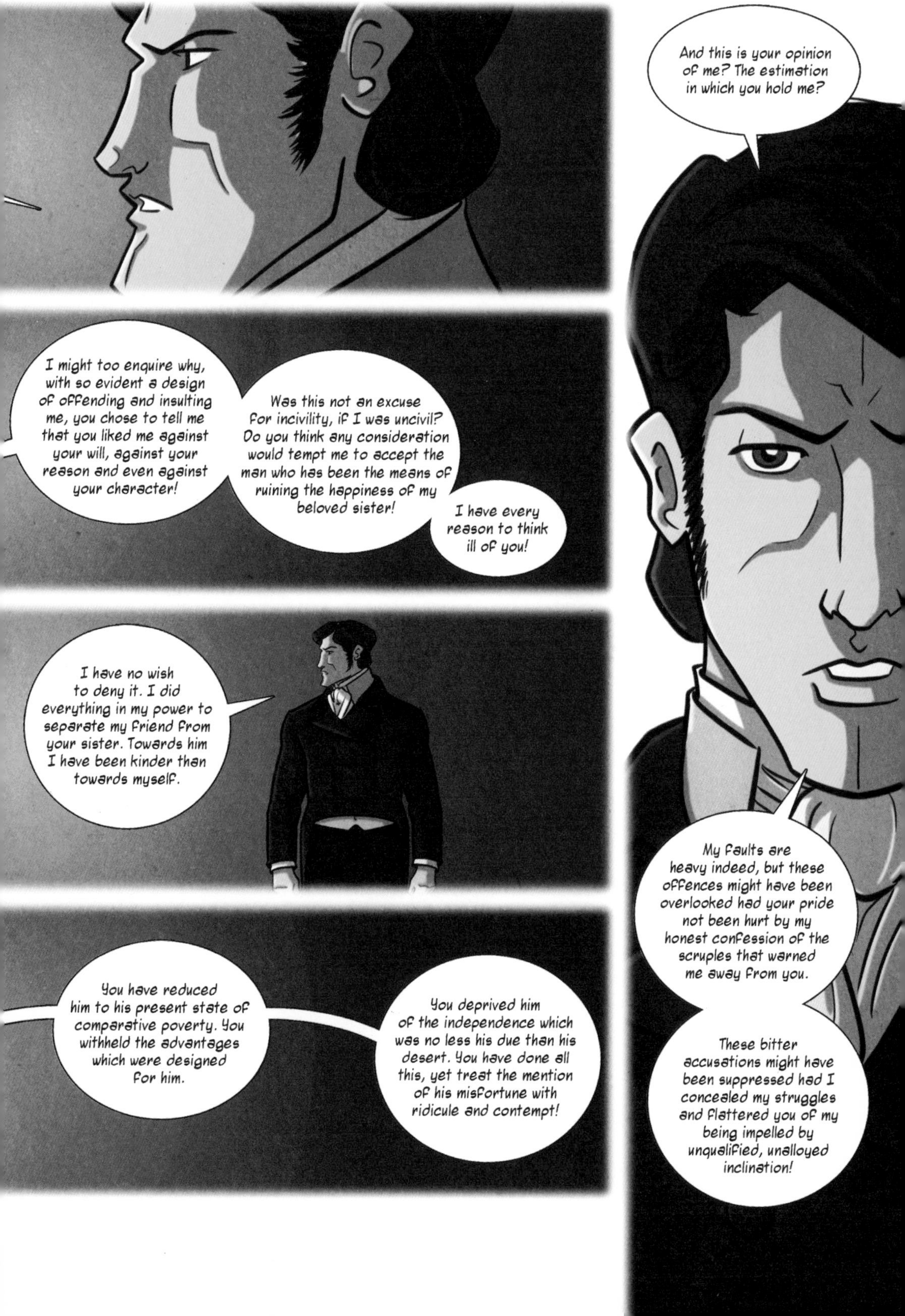
And this is your opinion of me? The estimation in which you hold me?
I might too enquire why, with so evident a design of offending and insulting me, you chose to tell me that you liked me against your will, against your reason and even against your character!
Was this not an excuse for incivility, if I was uncivil? Do you think any consideration would tempt me to accept the man who has been the means of ruining the happiness of my beloved sister!
I have every reason to think ill of you!
I have no wish to deny it. I did everything in my power to separate my friend from your sister. Towards him I have been kinder than towards myself.
You have reduced him to his present state of comparative poverty. You withheld the advantages which were designed for him.
You deprived him of the independence which was no less his due than his desert. You have done all this, yet treat the mention of his misfortune with ridicule and contempt!
My faults are heavy indeed, but these offences might have been overlooked had your pride not been hurt by my honest confession of the scruples that warned me away from you.
These bitter accusations might have been suppressed had I concealed my struggles and flattered you of my being impelled by unqualified, unalloyed inclination!

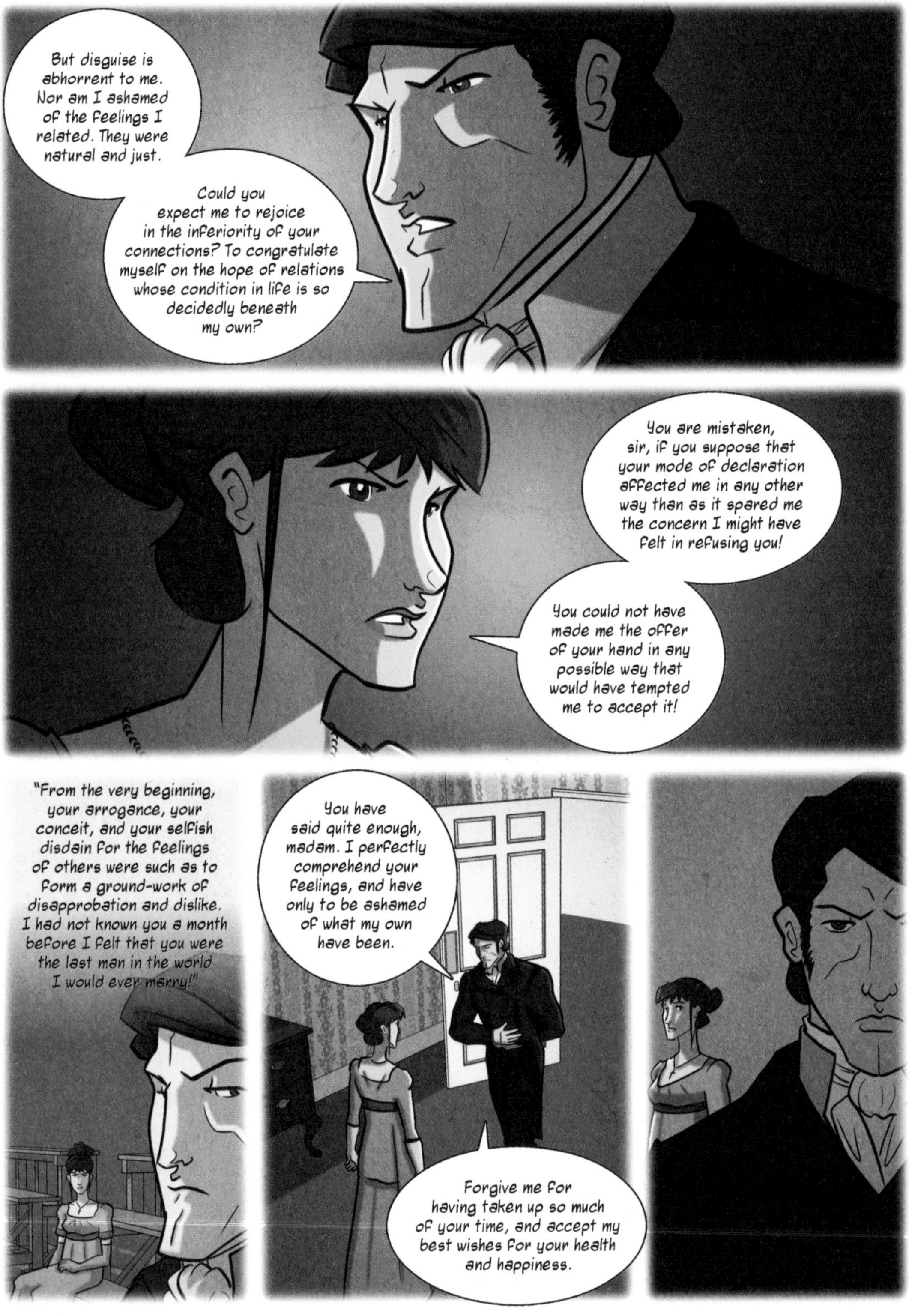
But disguise is abhorrent to me. Nor am I ashamed of the feelings I related. They were natural and just.
Could you expect me to rejoice in the inferiority of your connections? To congratulate myself on the hope of relations whose condition in life is so decidedly beneath my own?
You are mistaken, sir, if you suppose that your mode of declaration affected me in any other way than as it spared me the concern I might have felt in refusing you!
You could not have made me the offer of your hand in any possible way that would have tempted me to accept it!
"From the very beginning, your arrogance, your conceit, and your selfish disdain for the feelings of others were such as to form a ground-work of disapprobation and dislike. I had not known you a month before I felt that you were the last man in the world I would ever marry!"
You have said quite enough, madam. I perfectly comprehend your feelings, and have only to be ashamed of what my own have been.
Forgive me for having taken up so much of your time, and accept my best wishes for your health and happiness.

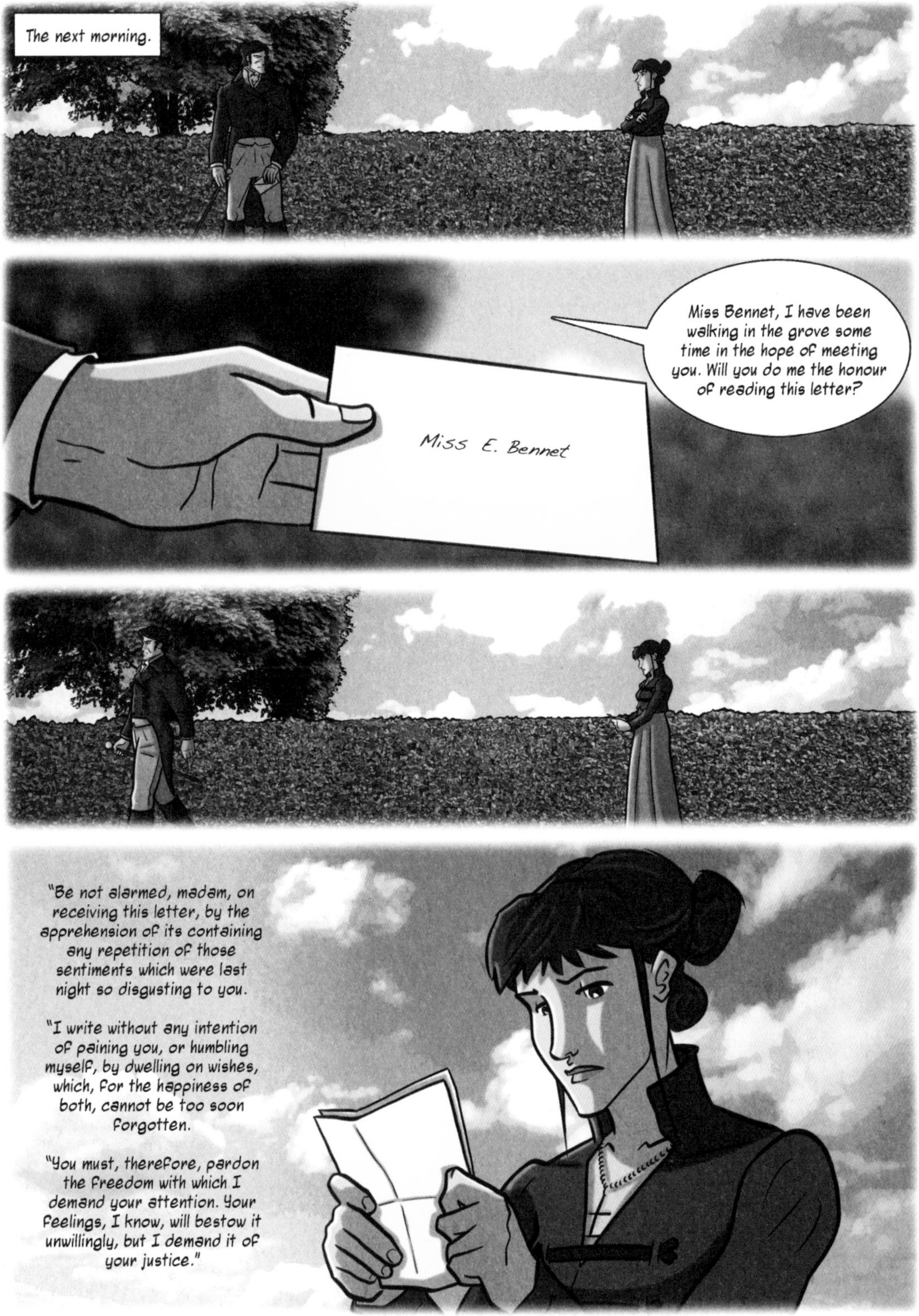
The next morning.
Miss Bennet, I have been walking in the grove some time in the hope of meeting you. Will you do me the honour of reading this letter?
Miss E. Bennet
"Be not alarmed, madam, on receiving this letter, by the apprehension of its containing any repetition of those sentiments which were last night so disgusting to you.
"I write without any intention of paining you, or humbling myself, by dwelling on wishes, which, for the happiness of both, cannot be too soon forgotten.
"You must, therefore, pardon the freedom with which I demand your attention. Your feelings, I know, will bestow it unwillingly, but I demand it of your justice."

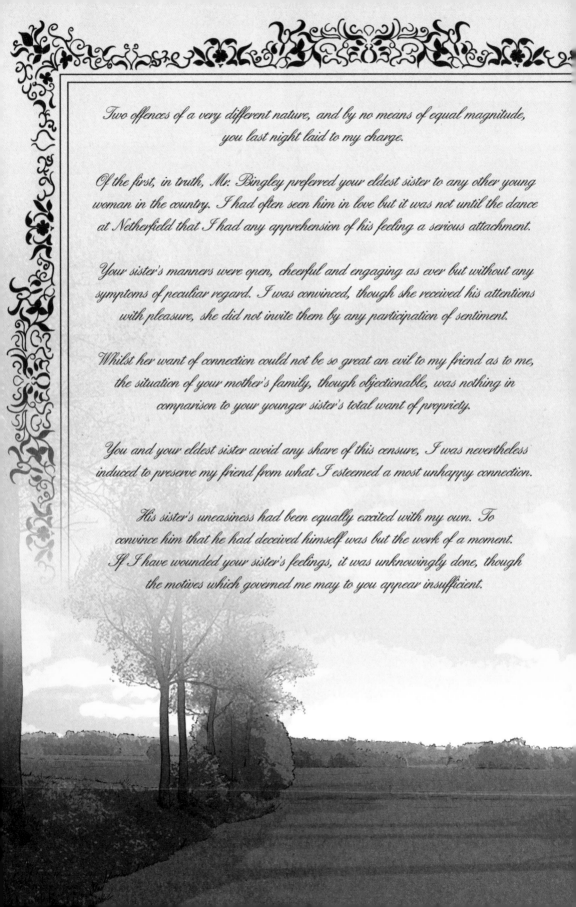

Two offences of a very different nature, and by no means of equal magnitude,
you last night laid to my charge.

Of the first, in truth, Mr. Bingley preferred your eldest sister to any other young
woman in the country. I had often seen him in love but it was not until the dance
at Netherfield that I had any apprehension of his feeling a serious attachment.

Your sister's manners were open, cheerful and engaging as ever but without any
symptoms of peculiar regard. I was convinced, though she received his attentions
with pleasure, she did not invite them by any participation of sentiment.

Whilst her want of connection could not be so great an evil to my friend as to me,
the situation of your mother's family, though objectionable, was nothing in
comparison to your younger sister's total want of propriety.

You and your eldest sister avoid any share of this censure, I was nevertheless
induced to preserve my friend from what I esteemed a most unhappy connection.

His sister's uneasiness had been equally excited with my own. To
convince him that he had deceived himself was but the work of a moment.
If I have wounded your sister's feelings, it was unknowingly done, though
the motives which governed me may to you appear insufficient.

With respect to the weightier accusation, of having injured Mr. Wickham, I can only refute it by laying before you the truth of his connection with my family.

My late father was fond of this young man and, in his will, assured him a living if he became ordained.

However, Wickham resolved against taking orders with an intention, instead, of studying the law. He wrote to ask me for three thousand pounds in lieu of his legacy, to which I acceded.

He found the law an unprofitable study and three years later asked for further funds which I not unreasonably refused. He was violent in his abuse of me. After that, every appearance of acquaintance was dropped.

Of what I say next, I must trust to your discretion and secrecy. About a year ago, my sister, who is ten years my junior, went to Ramsgate, followed by Mr. Wickham, undoubtedly by design. He so far recommended himself that she believed herself in love and consented to an elopement.

I am happy to add she admitted her imprudence to me a day or two beforehand. You may imagine how I felt and acted. Wickham left immediately. His objective was unquestionably my sister's fortune, though I cannot help supposing that the hope of revenging himself on me was a strong inducement.

I will only add, God bless you.

Fitzwilliam Darcy

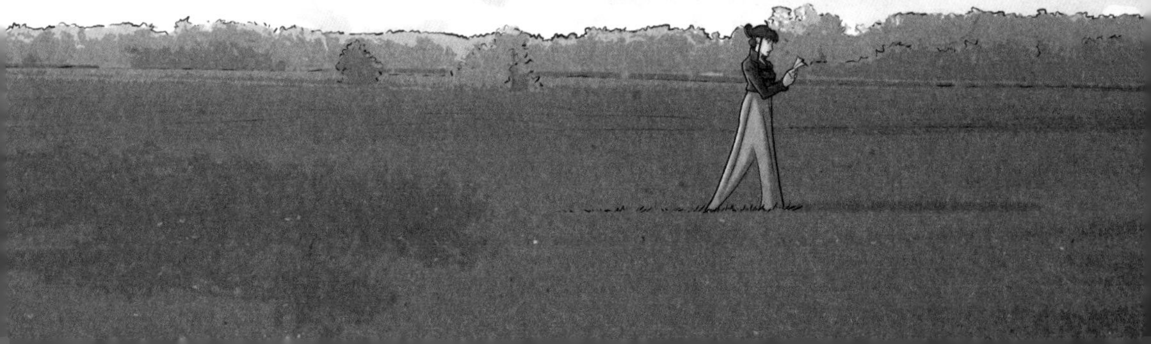

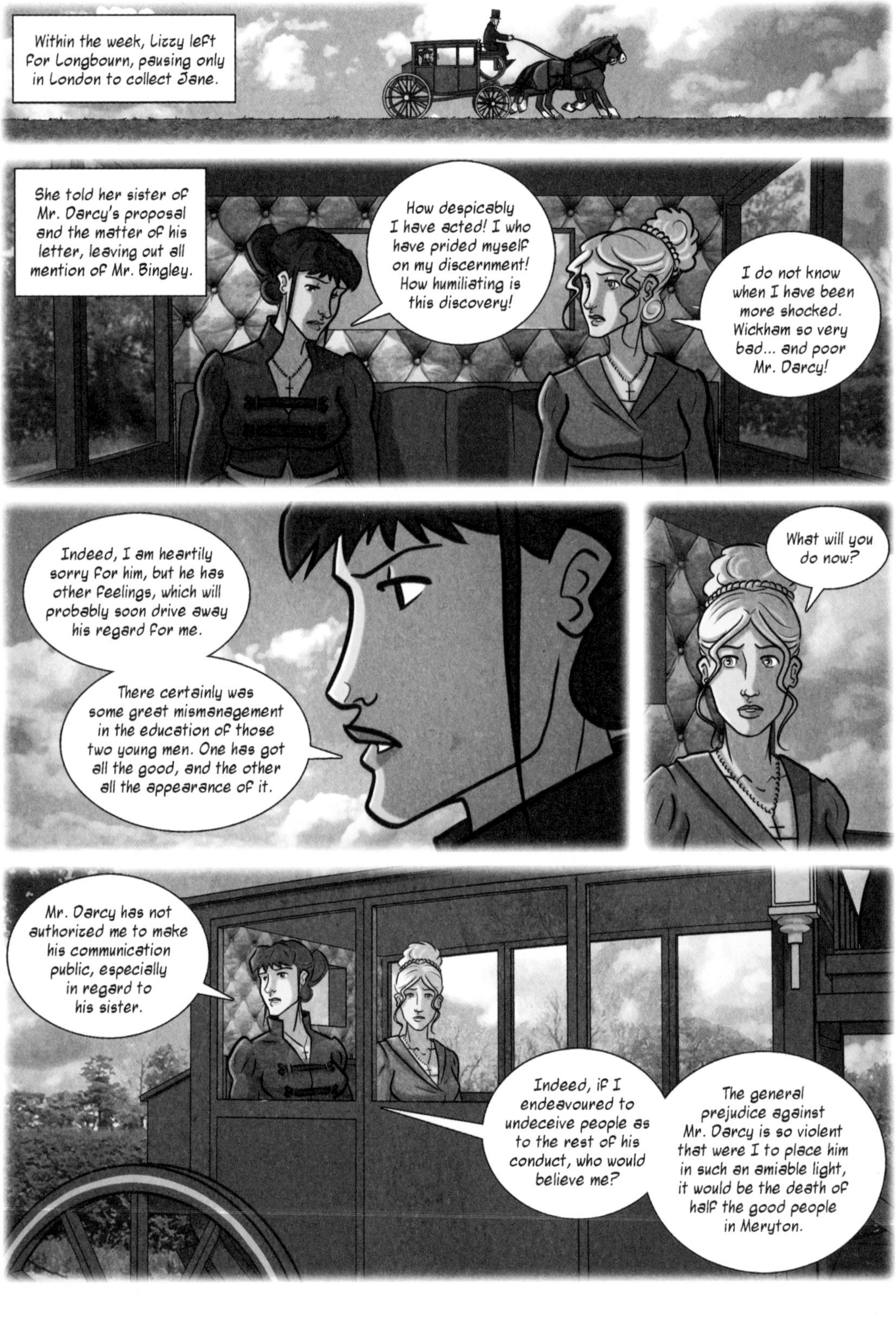

Within the week, Lizzy left for Longbourn, pausing only in London to collect Jane.
She told her sister of Mr. Darcy's proposal and the matter of his letter, leaving out all mention of Mr. Bingley.
How despicably I have acted! I who have prided myself on my discernment! How humiliating is this discovery!
I do not know when I have been more shocked. Wickham so very bad... and poor Mr. Darcy!
Indeed, I am heartily sorry for him, but he has other feelings, which will probably soon drive away his regard for me.
There certainly was some great mismanagement in the education of those two young men. One has got all the good, and the other all the appearance of it.
What will you do now?
Mr. Darcy has not authorized me to make his communication public, especially in regard to his sister.
Indeed, if I endeavoured to undeceive people as to the rest of his conduct, who would believe me?
The general prejudice against Mr. Darcy is so violent that were I to place him in such an amiable light, it would be the death of half the good people in Meryton.

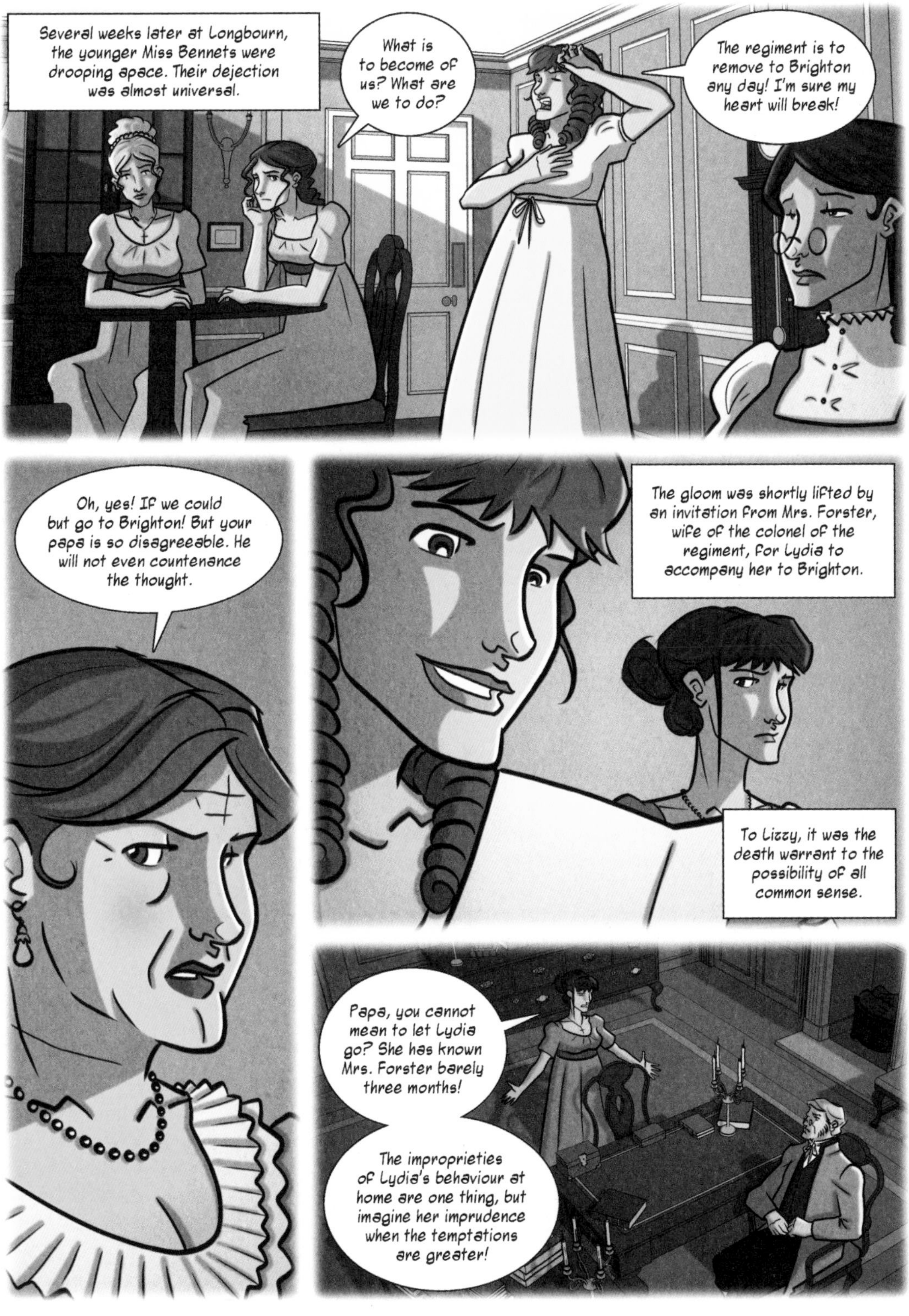

Several weeks later at Longbourn, the younger Miss Bennets were drooping apace. Their dejection was almost universal.
What is to become of us? What are we to do?
The regiment is to remove to Brighton any day! I'm sure my heart will break!
Oh, yes! If we could but go to Brighton! But your papa is so disagreeable. He will not even countenance the thought.
The gloom was shortly lifted by an invitation from Mrs. Forster, wife of the colonel of the regiment, for Lydia to accompany her to Brighton.
To Lizzy, it was the death warrant to the possibility of all common sense.
Papa, you cannot mean to let Lydia go? She has known Mrs. Forster barely three months!
The improprieties of Lydia's behaviour at home are one thing, but imagine her imprudence when the temptations are greater!

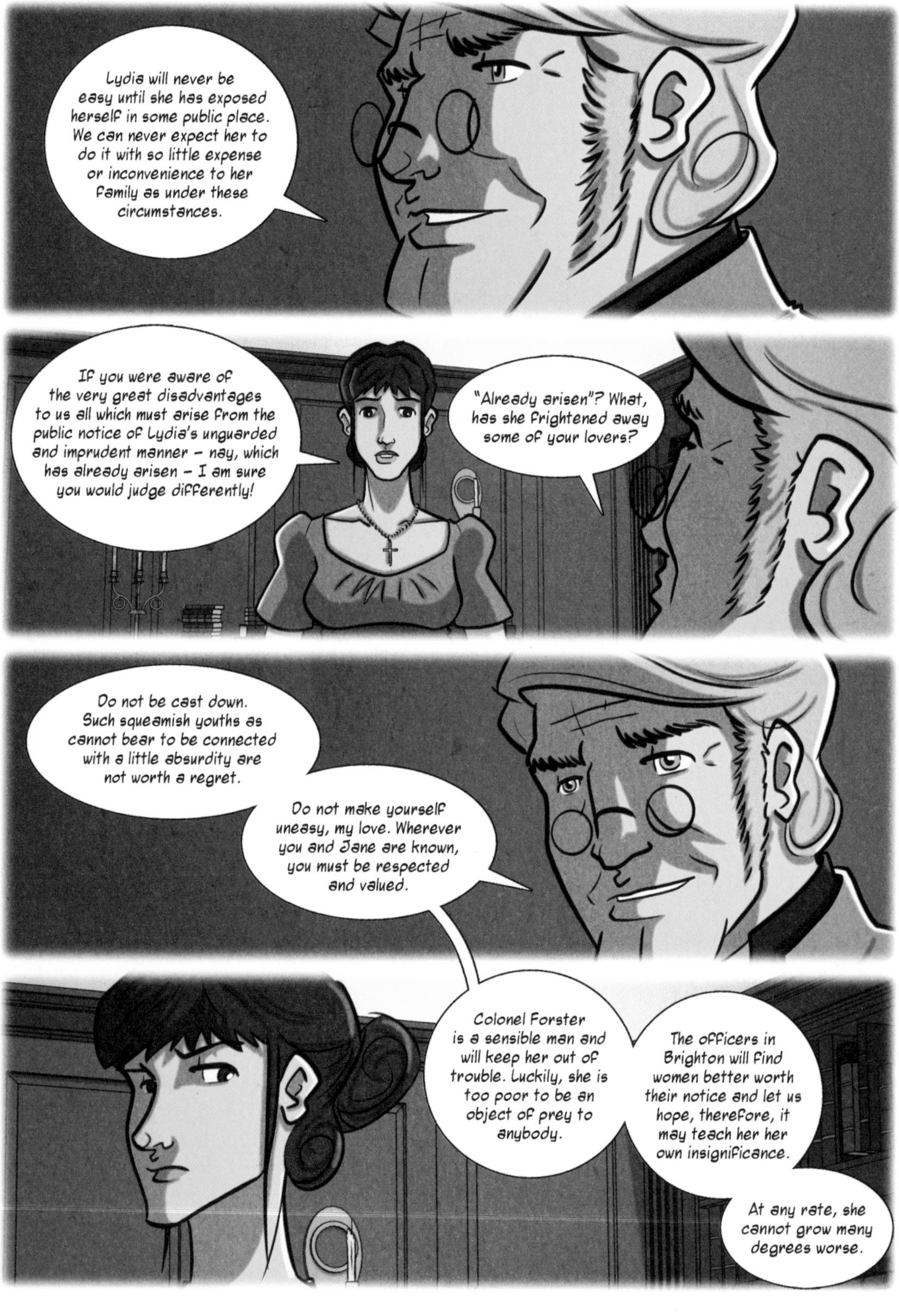
Lydia will never be easy until she has exposed herself in some public place. We can never expect her to do it with so little expense or inconvenience to her family as under these circumstances.
If you were aware of the very great disadvantages to us all which must arise from the public notice of Lydia's unguarded and imprudent manner – nay, which has already arisen – I am sure you would judge differently!
"Already arisen"? What, has she frightened away some of your lovers?
Do not be cast down. Such squeamish youths as cannot bear to be connected with a little absurdity are not worth a regret.
Do not make yourself uneasy, my love. Wherever you and Jane are known, you must be respected and valued.
Colonel Forster is a sensible man and will keep her out of trouble. Luckily, she is too poor to be an object of prey to anybody.
The officers in Brighton will find women better worth their notice and let us hope, therefore, it may teach her her own insignificance.
At any rate, she cannot grow many degrees worse.

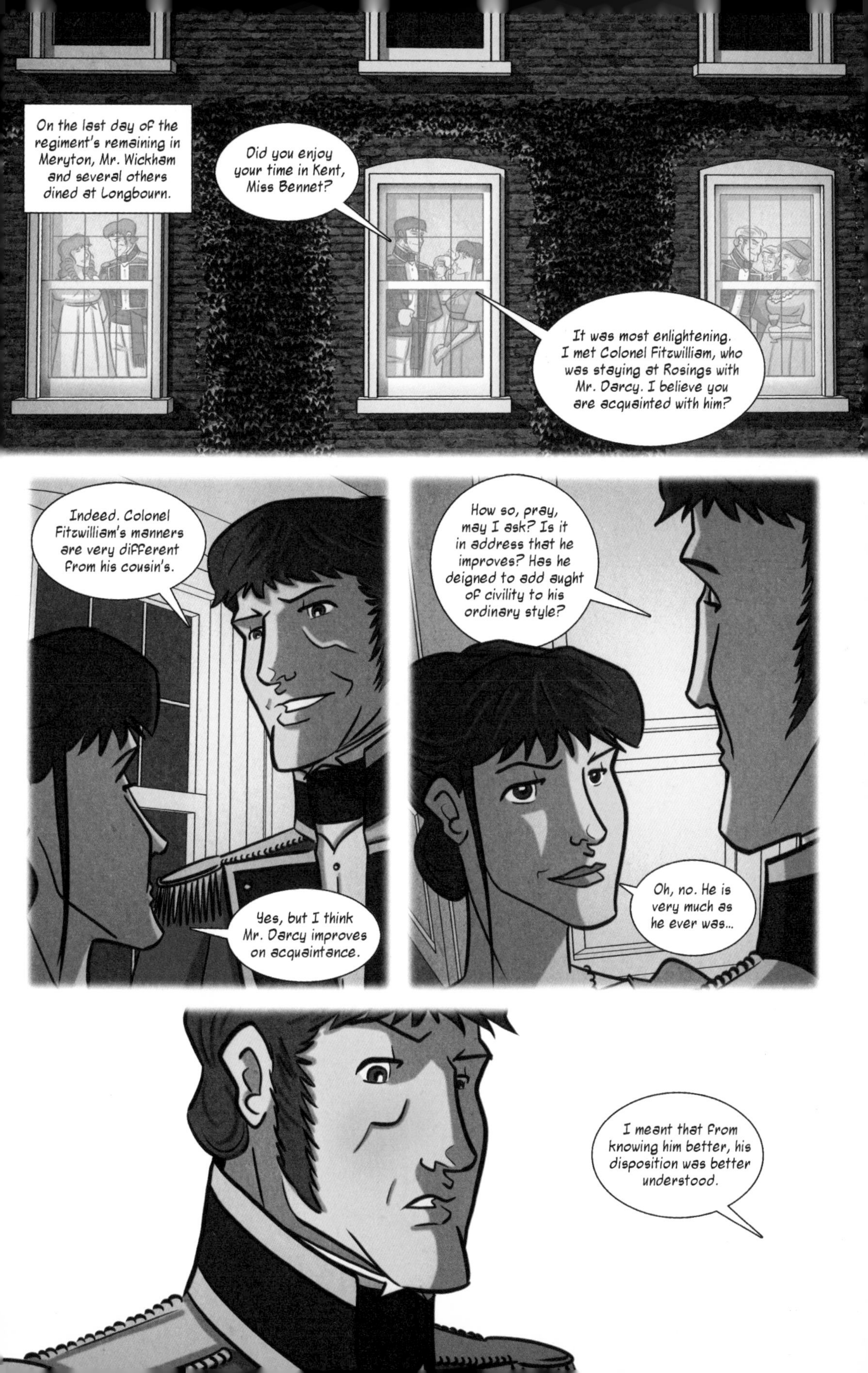
On the last day of the regiment's remaining in Meryton, Mr. Wickham and several others dined at Longbourn.
Did you enjoy your time in Kent, Miss Bennet?
It was most enlightening. I met Colonel Fitzwilliam, who was staying at Rosings with Mr. Darcy. I believe you are acquainted with him?
Indeed. Colonel Fitzwilliam's manners are very different from his cousin's.
Yes, but I think Mr. Darcy improves on acquaintance.
How so, pray, may I ask? Is it in address that he improves? Has he deigned to add aught of civility to his ordinary style?
Oh, no. He is very much as he ever was...
I meant that from knowing him better, his disposition was better understood.

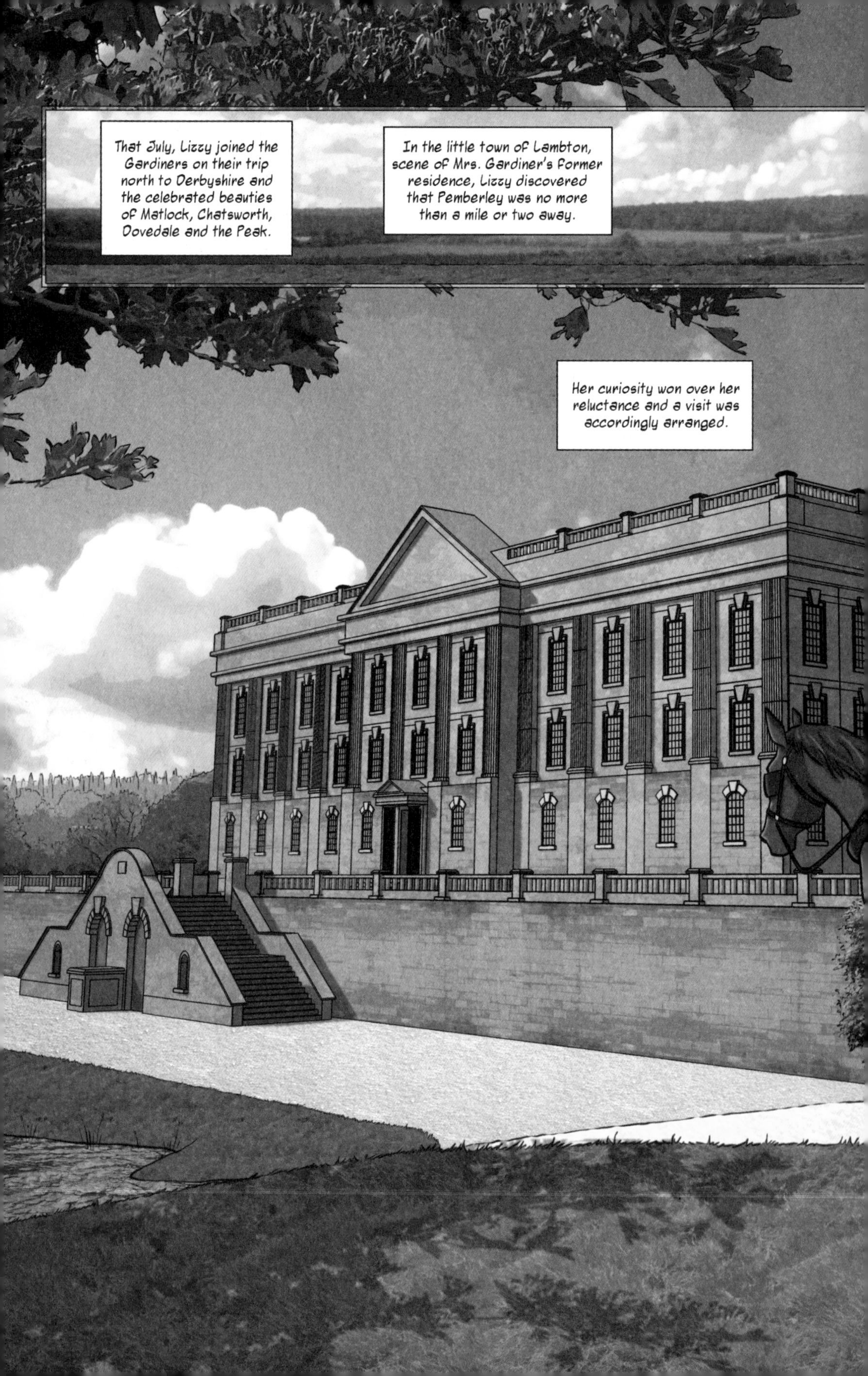
That July, Lizzy joined the Gardiners on their trip north to Derbyshire and the celebrated beauties of Matlock, Chatsworth, Dovedale and the Peak.
In the little town of Lambton, scene of Mrs. Gardiner's former residence, Lizzy discovered that Pemberley was no more than a mile or two away.
Her curiosity won over her reluctance and a visit was accordingly arranged.

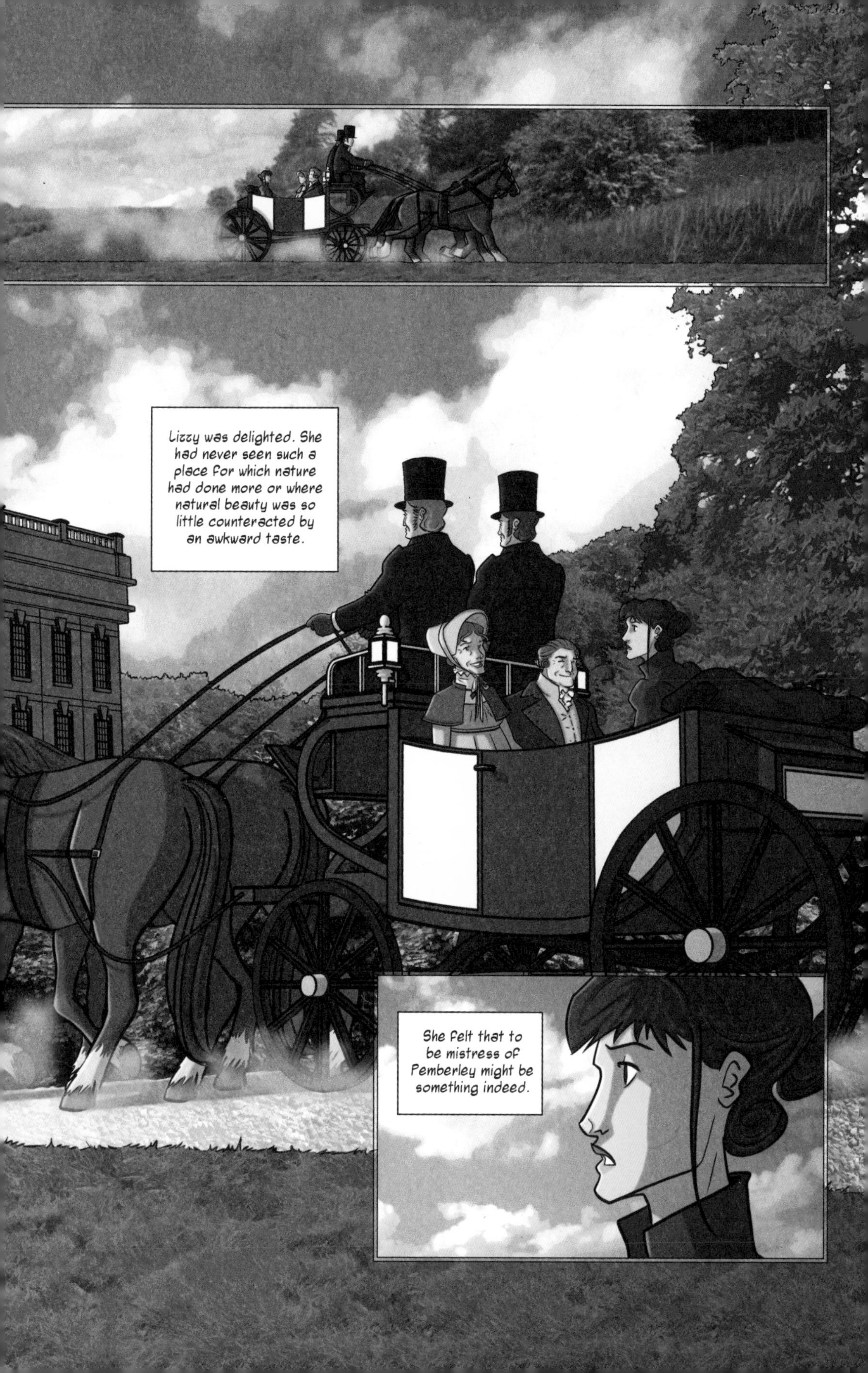
Lizzy was delighted. She had never seen such a place for which nature had done more or where natural beauty was so little counteracted by an awkward taste.
She felt that to be mistress of Pemberley might be something indeed.

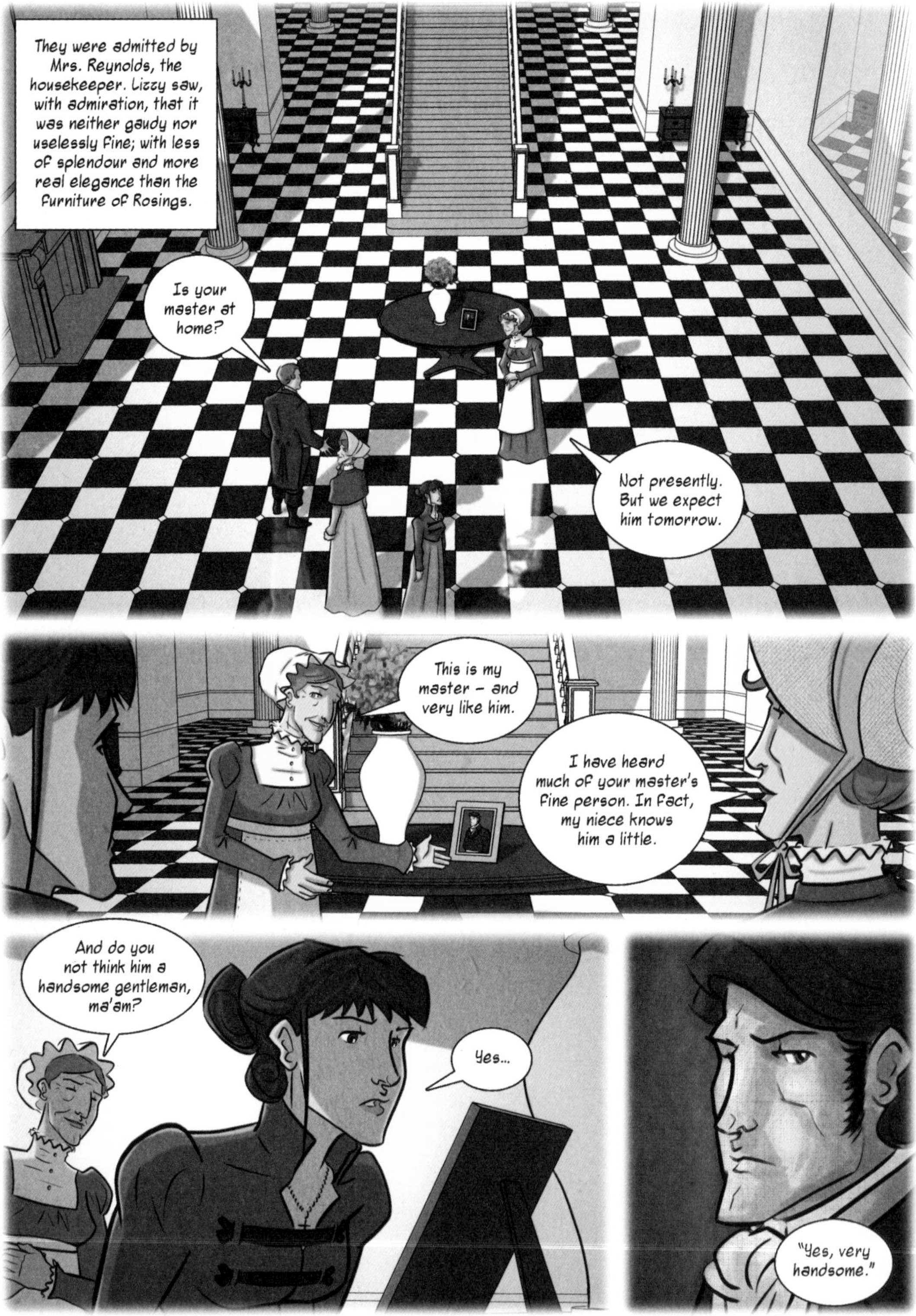
They were admitted by Mrs. Reynolds, the housekeeper. Lizzy saw, with admiration, that it was neither gaudy nor uselessly fine; with less of splendour and more real elegance than the furniture of Rosings.
Is your master at home?
Not presently. But we expect him tomorrow.
This is my master – and very like him.
I have heard much of your master's fine person. In fact, my niece knows him a little.
And do you not think him a handsome gentleman, ma'am?
Yes...
"Yes, very handsome."

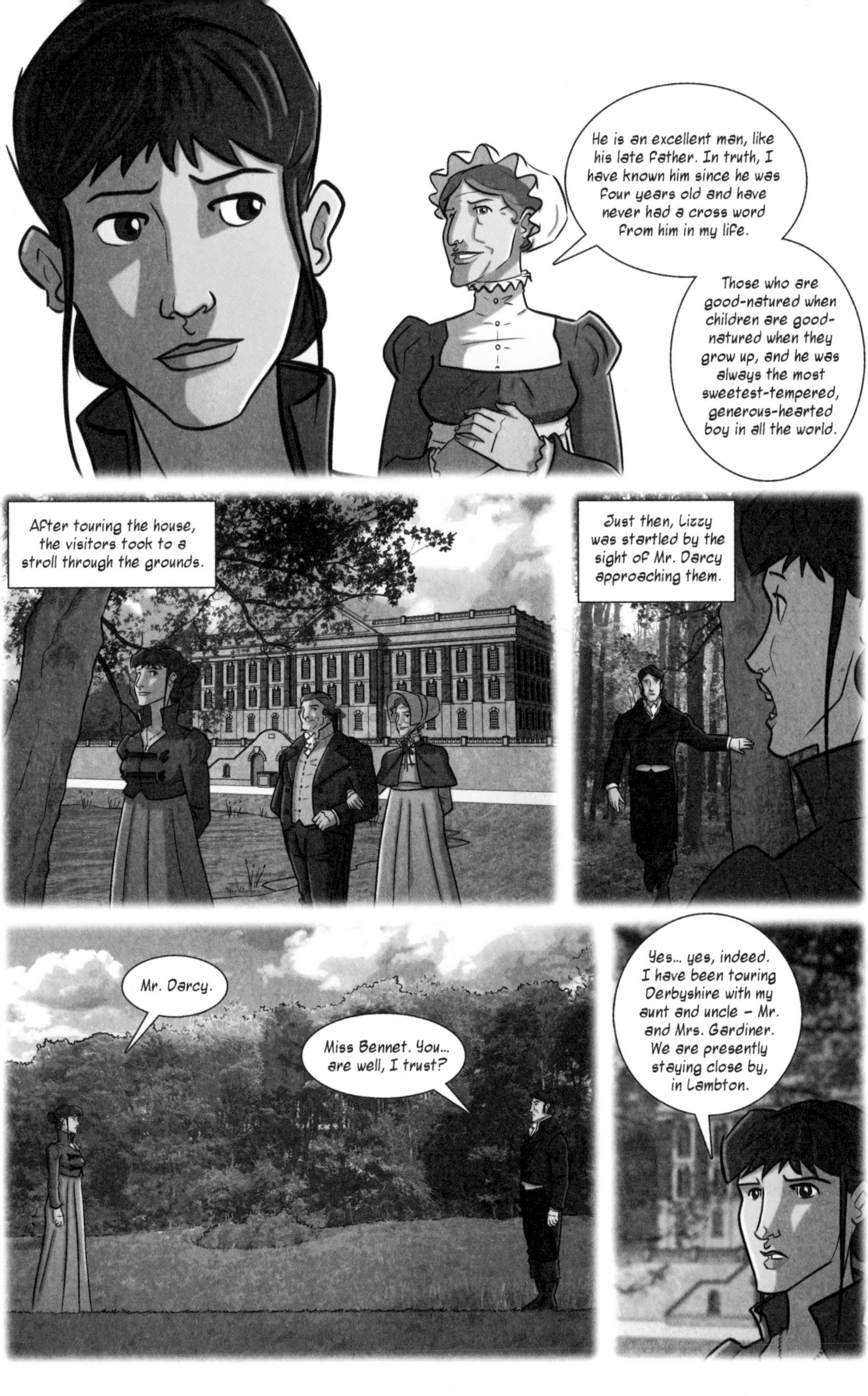
He is an excellent man, like his late father. In truth, I have known him since he was four years old and have never had a cross word from him in my life.
Those who are good-natured when children are good-natured when they grow up, and he was always the most sweetest-tempered, generous-hearted boy in all the world.
After touring the house, the visitors took to a stroll through the grounds.
Just then, Lizzy was startled by the sight of Mr. Darcy approaching them.
Mr. Darcy.
Miss Bennet. You... are well, I trust?
Yes... yes, indeed. I have been touring Derbyshire with my aunt and uncle – Mr. and Mrs. Gardiner. We are presently staying close by, in Lambton.

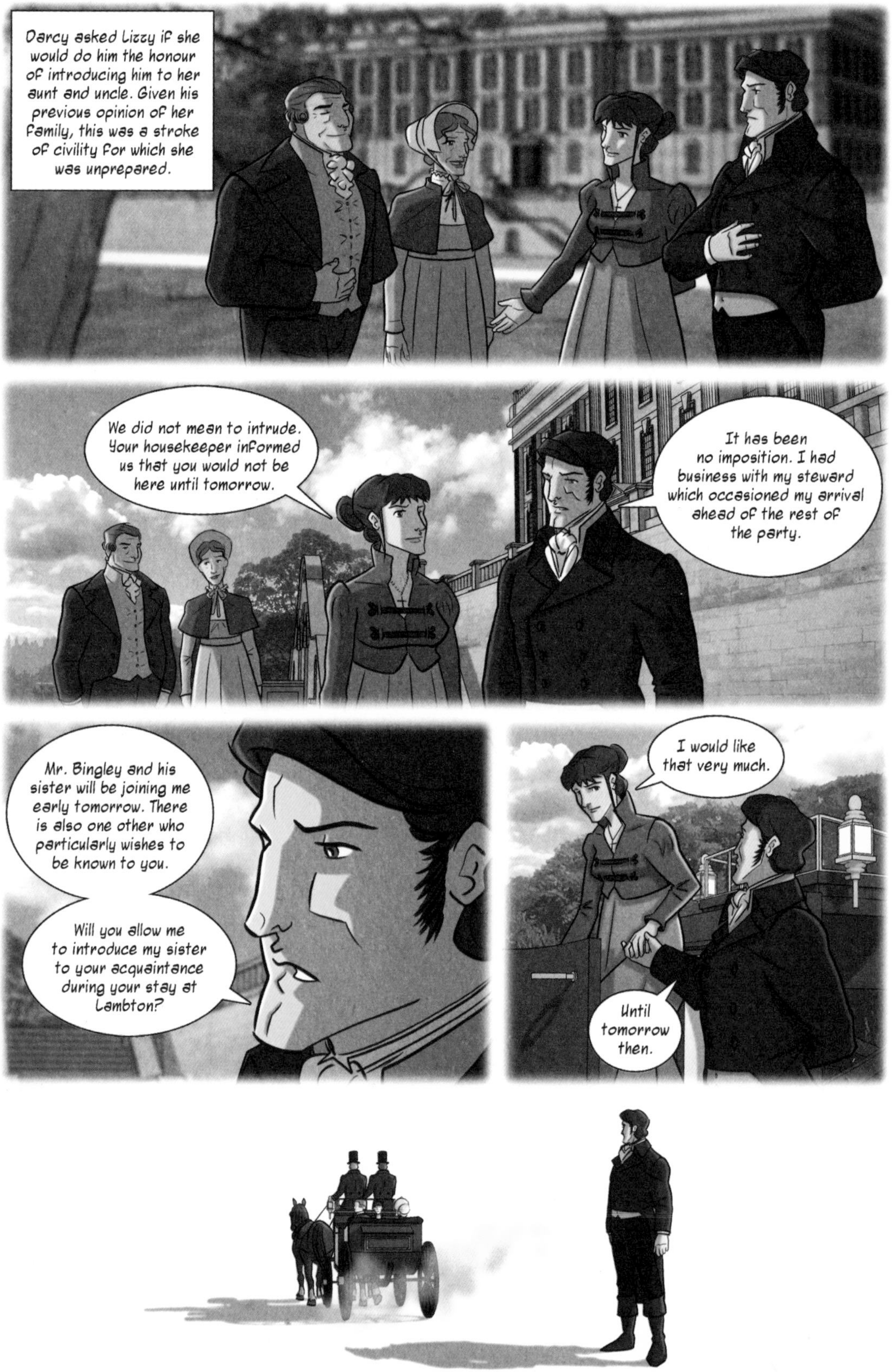

Darcy asked Lizzy if she would do him the honour of introducing him to her aunt and uncle. Given his previous opinion of her family, this was a stroke of civility for which she was unprepared.
We did not mean to intrude. Your housekeeper informed us that you would not be here until tomorrow.
It has been no imposition. I had business with my steward which occasioned my arrival ahead of the rest of the party.
Mr. Bingley and his sister will be joining me early tomorrow. There is also one other who particularly wishes to be known to you.
Will you allow me to introduce my sister to your acquaintance during your stay at Lambton?
I would like that very much.
Until tomorrow then.

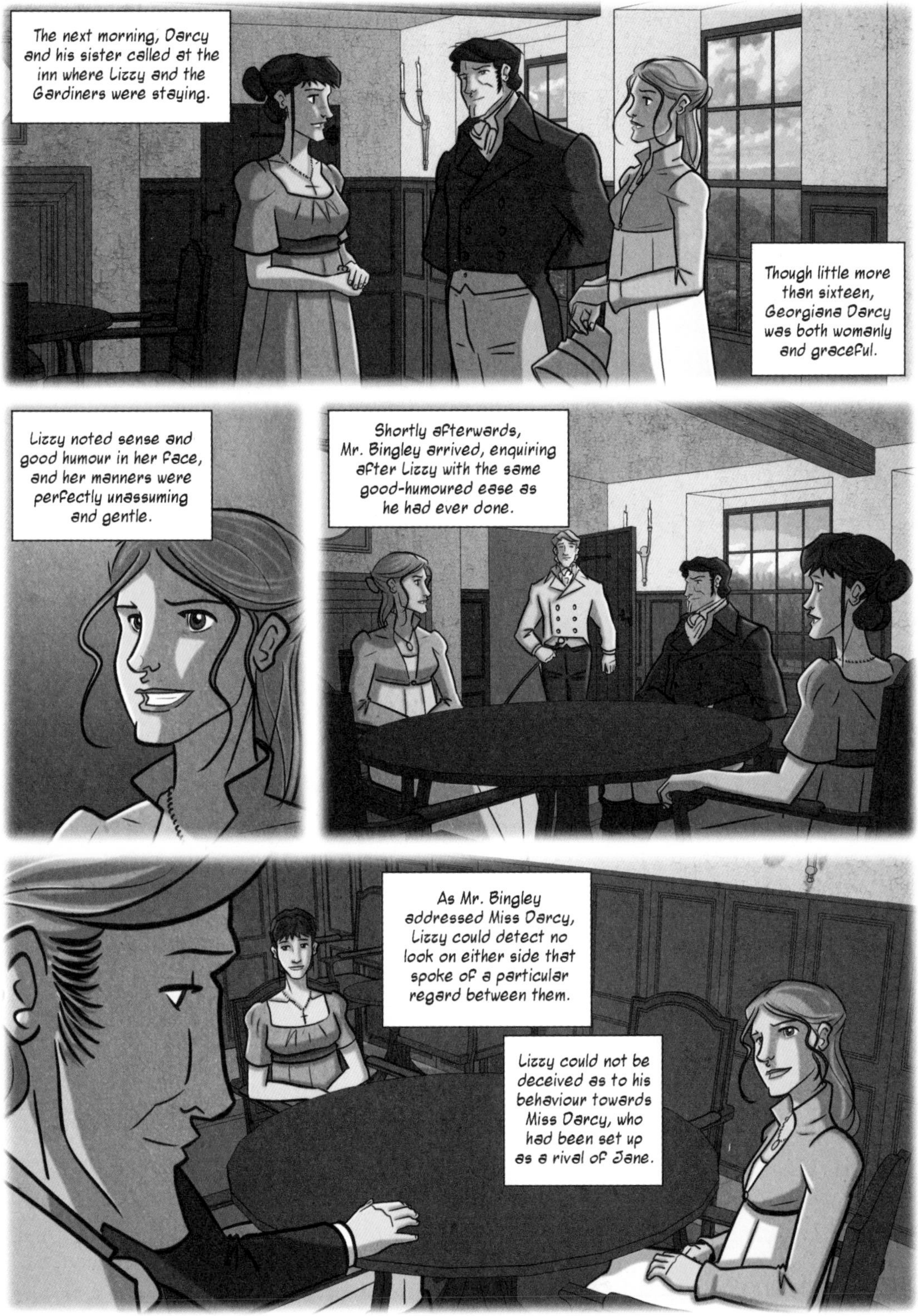
The next morning, Darcy and his sister called at the inn where Lizzy and the Gardiners were staying.
Though little more than sixteen, Georgiana Darcy was both womanly and graceful.
Lizzy noted sense and good humour in her face, and her manners were perfectly unassuming and gentle.
Shortly afterwards, Mr. Bingley arrived, enquiring after Lizzy with the same good-humoured ease as he had ever done.
As Mr. Bingley addressed Miss Darcy, Lizzy could detect no look on either side that spoke of a particular regard between them.
Lizzy could not be deceived as to his behaviour towards Miss Darcy, who had been set up as a rival of Jane.

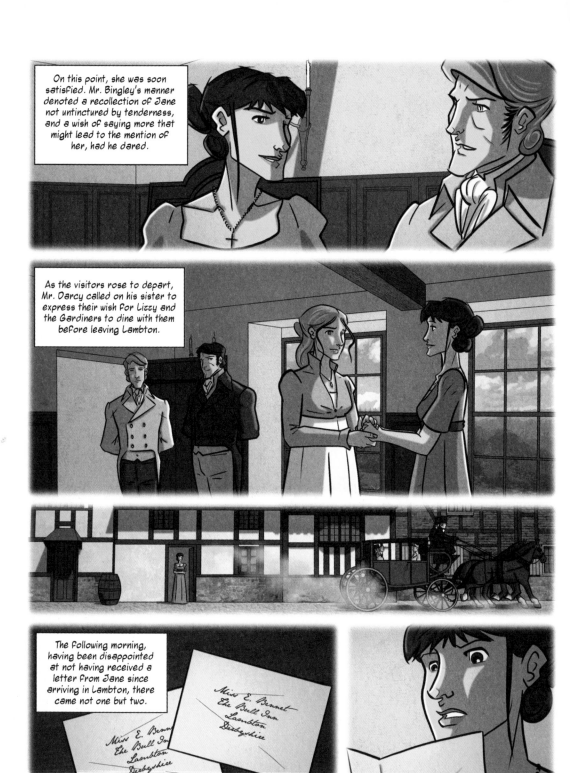

On this point, she was soon satisfied. Mr. Bingley's manner denoted a recollection of Jane not untinctured by tenderness, and a wish of saying more that might lead to the mention of her, had he dared.

As the visitors rose to depart, Mr. Darcy called on his sister to express their wish for Lizzy and the Gardiners to dine with them before leaving Lambton.

The following morning, having been disappointed at not having received a letter from Jane since arriving in Lambton, there came not one but two.

Miss E. Bennet
The Bull Inn
Lambton
Derbyshire

Miss E. Bennet
The Bull Inn
Lambton
Derbyshire

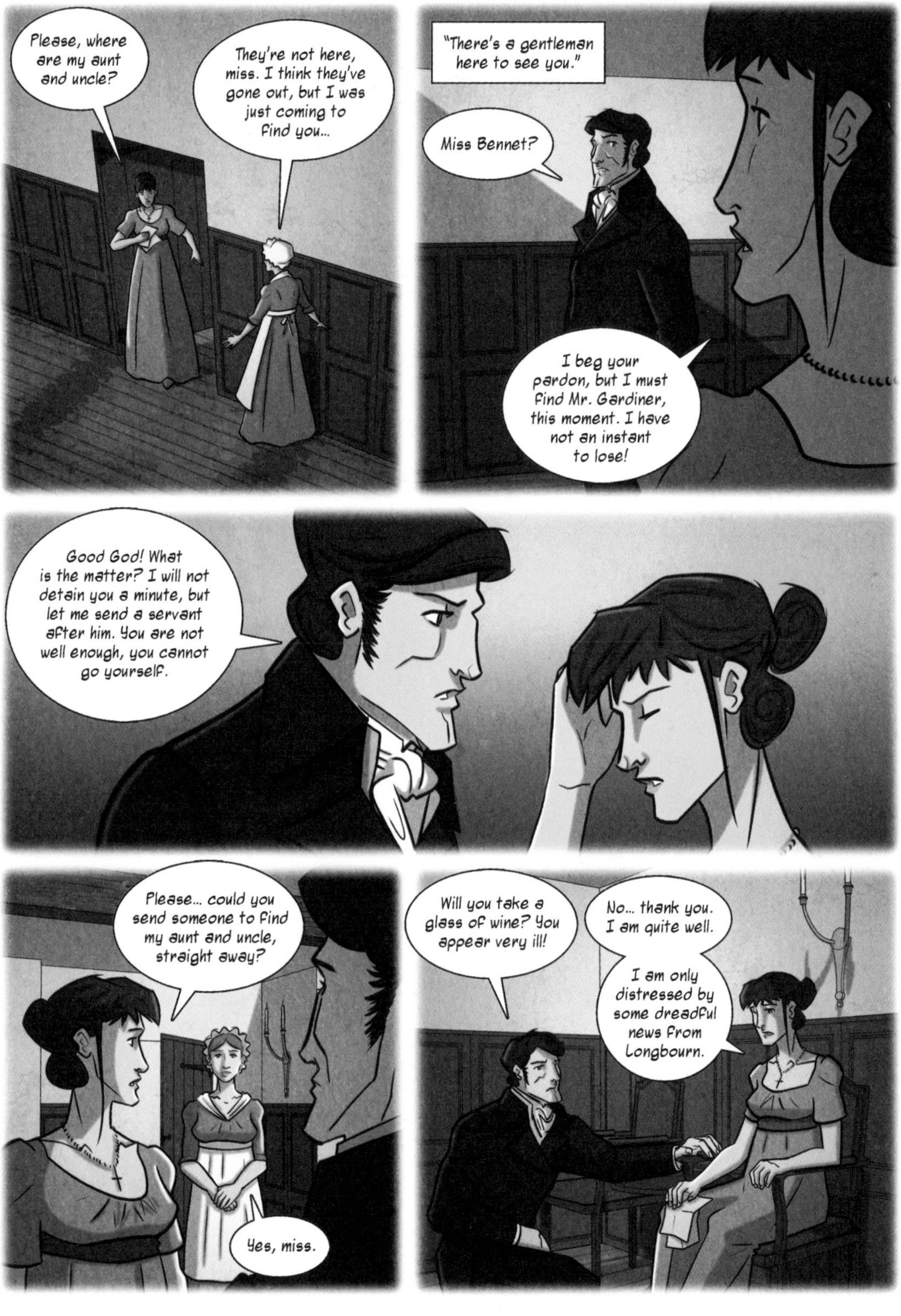
Please, where are my aunt and uncle?
They're not here, miss. I think they've gone out, but I was just coming to find you...
"There's a gentleman here to see you."
Miss Bennet?
I beg your pardon, but I must find Mr. Gardiner, this moment. I have not an instant to lose!
Good God! What is the matter? I will not detain you a minute, but let me send a servant after him. You are not well enough, you cannot go yourself.
Please... could you send someone to find my aunt and uncle, straight away?
Yes, miss.
Will you take a glass of wine? You appear very ill!
No... thank you. I am quite well.
I am only distressed by some dreadful news from Longbourn.

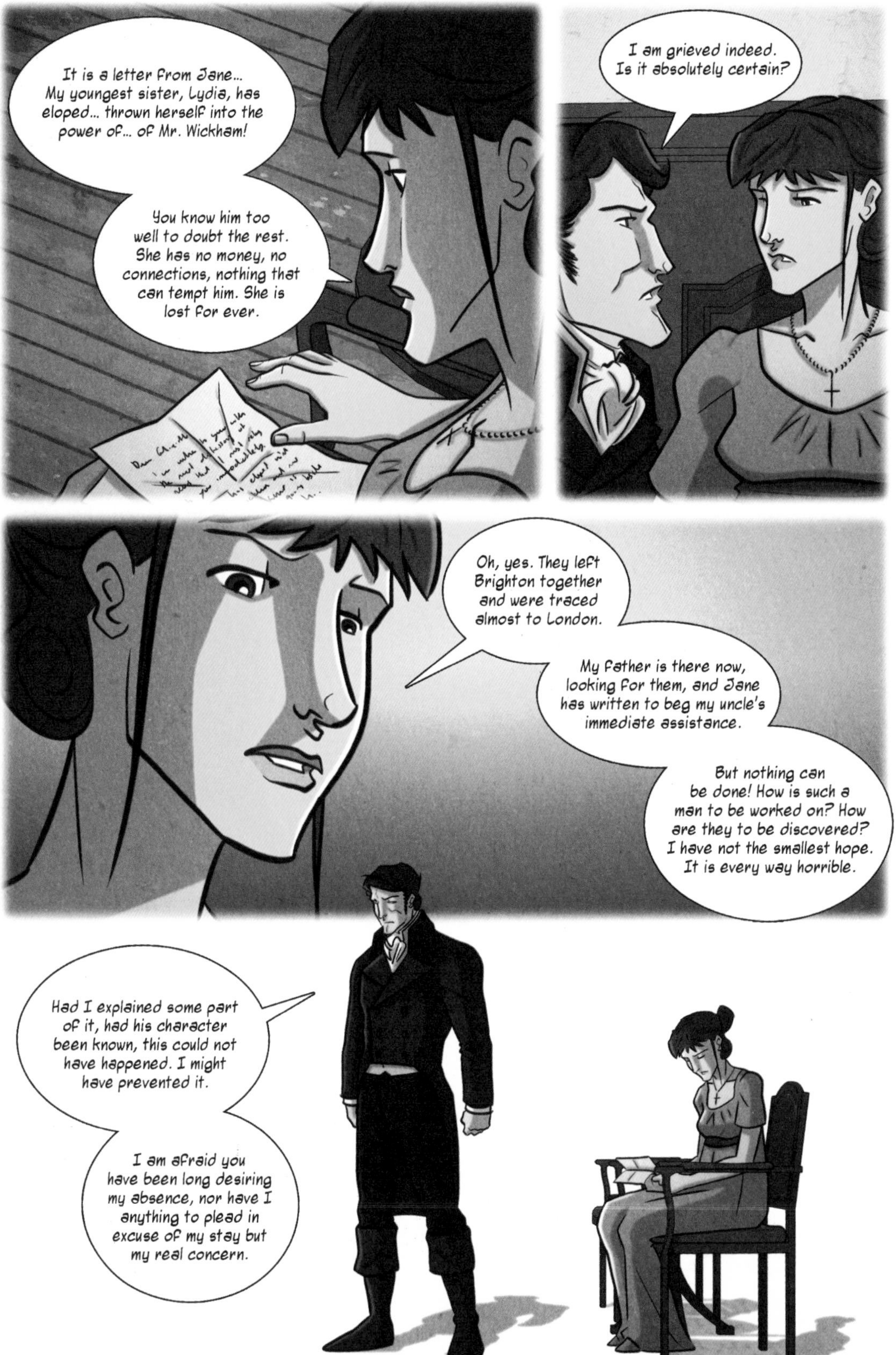
It is a letter from Jane... My youngest sister, Lydia, has eloped... thrown herself into the power of... of Mr. Wickham!
You know him too well to doubt the rest. She has no money, no connections, nothing that can tempt him. She is lost for ever.
I am grieved indeed. Is it absolutely certain?
Oh, yes. They left Brighton together and were traced almost to London.
My father is there now, looking for them, and Jane has written to beg my uncle's immediate assistance.
But nothing can be done! How is such a man to be worked on? How are they to be discovered? I have not the smallest hope. It is every way horrible.
Had I explained some part of it, had his character been known, this could not have happened. I might have prevented it.
I am afraid you have been long desiring my absence, nor have I anything to plead in excuse of my stay but my real concern.

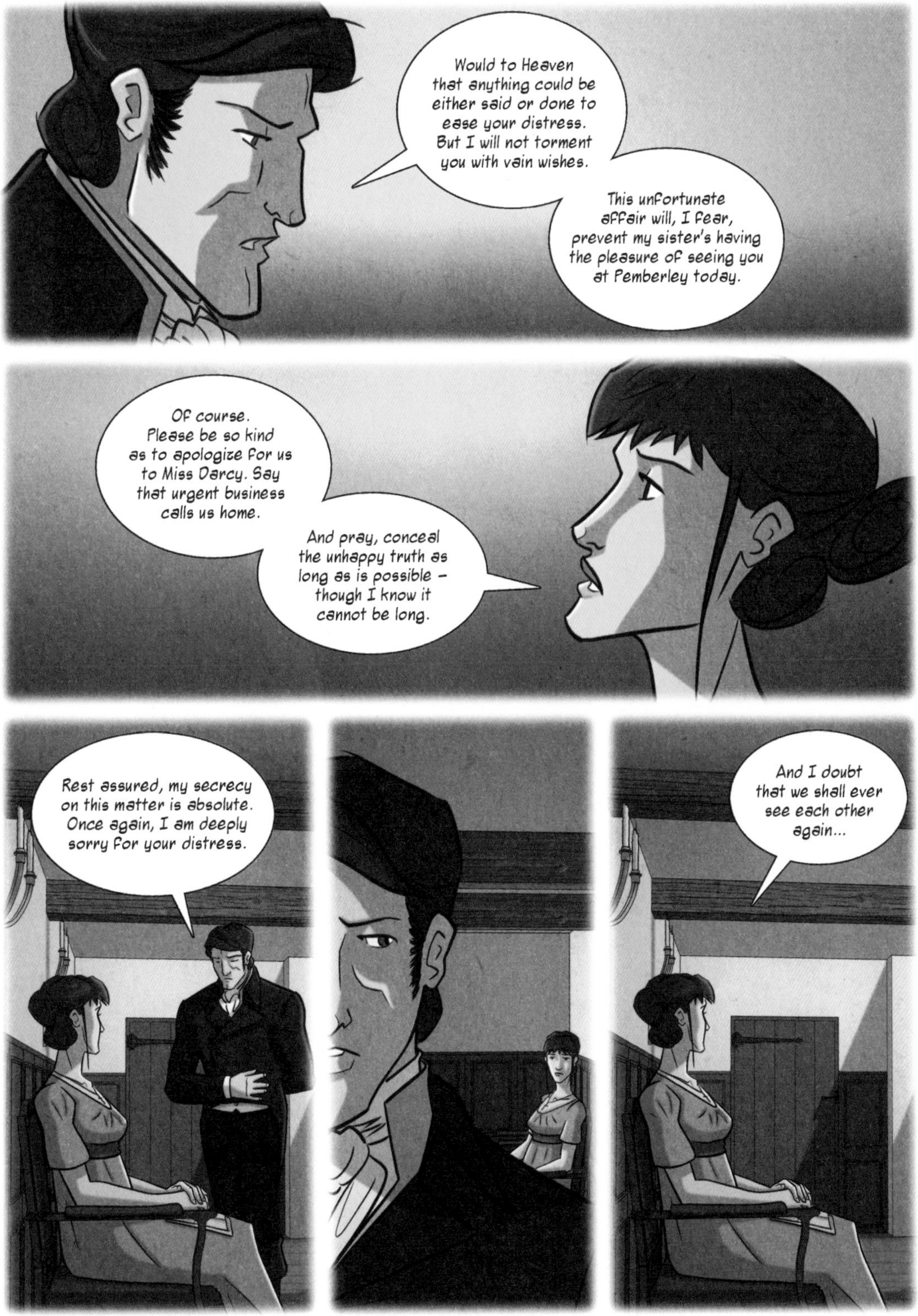
Would to Heaven that anything could be either said or done to ease your distress. But I will not torment you with vain wishes.
This unfortunate affair will, I fear, prevent my sister's having the pleasure of seeing you at Pemberley today.
Of course. Please be so kind as to apologize for us to Miss Darcy. Say that urgent business calls us home.
And pray, conceal the unhappy truth as long as is possible – though I know it cannot be long.
Rest assured, my secrecy on this matter is absolute. Once again, I am deeply sorry for your distress.
And I doubt that we shall ever see each other again...

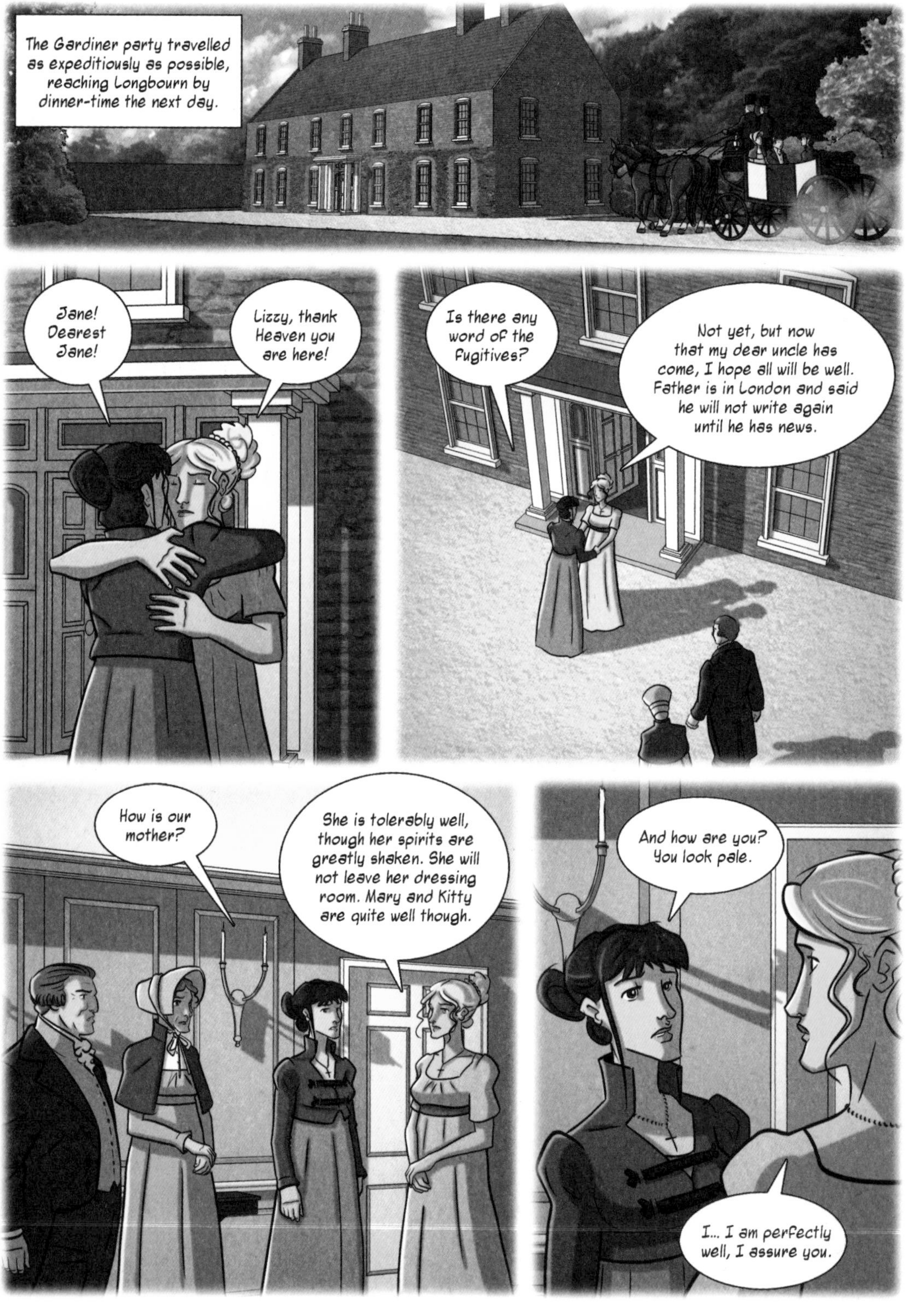
The Gardiner party travelled as expeditiously as possible, reaching Longbourn by dinner-time the next day.
Jane! Dearest Jane!
Lizzy, thank Heaven you are here!
Is there any word of the fugitives?
Not yet, but now that my dear uncle has come, I hope all will be well. Father is in London and said he will not write again until he has news.
How is our mother?
She is tolerably well, though her spirits are greatly shaken. She will not leave her dressing room. Mary and Kitty are quite well though.
And how are you? You look pale.
I... I am perfectly well, I assure you.

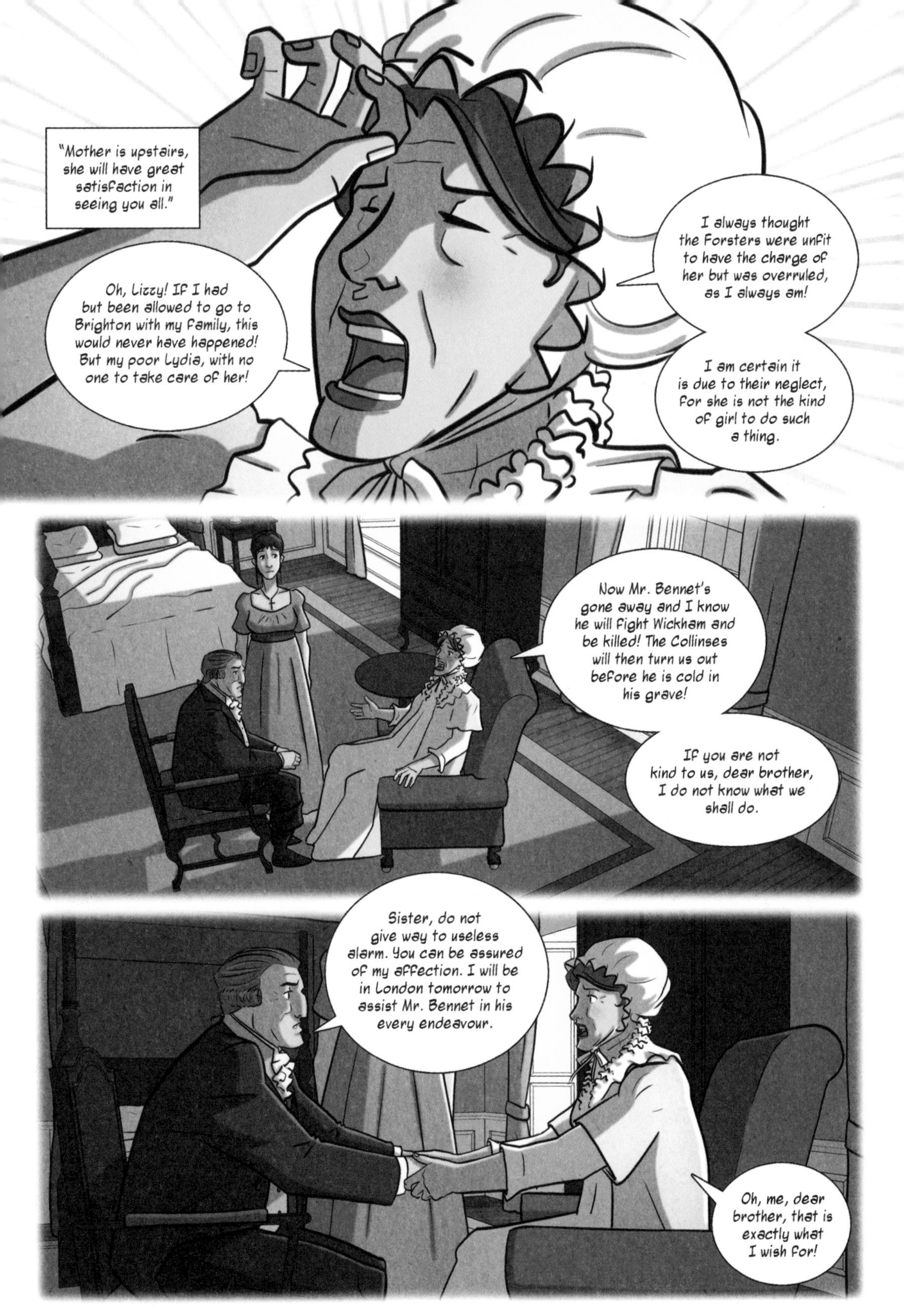

"Mother is upstairs, she will have great satisfaction in seeing you all."
Oh, Lizzy! If I had but been allowed to go to Brighton with my family, this would never have happened! But my poor Lydia, with no one to take care of her!
I always thought the Forsters were unfit to have the charge of her but was overruled, as I always am!
I am certain it is due to their neglect, for she is not the kind of girl to do such a thing.
Now Mr. Bennet's gone away and I know he will fight Wickham and be killed! The Collinses will then turn us out before he is cold in his grave!
If you are not kind to us, dear brother, I do not know what we shall do.
Sister, do not give way to useless alarm. You can be assured of my affection. I will be in London tomorrow to assist Mr. Bennet in his every endeavour.
Oh, me, dear brother, that is exactly what I wish for!

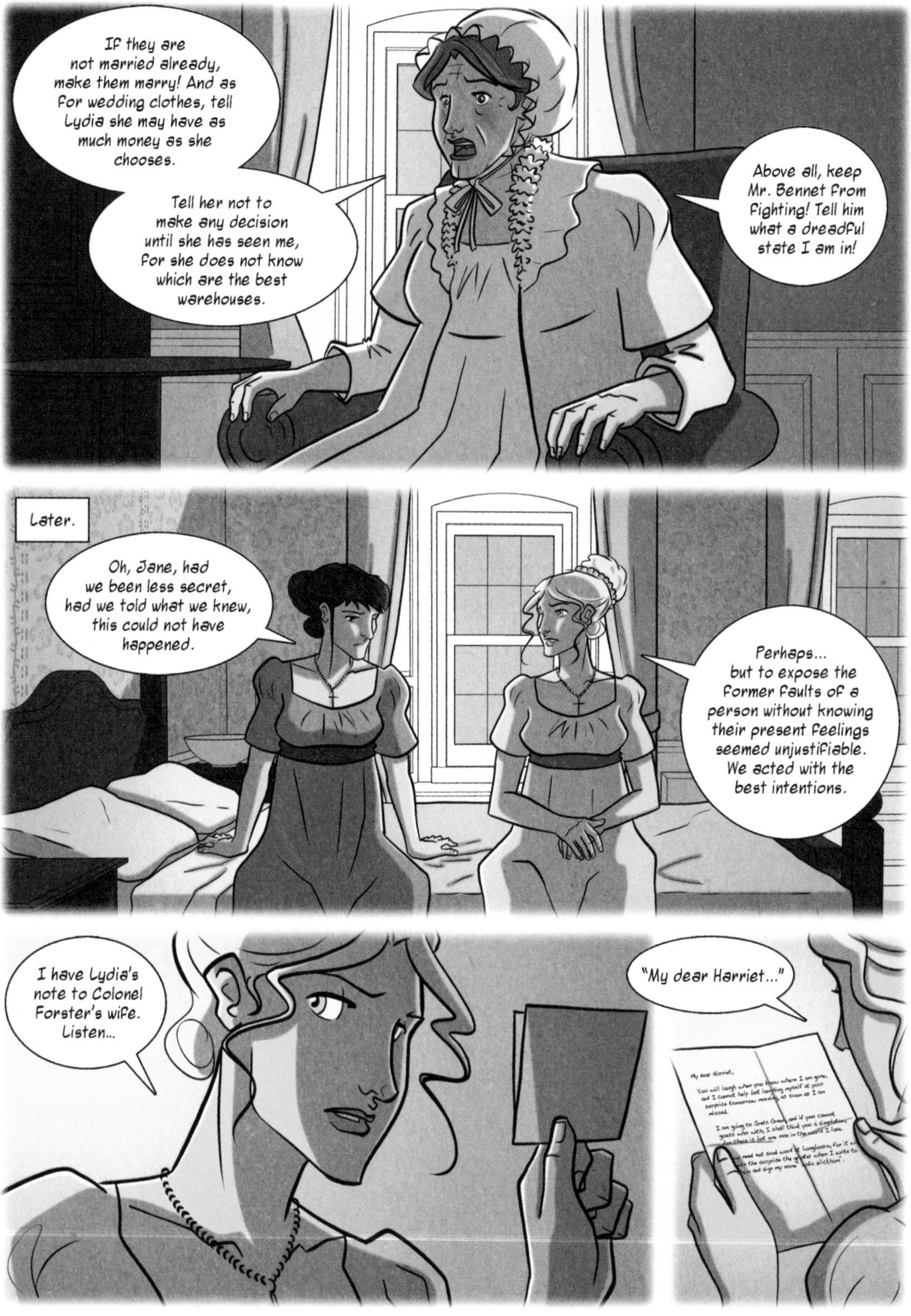
If they are not married already, make them marry! And as for wedding clothes, tell Lydia she may have as much money as she chooses.
Tell her not to make any decision until she has seen me, for she does not know which are the best warehouses.
Above all, keep Mr. Bennet from fighting! Tell him what a dreadful state I am in!
Later.
Oh, Jane, had we been less secret, had we told what we knew, this could not have happened.
Perhaps... but to expose the former faults of a person without knowing their present feelings seemed unjustifiable. We acted with the best intentions.
I have Lydia's note to Colonel Forster's wife. Listen...
"My dear Harriet..."

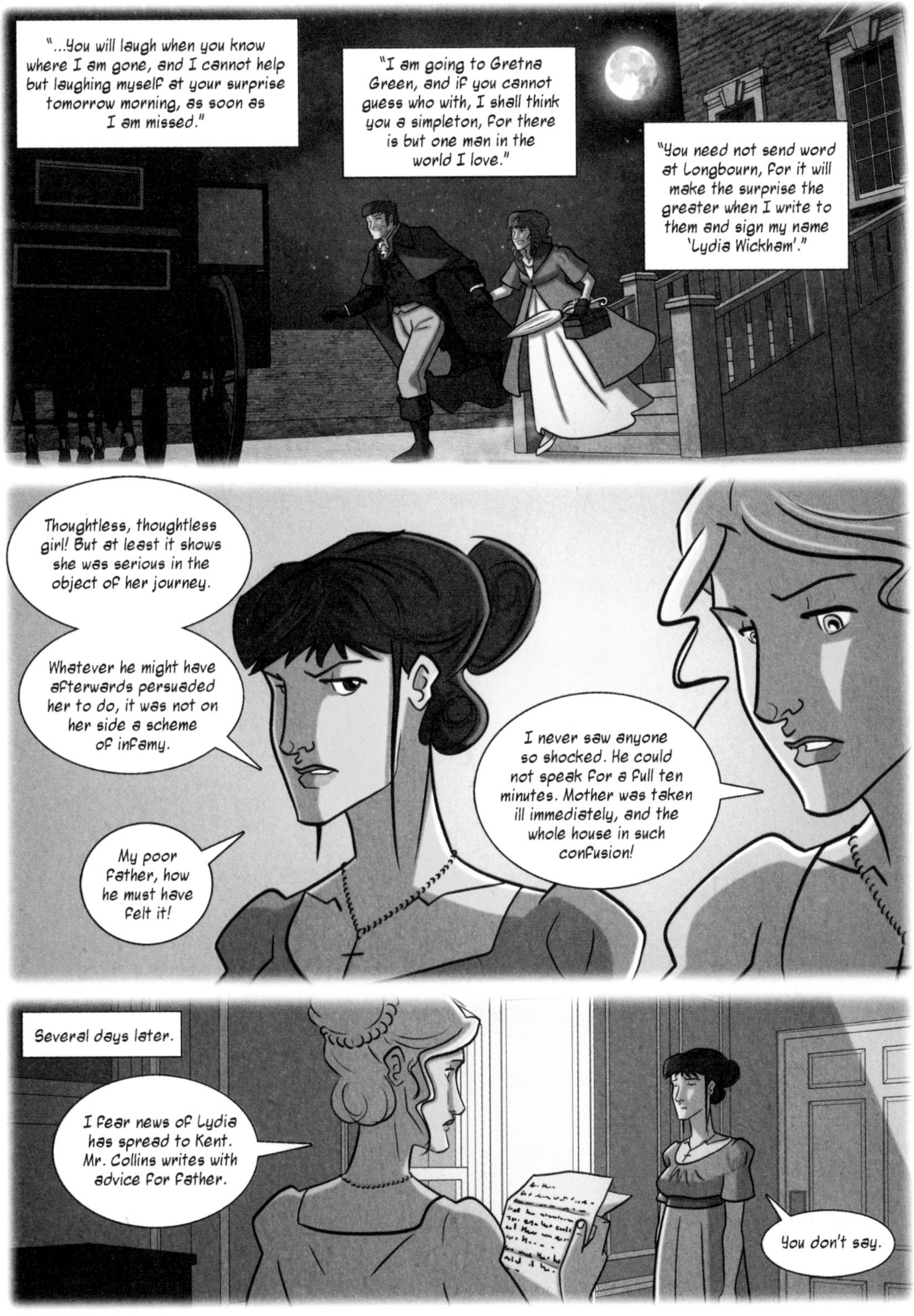
"...You will laugh when you know where I am gone, and I cannot help but laughing myself at your surprise tomorrow morning, as soon as I am missed."
"I am going to Gretna Green, and if you cannot guess who with, I shall think you a simpleton, for there is but one man in the world I love."
"You need not send word at Longbourn, for it will make the surprise the greater when I write to them and sign my name 'Lydia Wickham'."
Thoughtless, thoughtless girl! But at least it shows she was serious in the object of her journey.
Whatever he might have afterwards persuaded her to do, it was not on her side a scheme of infamy.
I never saw anyone so shocked. He could not speak for a full ten minutes. Mother was taken ill immediately, and the whole house in such confusion!
My poor father, how he must have felt it!
Several days later.
I fear news of Lydia has spread to Kent. Mr. Collins writes with advice for father.
You don't say.

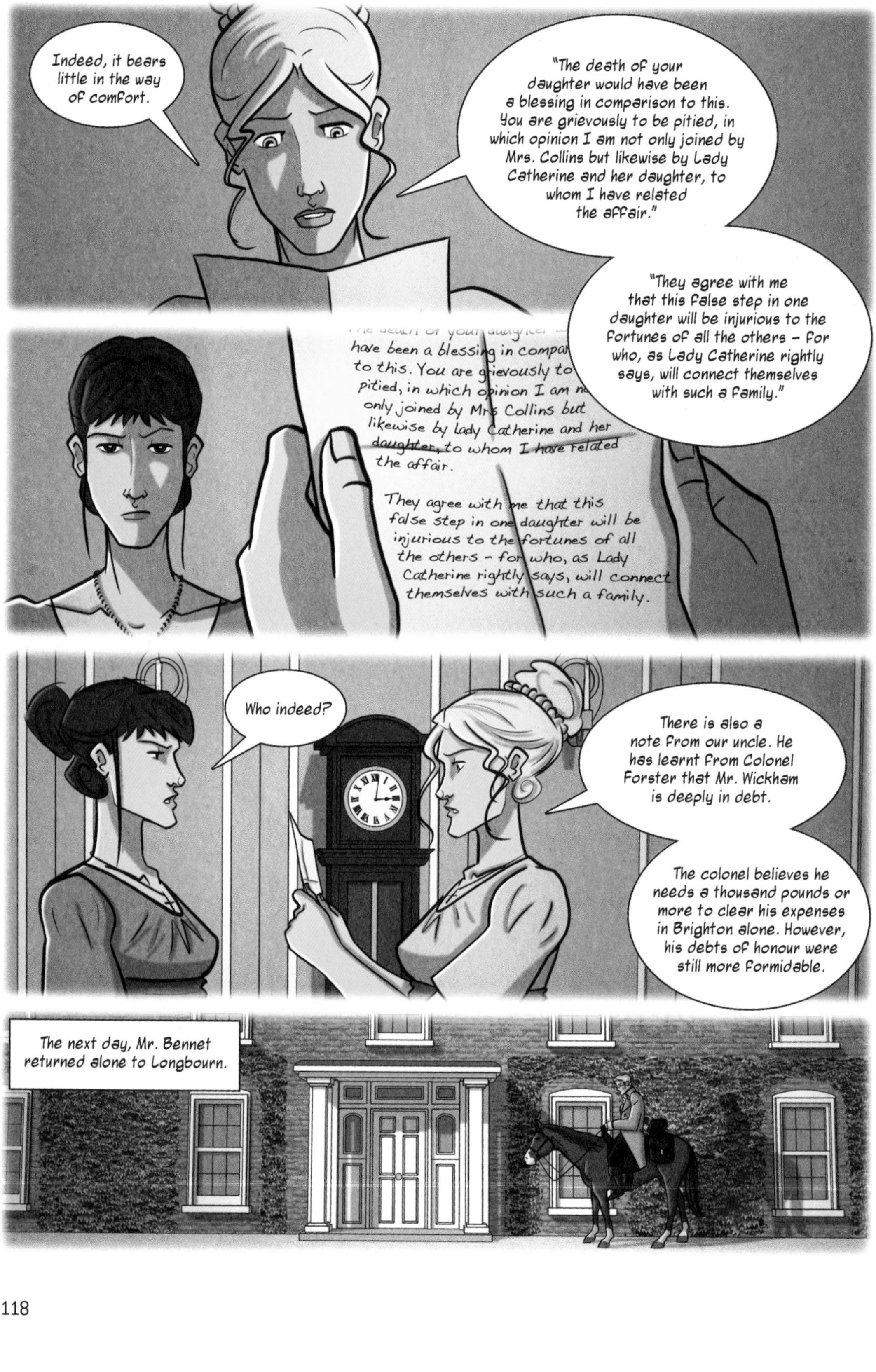
Indeed, it bears little in the way of comfort.
"The death of your daughter would have been a blessing in comparison to this. You are grievously to be pitied, in which opinion I am not only joined by Mrs. Collins but likewise by Lady Catherine and her daughter, to whom I have related the affair."
"They agree with me that this false step in one daughter will be injurious to the fortunes of all the others – for who, as Lady Catherine rightly says, will connect themselves with such a family."
have been a blessing in compar
to this. You are grievously to
pitied, in which opinion I am n
only joined by Mrs Collins but
likewise by Lady Catherine and her
daughter, to whom I have related
the affair.
They agree with me that this
false step in one daughter will be
injurious to the fortunes of all
the others – for who, as Lady
Catherine rightly says, will connect
themselves with such a family.
Who indeed?
There is also a note from our uncle. He has learnt from Colonel Forster that Mr. Wickham is deeply in debt.
The colonel believes he needs a thousand pounds or more to clear his expenses in Brighton alone. However, his debts of honour were still more formidable.
The next day, Mr. Bennet returned alone to Longbourn.

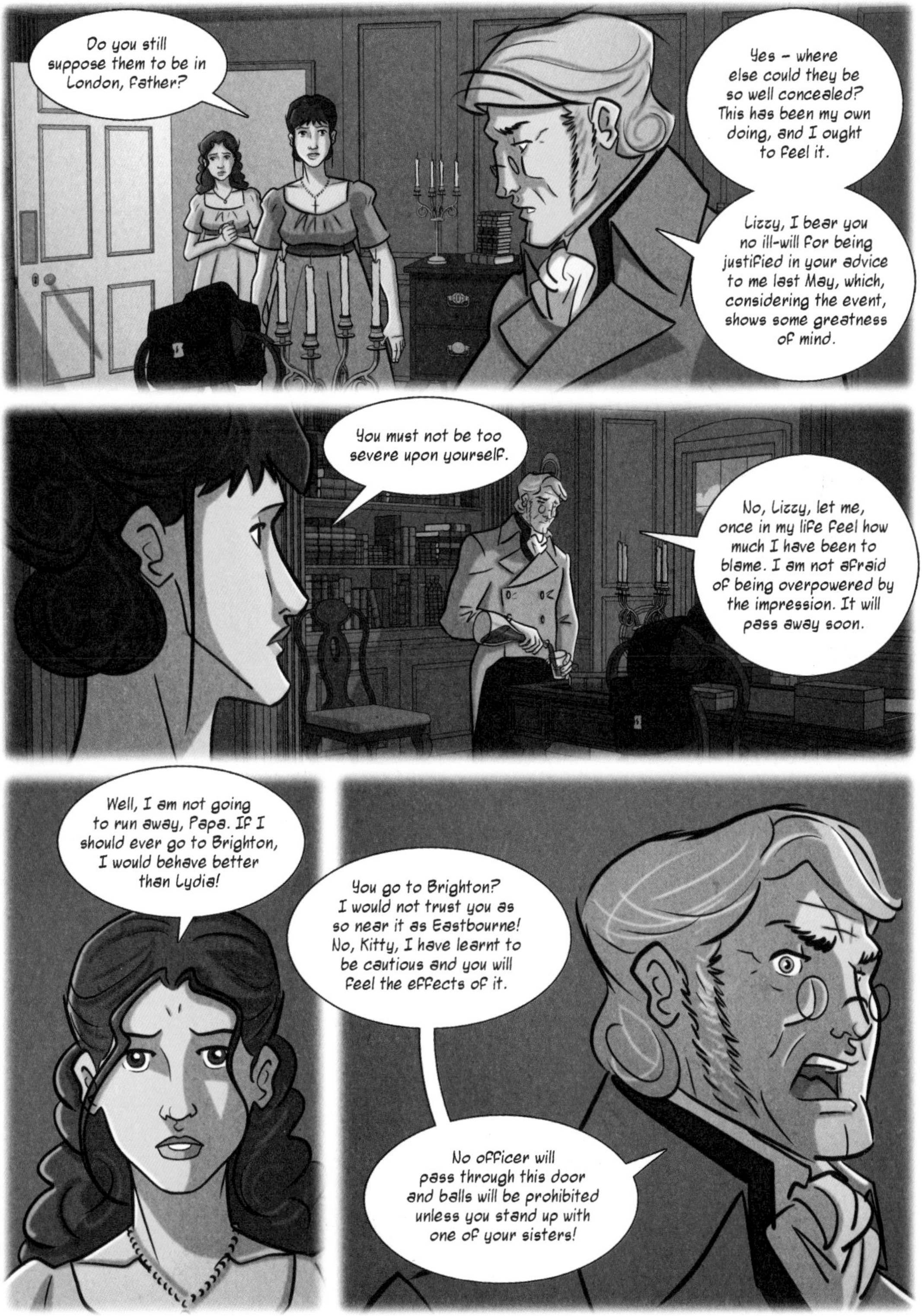
Do you still suppose them to be in London, father?
Yes – where else could they be so well concealed? This has been my own doing, and I ought to feel it.
Lizzy, I bear you no ill-will for being justified in your advice to me last May, which, considering the event, shows some greatness of mind.
You must not be too severe upon yourself.
No, Lizzy, let me, once in my life feel how much I have been to blame. I am not afraid of being overpowered by the impression. It will pass away soon.
Well, I am not going to run away, Papa. If I should ever go to Brighton, I would behave better than Lydia!
You go to Brighton? I would not trust you as so near it as Eastbourne! No, Kitty, I have learnt to be cautious and you will feel the effects of it.
No officer will pass through this door and balls will be prohibited unless you stand up with one of your sisters!

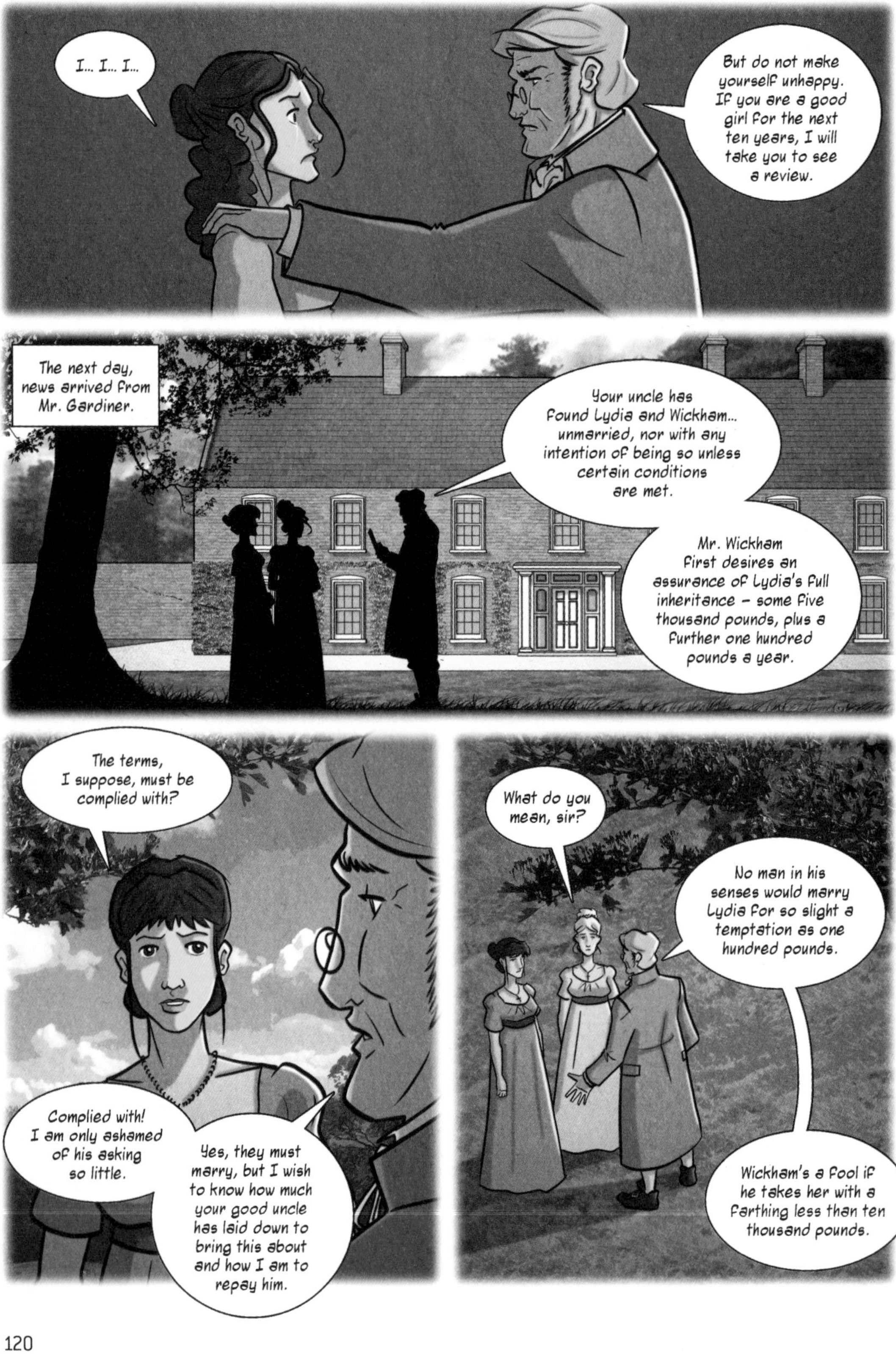
I... I... I...
But do not make yourself unhappy. If you are a good girl for the next ten years, I will take you to see a review.
The next day, news arrived from Mr. Gardiner.
Your uncle has found Lydia and Wickham... unmarried, nor with any intention of being so unless certain conditions are met.
Mr. Wickham first desires an assurance of Lydia's full inheritance – some five thousand pounds, plus a further one hundred pounds a year.
The terms, I suppose, must be complied with?
Complied with! I am only ashamed of his asking so little.
Yes, they must marry, but I wish to know how much your good uncle has laid down to bring this about and how I am to repay him.
What do you mean, sir?
No man in his senses would marry Lydia for so slight a temptation as one hundred pounds.
Wickham's a fool if he takes her with a farthing less than ten thousand pounds.

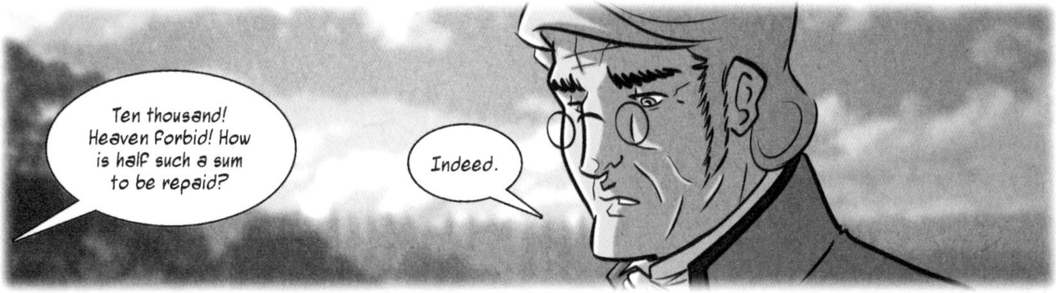
Ten thousand! Heaven forbid! How is half such a sum to be repaid?
Indeed.

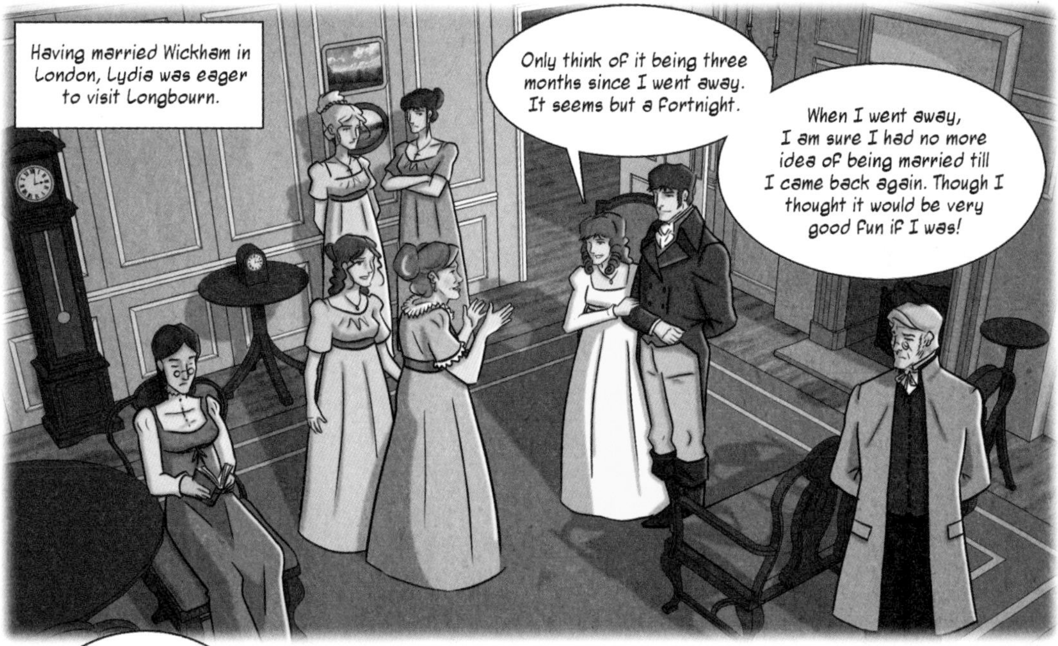
Having married Wickham in London, Lydia was eager to visit Longbourn.
Only think of it being three months since I went away. It seems but a fortnight.
When I went away, I am sure I had no more idea of being married till I came back again. Though I thought it would be very good fun if I was!

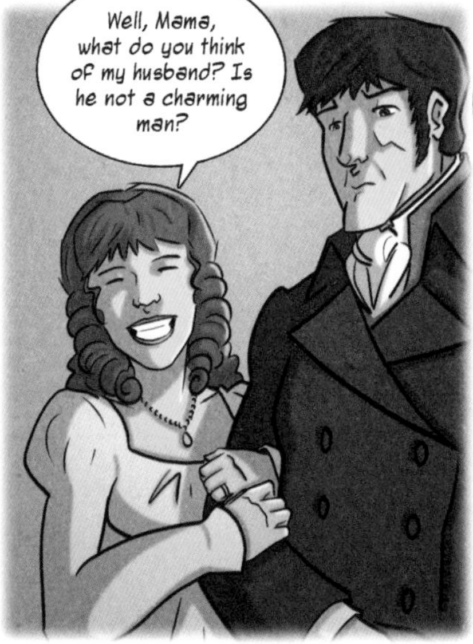
Well, Mama, what do you think of my husband? Is he not a charming man?

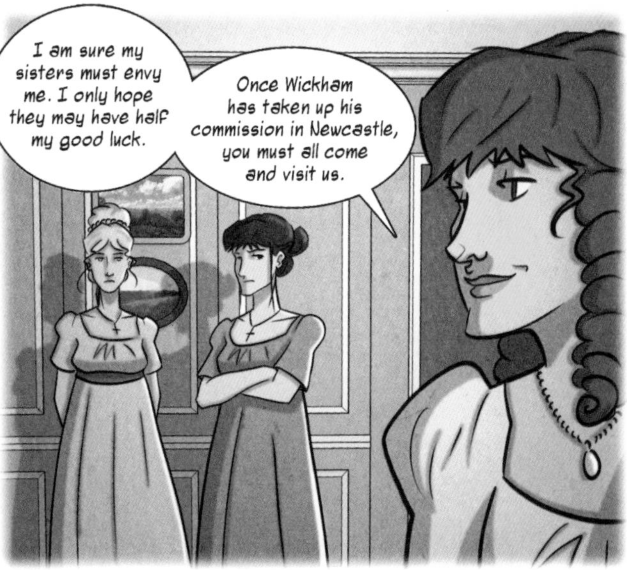
I am sure my sisters must envy me. I only hope they may have half my good luck.
Once Wickham has taken up his commission in Newcastle, you must all come and visit us.

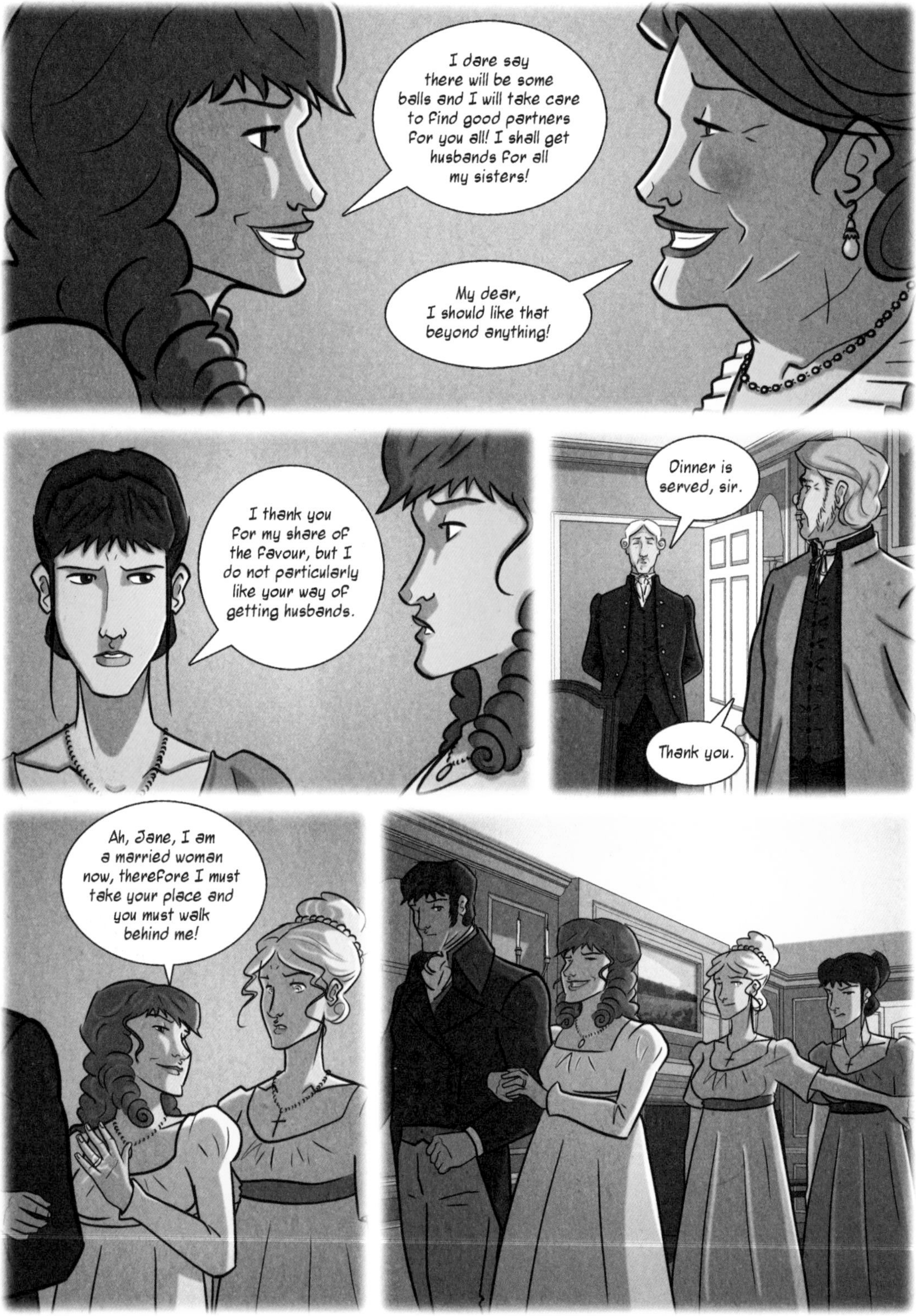

I dare say there will be some balls and I will take care to find good partners for you all! I shall get husbands for all my sisters!
My dear, I should like that beyond anything!
I thank you for my share of the favour, but I do not particularly like your way of getting husbands.
Dinner is served, sir.
Thank you.
Ah, Jane, I am a married woman now, therefore I must take your place and you must walk behind me!

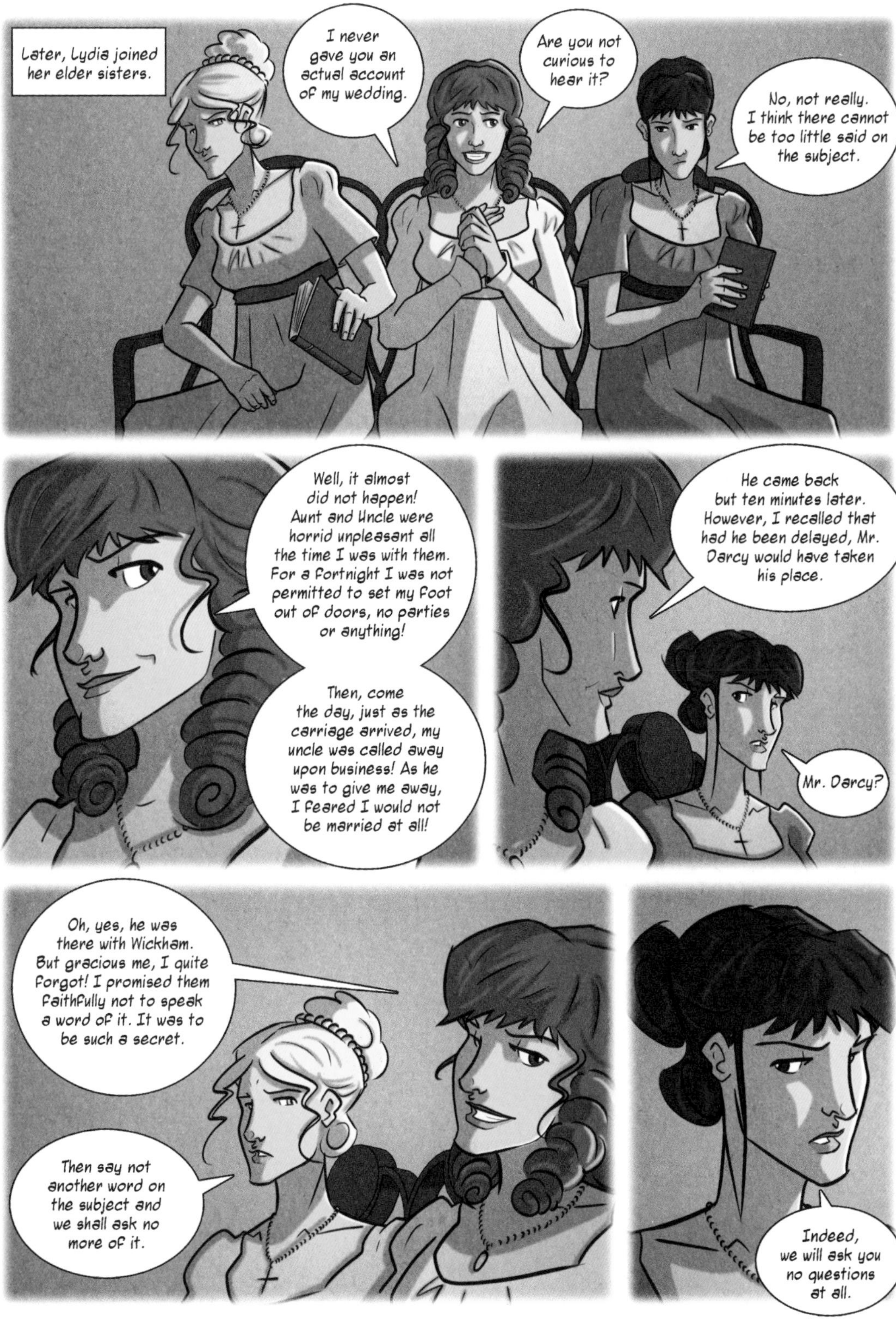
Later, Lydia joined her elder sisters.
I never gave you an actual account of my wedding.
Are you not curious to hear it?
No, not really. I think there cannot be too little said on the subject.
Well, it almost did not happen! Aunt and Uncle were horrid unpleasant all the time I was with them. For a fortnight I was not permitted to set my foot out of doors, no parties or anything!
Then, come the day, just as the carriage arrived, my uncle was called away upon business! As he was to give me away, I feared I would not be married at all!
He came back but ten minutes later. However, I recalled that had he been delayed, Mr. Darcy would have taken his place.
Mr. Darcy?
Oh, yes, he was there with Wickham. But gracious me, I quite forgot! I promised them faithfully not to speak a word of it. It was to be such a secret.
Then say not another word on the subject and we shall ask no more of it.
Indeed, we will ask you no questions at all.

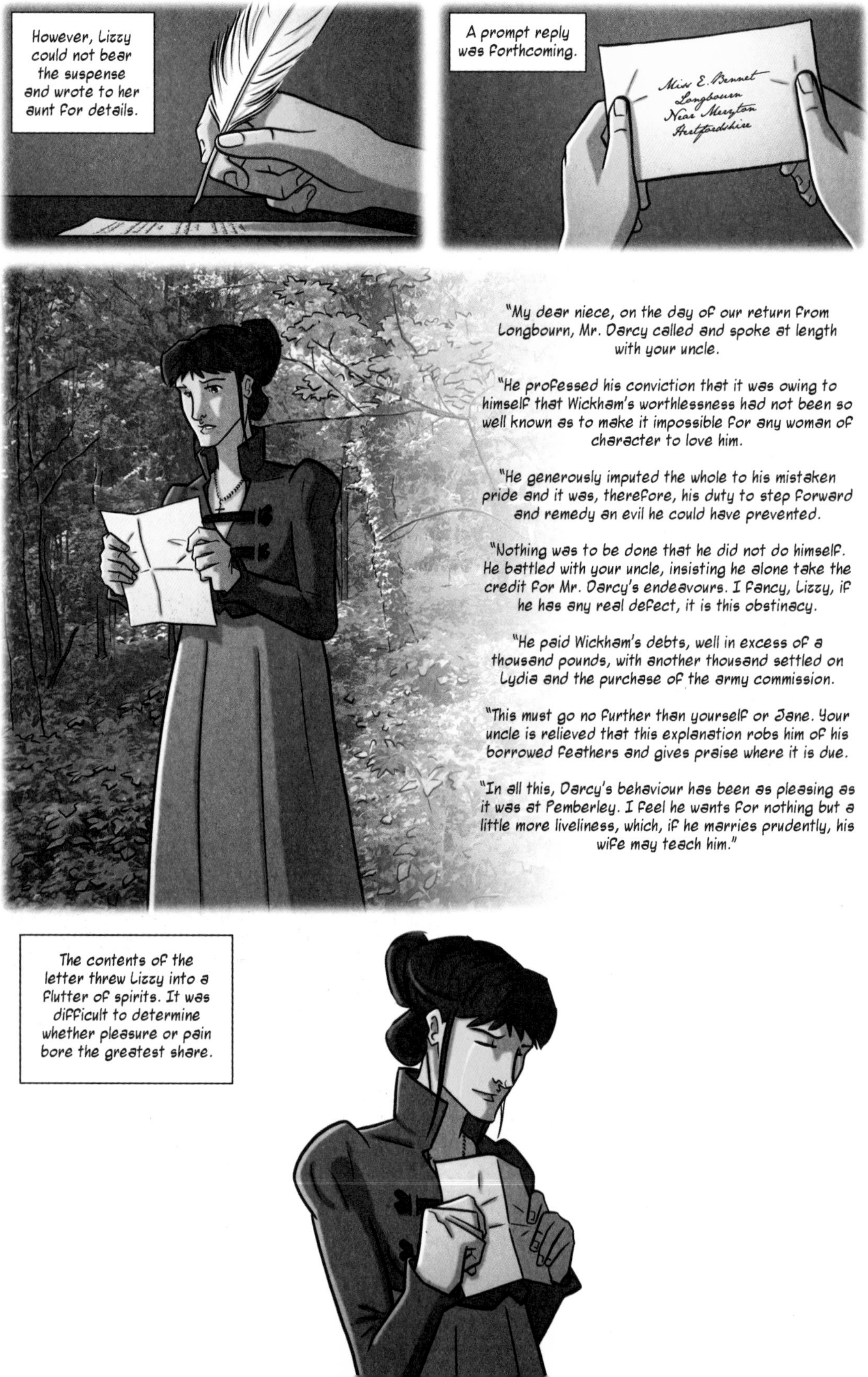
However, Lizzy could not bear the suspense and wrote to her aunt for details.
A prompt reply was forthcoming.
Miss E. Bennet
Longbourn
Near Meryton
Hertfordshire
"My dear niece, on the day of our return from Longbourn, Mr. Darcy called and spoke at length with your uncle.
"He professed his conviction that it was owing to himself that Wickham's worthlessness had not been so well known as to make it impossible for any woman of character to love him.
"He generously imputed the whole to his mistaken pride and it was, therefore, his duty to step forward and remedy an evil he could have prevented.
"Nothing was to be done that he did not do himself. He battled with your uncle, insisting he alone take the credit for Mr. Darcy's endeavours. I fancy, Lizzy, if he has any real defect, it is this obstinacy.
"He paid Wickham's debts, well in excess of a thousand pounds, with another thousand settled on Lydia and the purchase of the army commission.
"This must go no further than yourself or Jane. Your uncle is relieved that this explanation robs him of his borrowed feathers and gives praise where it is due.
"In all this, Darcy's behaviour has been as pleasing as it was at Pemberley. I feel he wants for nothing but a little more liveliness, which, if he marries prudently, his wife may teach him."
The contents of the letter threw Lizzy into a flutter of spirits. It was difficult to determine whether pleasure or pain bore the greatest share.

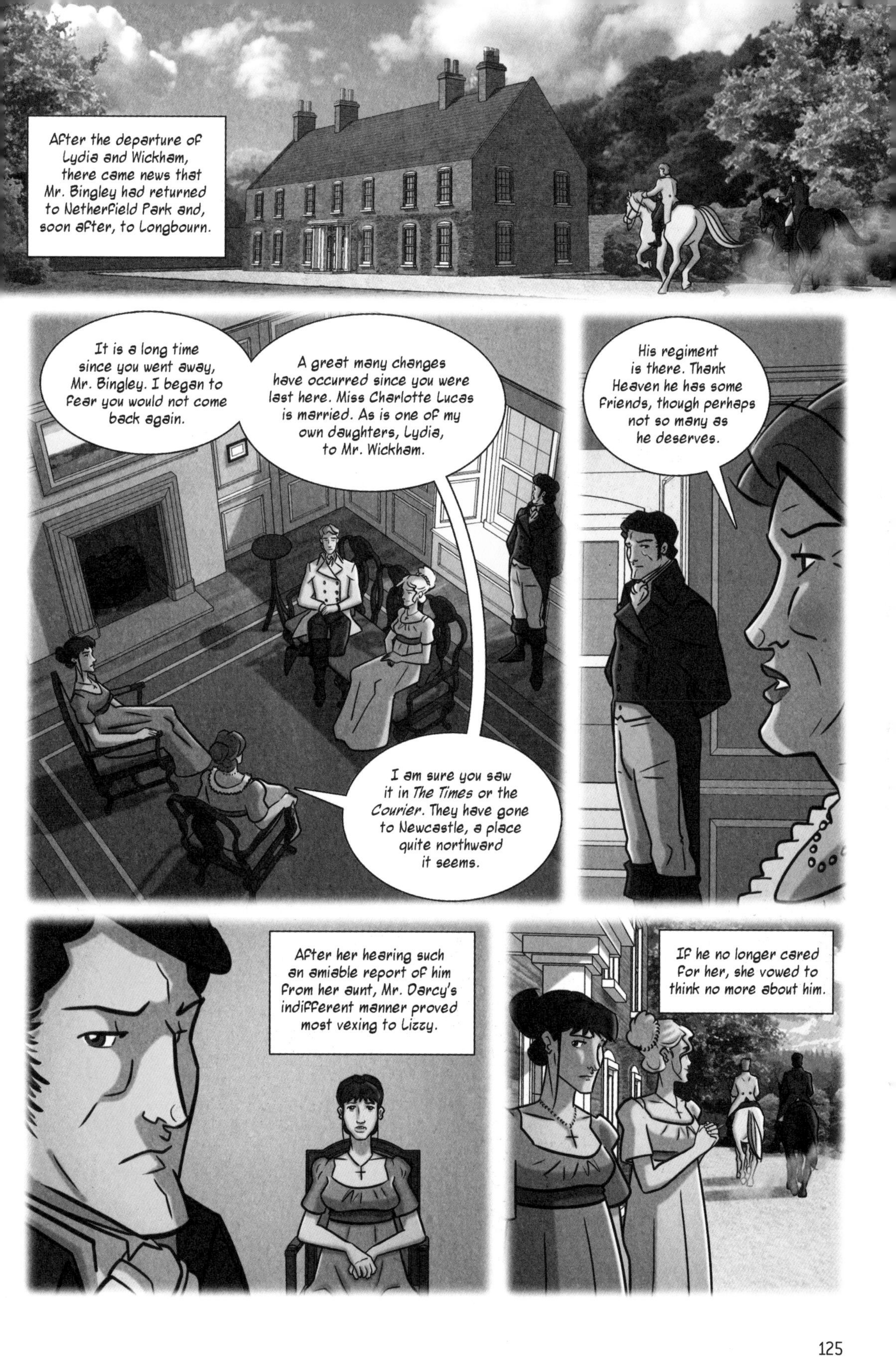
After the departure of Lydia and Wickham, there came news that Mr. Bingley had returned to Netherfield Park and, soon after, to Longbourn.
It is a long time since you went away, Mr. Bingley. I began to fear you would not come back again.
A great many changes have occurred since you were last here. Miss Charlotte Lucas is married. As is one of my own daughters, Lydia, to Mr. Wickham.
I am sure you saw it in *The Times* or the *Courier*. They have gone to Newcastle, a place quite northward it seems.
His regiment is there. Thank Heaven he has some friends, though perhaps not so many as he deserves.
After her hearing such an amiable report of him from her aunt, Mr. Darcy's indifferent manner proved most vexing to Lizzy.
If he no longer cared for her, she vowed to think no more about him.

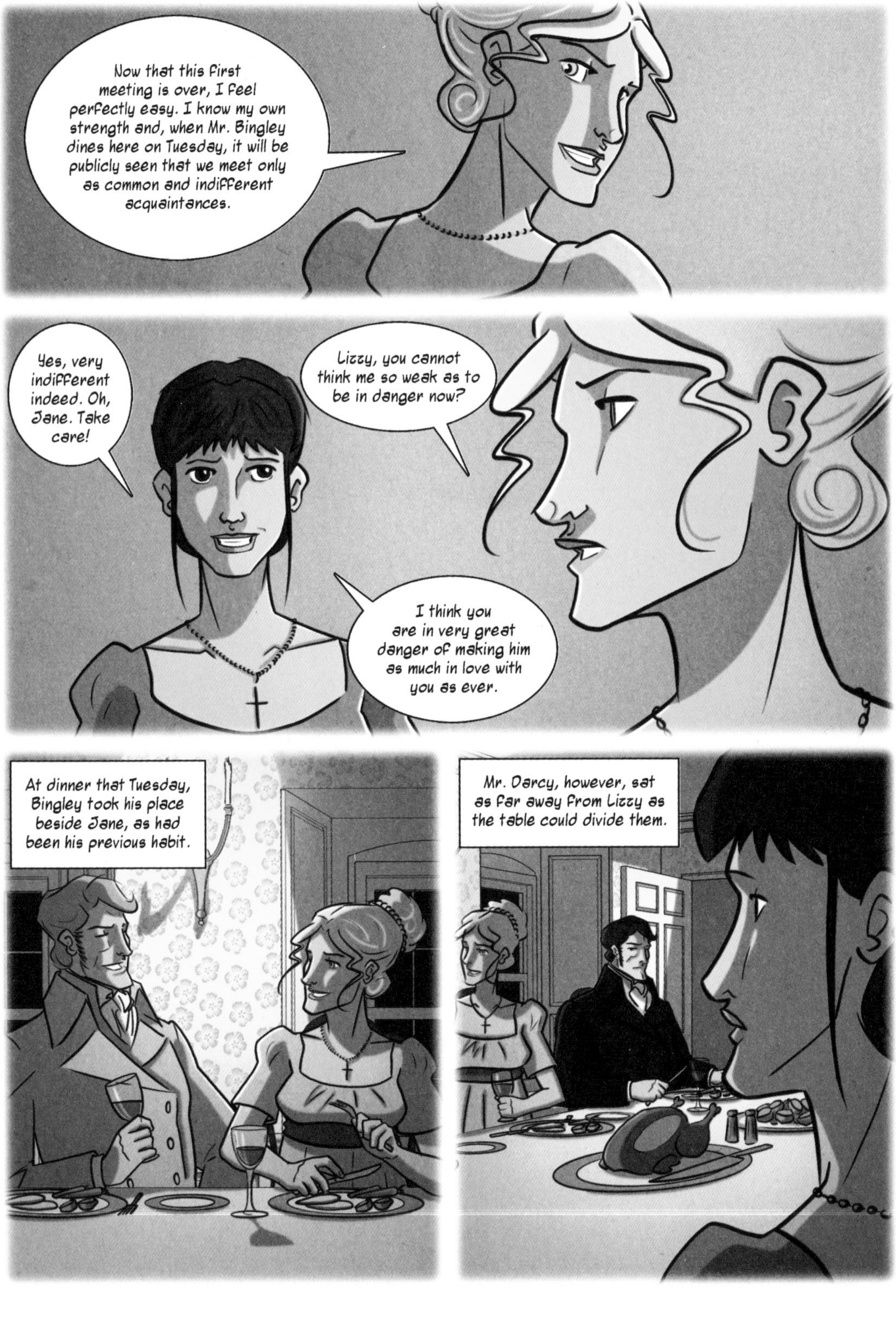
Now that this first meeting is over, I feel perfectly easy. I know my own strength and, when Mr. Bingley dines here on Tuesday, it will be publicly seen that we meet only as common and indifferent acquaintances.
Yes, very indifferent indeed. Oh, Jane. Take care!
Lizzy, you cannot think me so weak as to be in danger now?
I think you are in very great danger of making him as much in love with you as ever.
At dinner that Tuesday, Bingley took his place beside Jane, as had been his previous habit.
Mr. Darcy, however, sat as far away from Lizzy as the table could divide them.

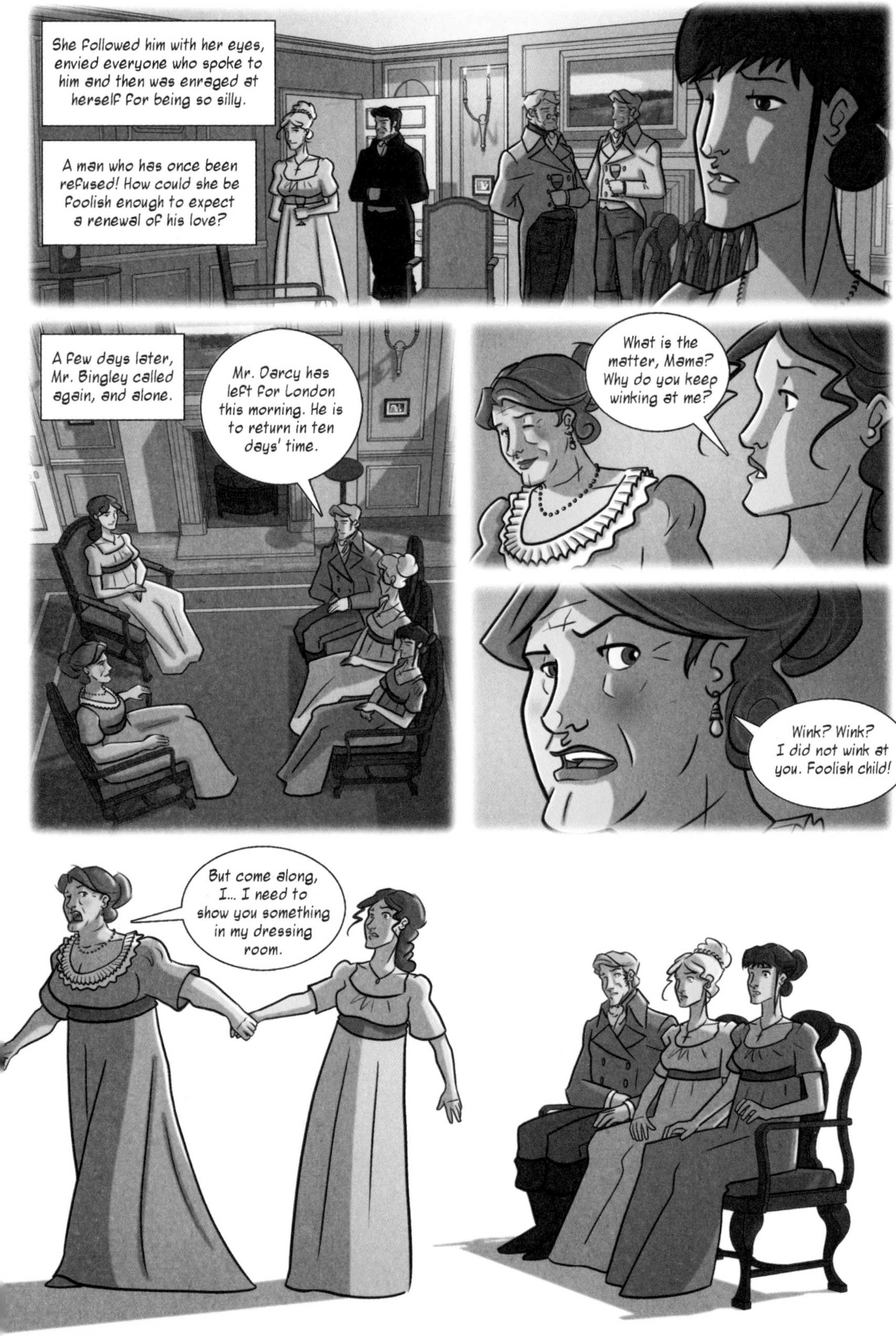
She followed him with her eyes, envied everyone who spoke to him and then was enraged at herself for being so silly.
A man who has once been refused! How could she be foolish enough to expect a renewal of his love?
A few days later, Mr. Bingley called again, and alone.
Mr. Darcy has left for London this morning. He is to return in ten days' time.
What is the matter, Mama? Why do you keep winking at me?
Wink? Wink? I did not wink at you. Foolish child!
But come along, I... I need to show you something in my dressing room.

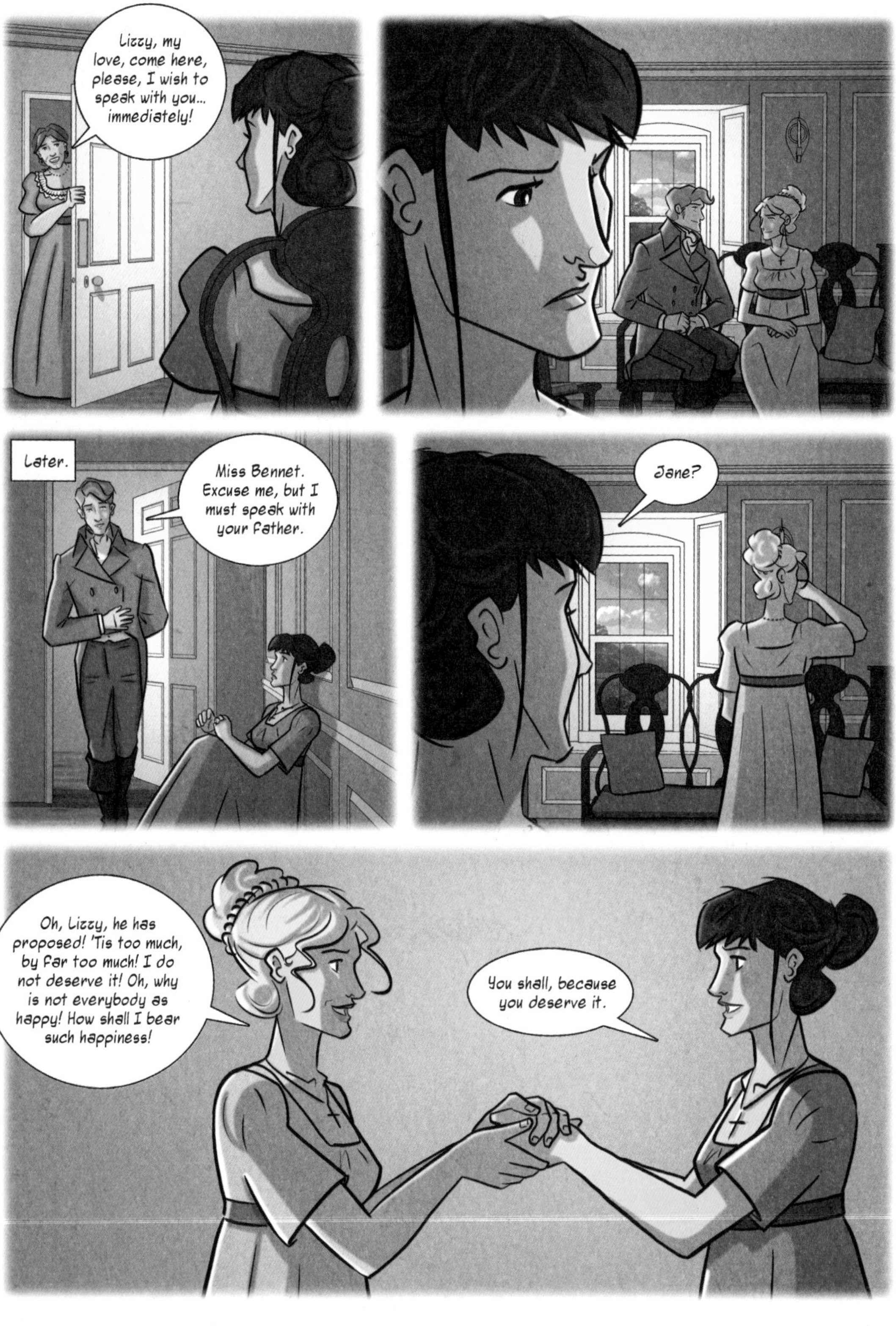
Lizzy, my love, come here, please, I wish to speak with you... immediately!
Later.
Miss Bennet. Excuse me, but I must speak with your father.
Jane?
Oh, Lizzy, he has proposed! 'Tis too much, by far too much! I do not deserve it! Oh, why is not everybody as happy! How shall I bear such happiness!
You shall, because you deserve it.

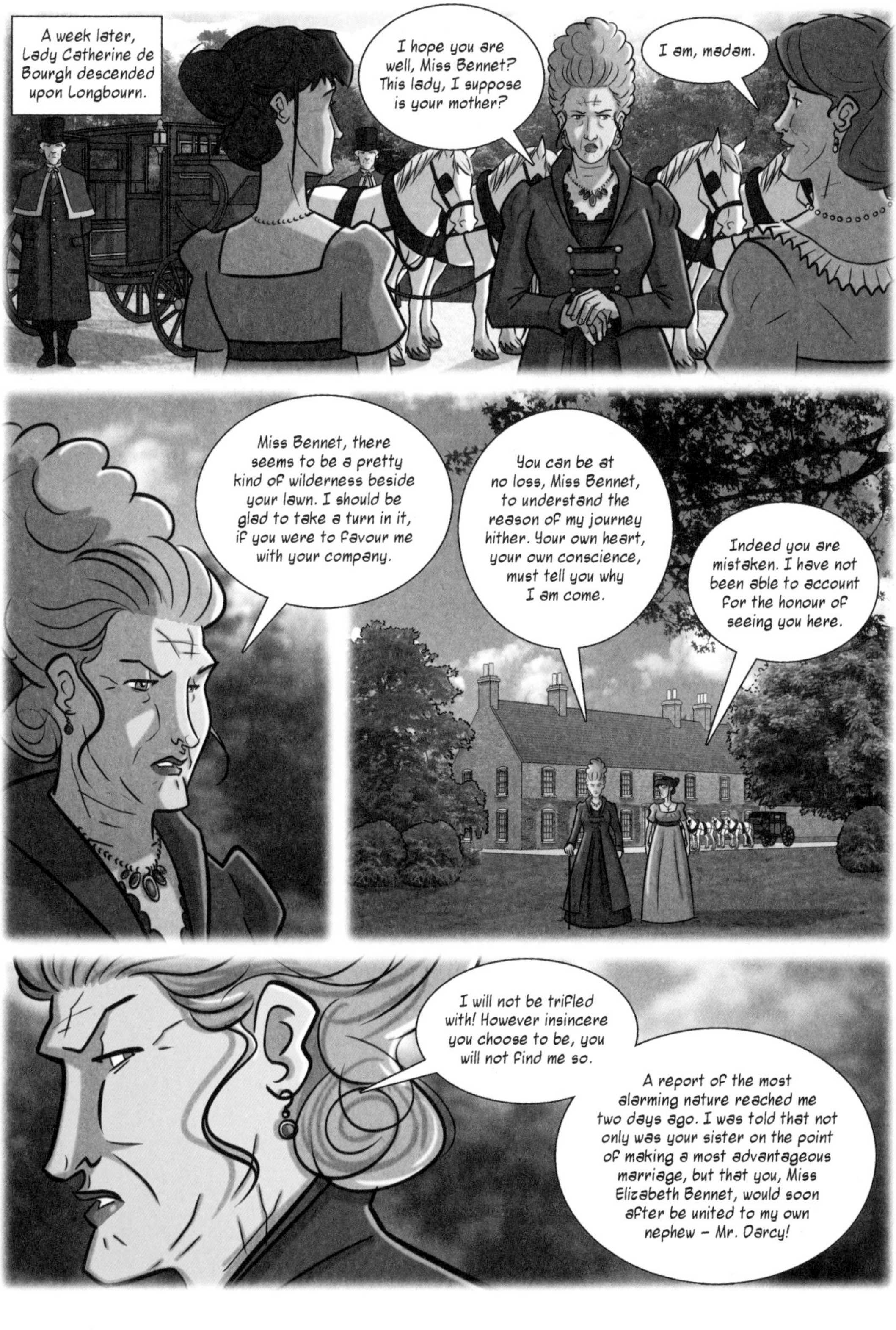

A week later, Lady Catherine de Bourgh descended upon Longbourn.
I hope you are well, Miss Bennet? This lady, I suppose is your mother?
I am, madam.
Miss Bennet, there seems to be a pretty kind of wilderness beside your lawn. I should be glad to take a turn in it, if you were to favour me with your company.
You can be at no loss, Miss Bennet, to understand the reason of my journey hither. Your own heart, your own conscience, must tell you why I am come.
Indeed you are mistaken. I have not been able to account for the honour of seeing you here.
I will not be trifled with! However insincere you choose to be, you will not find me so.
A report of the most alarming nature reached me two days ago. I was told that not only was your sister on the point of making a most advantageous marriage, but that you, Miss Elizabeth Bennet, would soon after be united to my own nephew – Mr. Darcy!

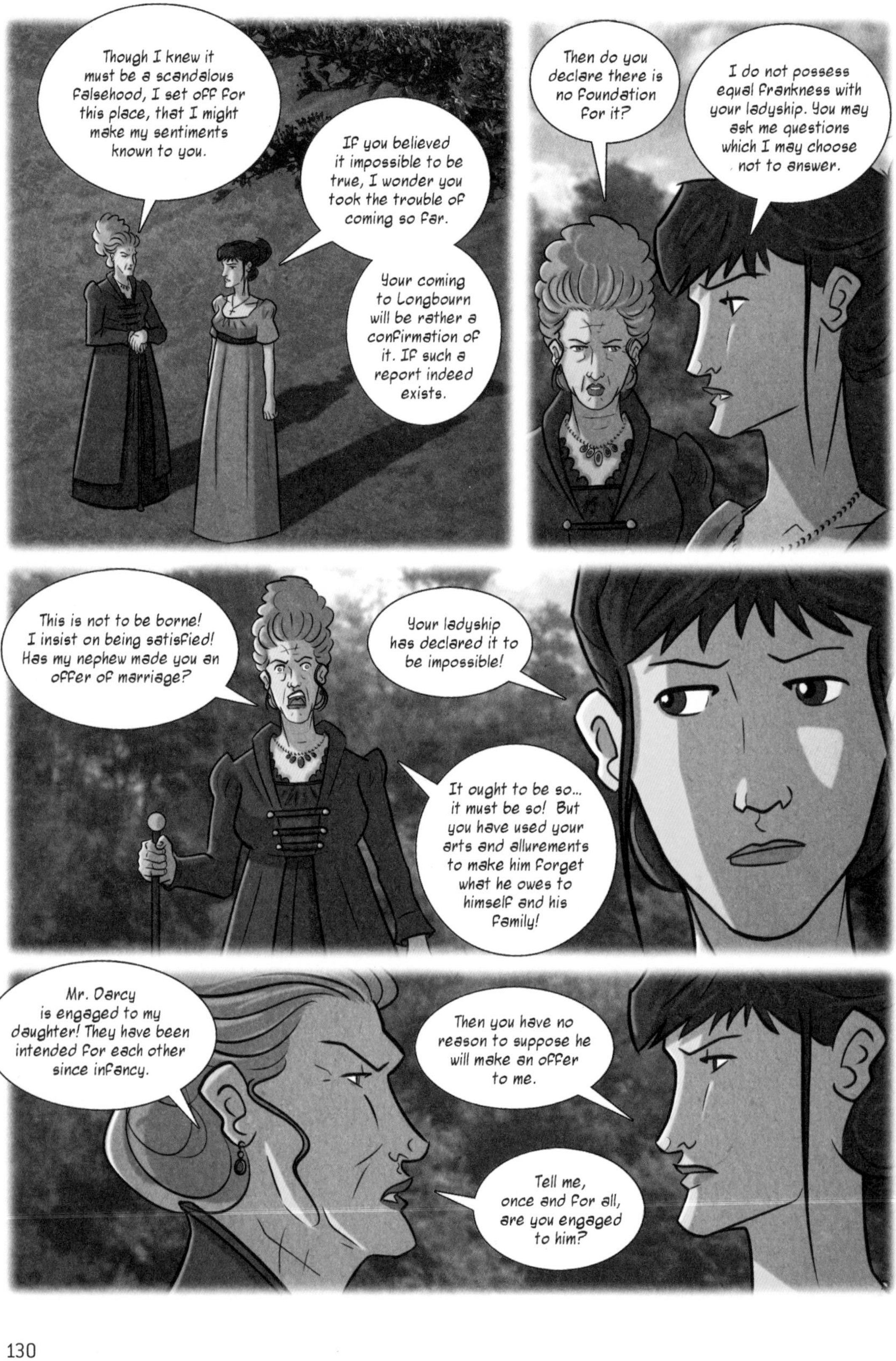
Though I knew it must be a scandalous falsehood, I set off for this place, that I might make my sentiments known to you.
If you believed it impossible to be true, I wonder you took the trouble of coming so far.
Your coming to Longbourn will be rather a confirmation of it. If such a report indeed exists.
Then do you declare there is no foundation for it?
I do not possess equal frankness with your ladyship. You may ask me questions which I may choose not to answer.
This is not to be borne! I insist on being satisfied! Has my nephew made you an offer of marriage?
Your ladyship has declared it to be impossible!
It ought to be so... it must be so! But you have used your arts and allurements to make him forget what he owes to himself and his family!
Mr. Darcy is engaged to my daughter! They have been intended for each other since infancy.
Then you have no reason to suppose he will make an offer to me.
Tell me, once and for all, are you engaged to him?

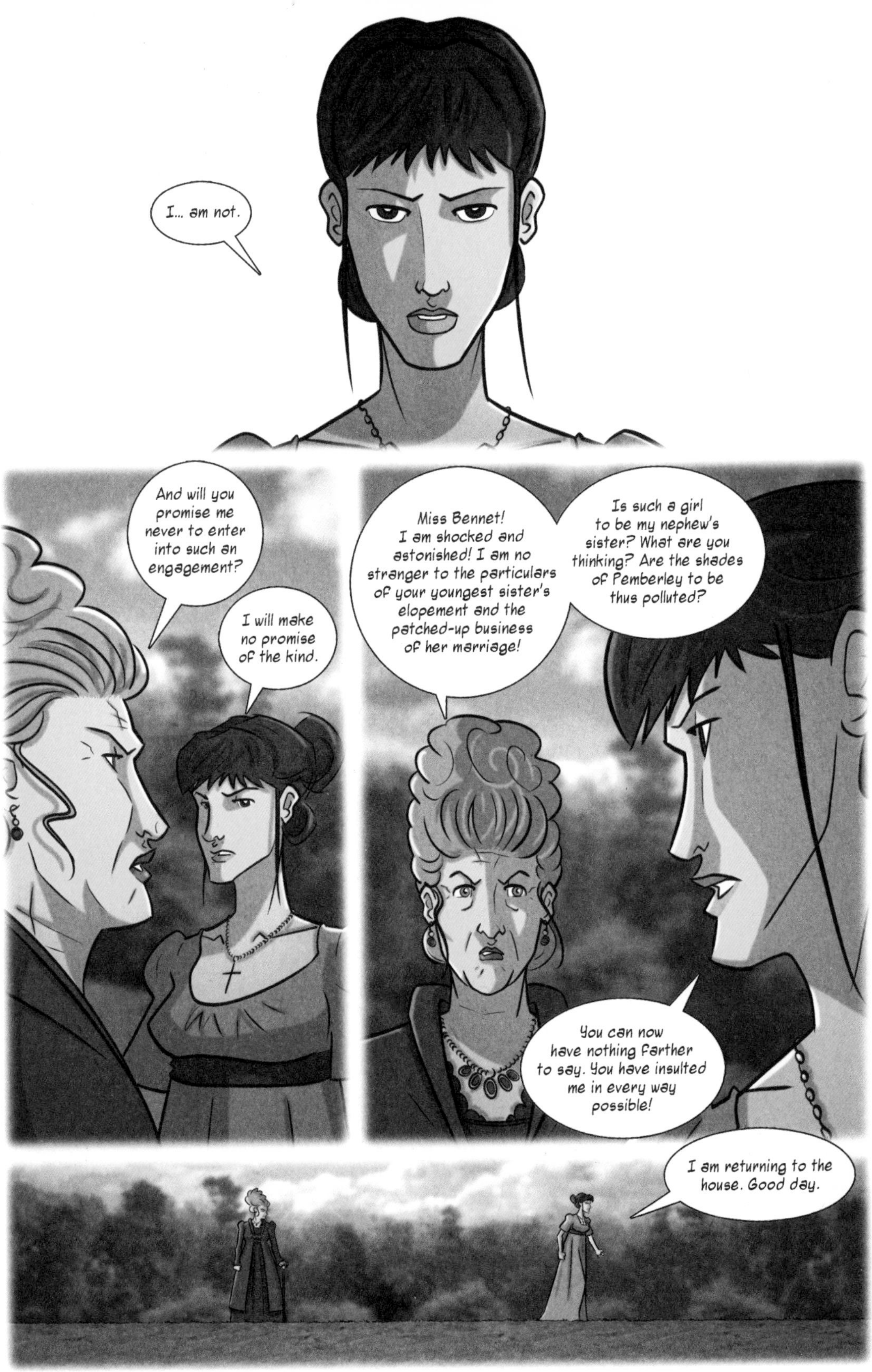
I... am not.
And will you promise me never to enter into such an engagement?
I will make no promise of the kind.
Miss Bennet! I am shocked and astonished! I am no stranger to the particulars of your youngest sister's elopement and the patched-up business of her marriage!
Is such a girl to be my nephew's sister? What are you thinking? Are the shades of Pemberley to be thus polluted?
You can now have nothing farther to say. You have insulted me in every way possible!
I am returning to the house. Good day.

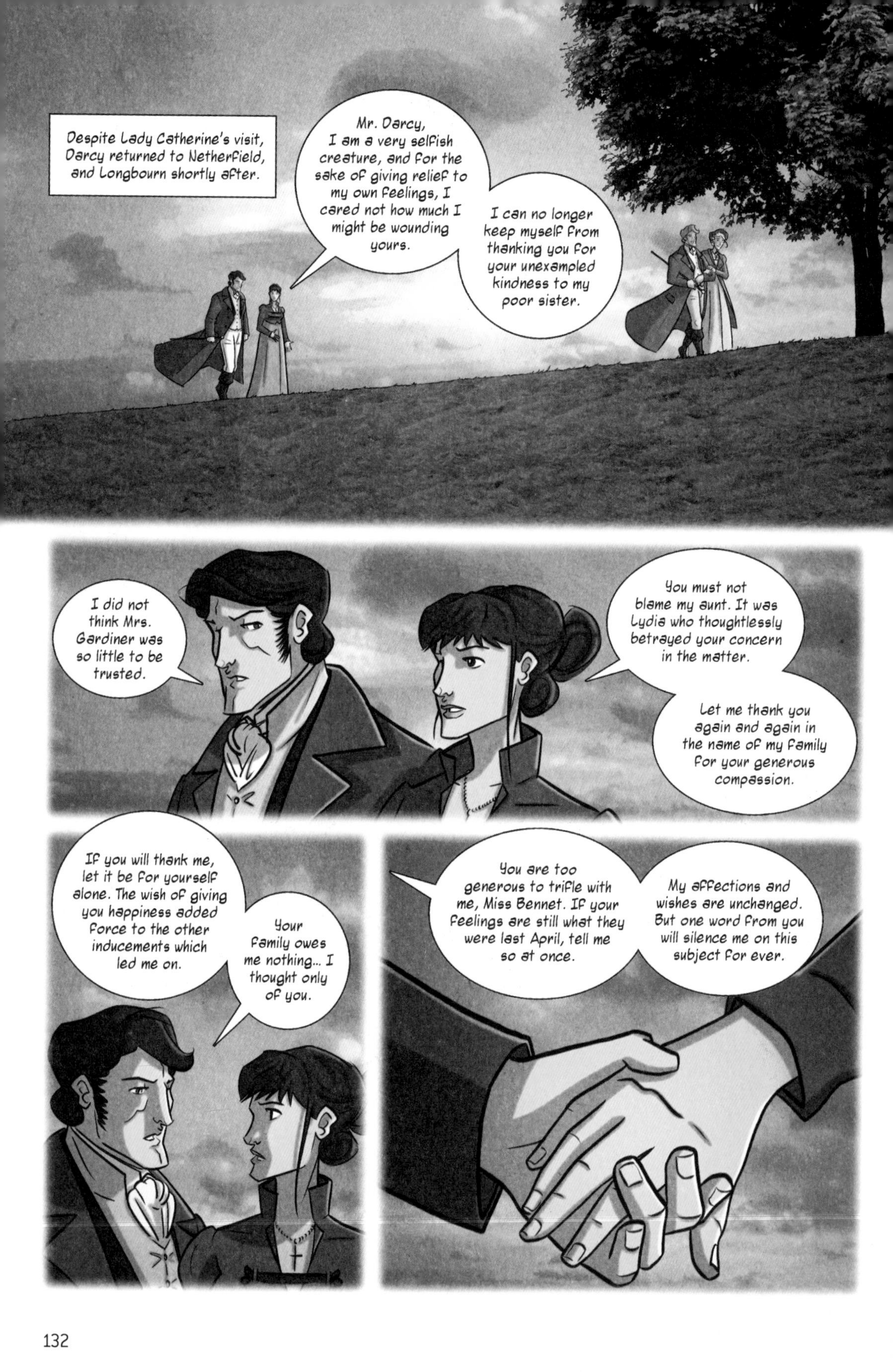
Despite Lady Catherine's visit, Darcy returned to Netherfield, and Longbourn shortly after.
Mr. Darcy, I am a very selfish creature, and for the sake of giving relief to my own feelings, I cared not how much I might be wounding yours.
I can no longer keep myself from thanking you for your unexampled kindness to my poor sister.
I did not think Mrs. Gardiner was so little to be trusted.
You must not blame my aunt. It was Lydia who thoughtlessly betrayed your concern in the matter.
Let me thank you again and again in the name of my family for your generous compassion.
If you will thank me, let it be for yourself alone. The wish of giving you happiness added force to the other inducements which led me on.
Your family owes me nothing... I thought only of you.
You are too generous to trifle with me, Miss Bennet. If your feelings are still what they were last April, tell me so at once.
My affections and wishes are unchanged. But one word from you will silence me on this subject for ever.

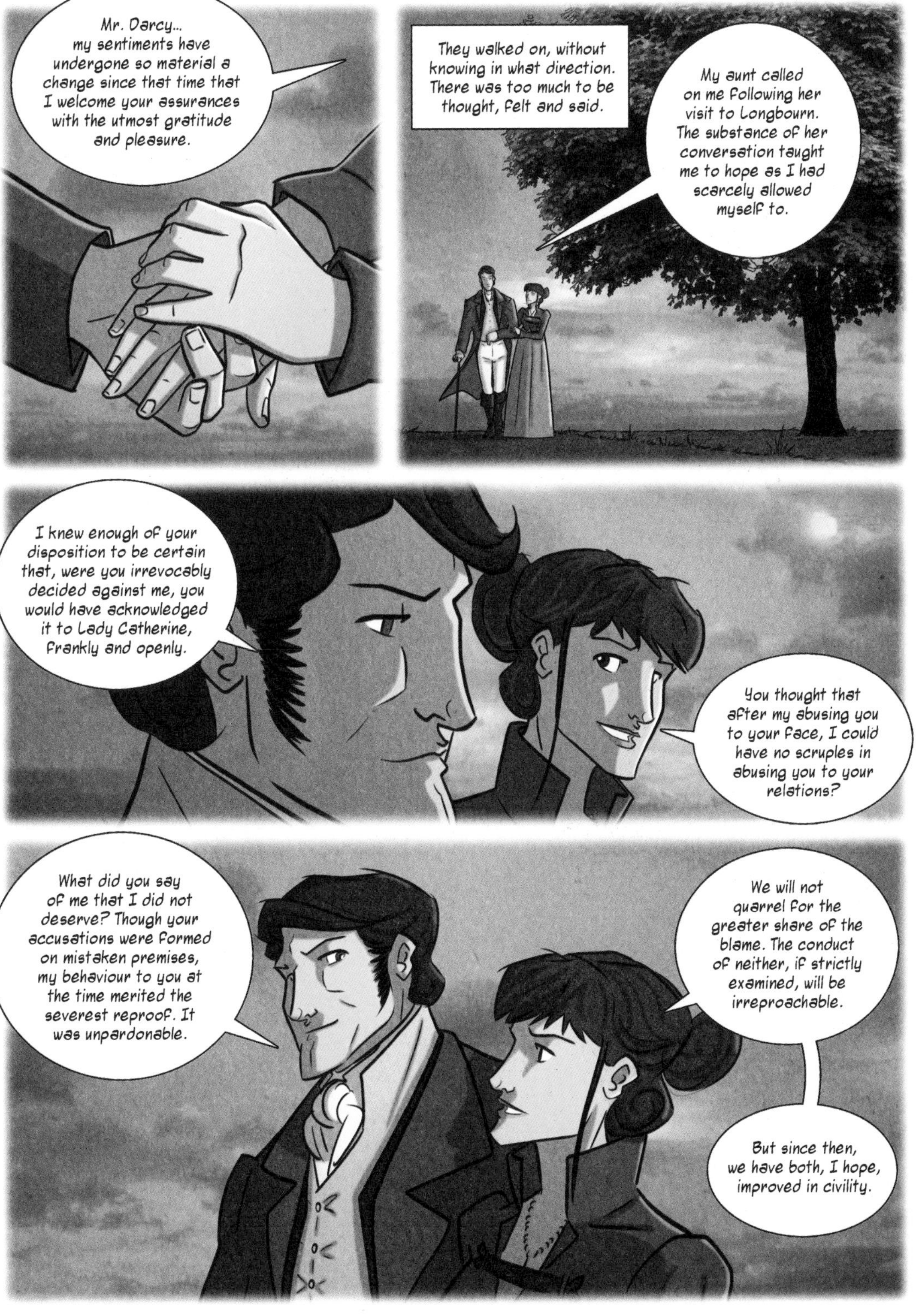
Mr. Darcy... my sentiments have undergone so material a change since that time that I welcome your assurances with the utmost gratitude and pleasure.
They walked on, without knowing in what direction. There was too much to be thought, felt and said.
My aunt called on me following her visit to Longbourn. The substance of her conversation taught me to hope as I had scarcely allowed myself to.
I knew enough of your disposition to be certain that, were you irrevocably decided against me, you would have acknowledged it to Lady Catherine, frankly and openly.
You thought that after my abusing you to your face, I could have no scruples in abusing you to your relations?
What did you say of me that I did not deserve? Though your accusations were formed on mistaken premises, my behaviour to you at the time merited the severest reproof. It was unpardonable.
We will not quarrel for the greater share of the blame. The conduct of neither, if strictly examined, will be irreproachable.
But since then, we have both, I hope, improved in civility.

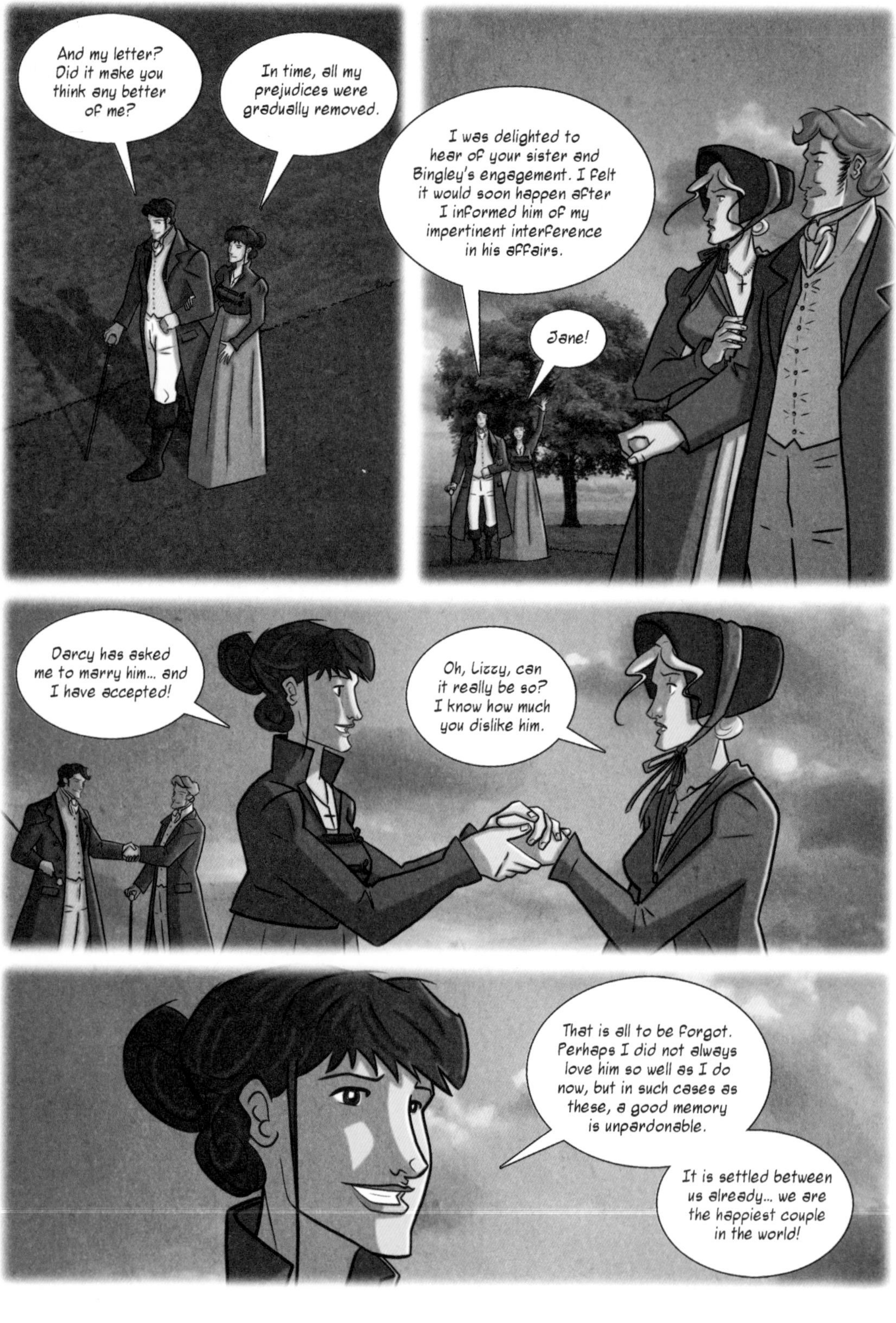
And my letter? Did it make you think any better of me?
In time, all my prejudices were gradually removed.
I was delighted to hear of your sister and Bingley's engagement. I felt it would soon happen after I informed him of my impertinent interference in his affairs.
Jane!
Darcy has asked me to marry him... and I have accepted!
Oh, Lizzy, can it really be so? I know how much you dislike him.
That is all to be forgot. Perhaps I did not always love him so well as I do now, but in such cases as these, a good memory is unpardonable.
It is settled between us already... we are the happiest couple in the world!

Epilogue:

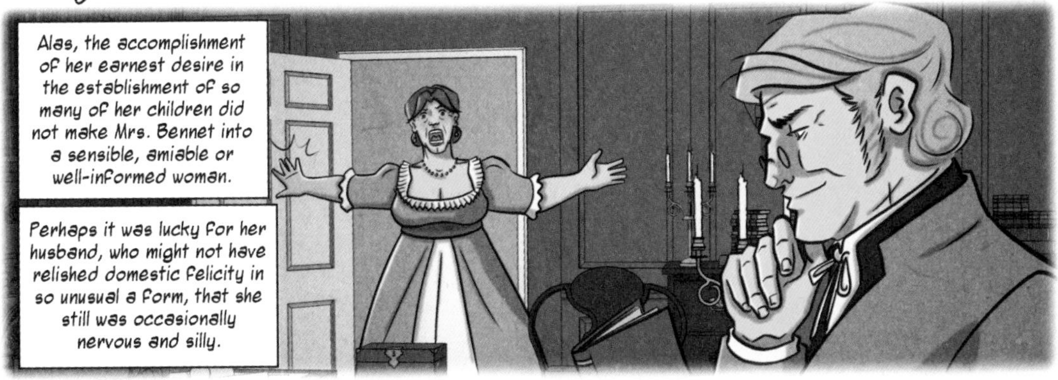
Alas, the accomplishment of her earnest desire in the establishment of so many of her children did not make Mrs. Bennet into a sensible, amiable or well-informed woman.
Perhaps it was lucky for her husband, who might not have relished domestic felicity in so unusual a form, that she still was occasionally nervous and silly.

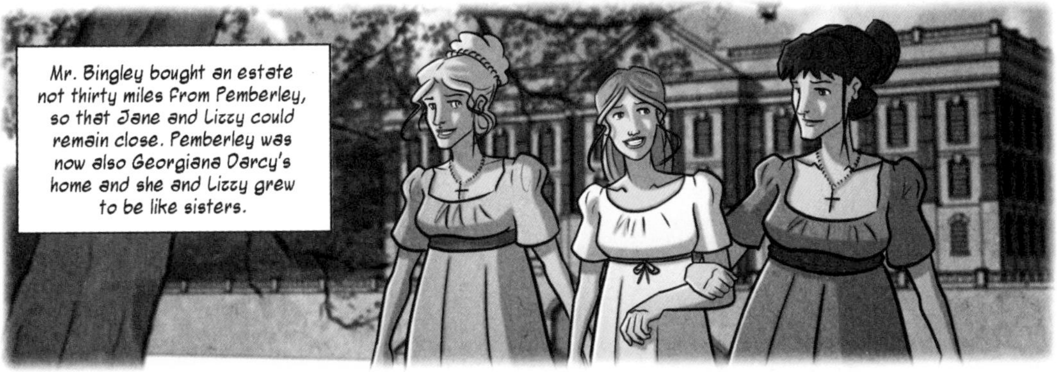
Mr. Bingley bought an estate not thirty miles from Pemberley, so that Jane and Lizzy could remain close. Pemberley was now also Georgiana Darcy's home and she and Lizzy grew to be like sisters.

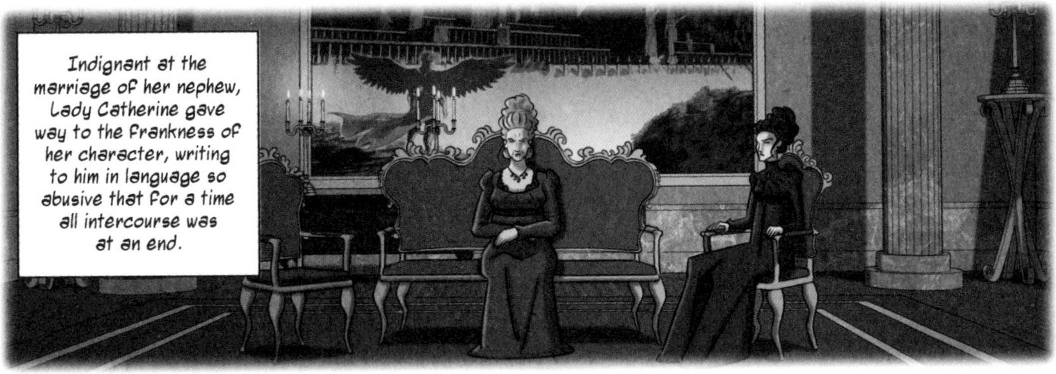
Indignant at the marriage of her nephew, Lady Catherine gave way to the frankness of her character, writing to him in language so abusive that for a time all intercourse was at an end.

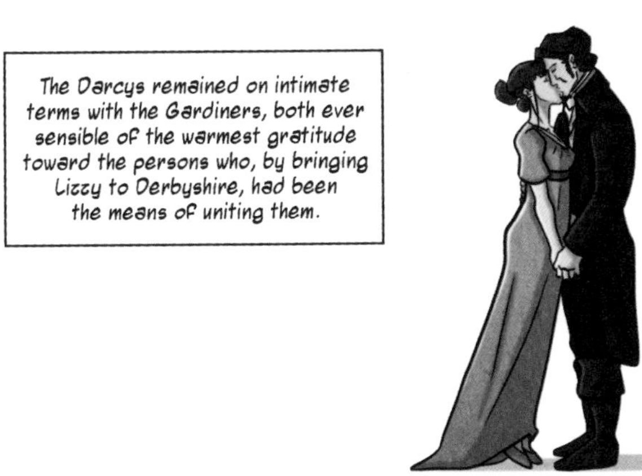
The Darcys remained on intimate terms with the Gardiners, both ever sensible of the warmest gratitude toward the persons who, by bringing Lizzy to Derbyshire, had been the means of uniting them.

The End

Other graphic novels in the Eye Classics series from SelfMadeHero:

The Master and Margarita, by Mikhail Bulgakov.
Adapted and illustrated by Andrzej Klimowski and Danusia Schejbal

Heart of Darkness, by Joseph Conrad
Adapted and illustrated by David Zane Mairowitz and Catherine Anyango

A Tale of Two Cities, by Charles Dickens
Adapted, illustrated and coloured by David Zane Mairowitz, Ryuta Osada and Robert Deas

Crime and Punishment, by Fyodor Dostoevsky
Adapted and illustrated by David Zane Mairowitz and Alain Korkos

The Trial, by Franz Kafka
Adapted and illustrated by David Zane Mairowitz and Chantal Montellier

At the Mountains of Madness, by H.P. Lovecraft. Adapted and illustrated by I.N.J Culbard

The Lovecraft Anthology: Volume 1, by H.P. Lovecraft. Edited by Dan Lockwood

Le Morte D'Arthur, by Sir Thomas Malory
Adapted, illustrated and coloured by John Matthews, Will Sweeney and Robert Deas

Nevermore, by Edgar Allan Poe. Edited by Dan Whitehead

Dr. Jekyll and Mr. Hyde, by R.L. Stevenson
Adapted and illustrated by Andrzej Klimowski and Danusia Schejbal

The Life and Opinions of Tristram Shandy, Gentleman, by Laurence Sterne
Adapted and illustrated by Martin Rowson

The Picture of Dorian Gray, by Oscar Wilde
Adapted and illustrated by Ian Edginton and I.N.J Culbard